THE SKULL OF SWIFT

Dean Swift

After a painting by Jervas, National Portrait Gallery

THE SKULL OF
SWIFT

—

An Extempore Exhumation

by

SHANE LESLIE

BOOKS FOR LIBRARIES PRESS
FREEPORT, NEW YORK

INTERNATIONAL STANDARD BOOK NUMBER:
0-8369-5987-6

LIBRARY OF CONGRESS CATALOG CARD NUMBER:
79-169767

PRINTED IN THE UNITED STATES OF AMERICA
BY
NEW WORLD BOOK MANUFACTURING CO., INC.
HALLANDALE, FLORIDA 33009

STELLAE MEAE

'Tis odd

None could explain the Word of God
Till I, the Top of Irish Deans
Have made it out with wondrous pains.
I've read the Devil and all of books
The world may read in my looks,
Above ten waggon load at least
Within my Skull in order placed.

—The Intelligencer, No. 11

Let Ireland tell how wit upheld her cause,
Her trade supported and supplied her laws;
And leave on Swift this grateful verse engraved,
The rights a Court attacked a poet saved.

—Alexander Pope on Dean Swift

To whom wit served for reason, and passion for zeal,
Who had teeth like a viper and tail like an eel;
Had a knack to laugh luckily, never thought twice
And with coarseness of heart had a taste that was nice.
He would quarrel with virtue because 'twas his foes
And was hardly a friend to the vice which he chose.

—Dean Jonathan Smedley on Dean Jonathan Swift

Perhaps I may allow the Dean
Had too much satire in his vein;
And seem'd determined not to starve it,
Because no age could more deserve it.
Yet malice never was his aim;
He lashed the vice, but spared the name;
No individual could resent,
Where thousands equally were meant.

—Dean Swift on Dean Swift.

CONTENTS

LIST OF ILLUSTRATIONS

THE SKULL OF SWIFT

THE SKULL OF SWIFT

I

(1835)

IN THE year of Grace 1835 some graceless ghouls excavated a pair of skulls in the Cathedral Church of Saint Patrick the Apostle of Ireland within the Metropolitan City of Dublin. One skull was that of a woman, frail tabernacle of the frail, in which the late Sir William Wilde, an Irish physician and antiquary of repute, discerned "perfect model of symmetry and beauty" and added that "the teeth were perhaps the most perfect ever witnessed in a skull." The inscribed stone testified the mortal name of Mrs. Hester Johnson, but gave no clue whether she was really wife, widow or maid. But among the immortals she appeared to bear another name, as it were in Homer, who attributed characters with both earthly and divine names. Mrs.

1

Johnson to men, to the gods she was apparently known as STELLA.

In close proximity lay the skull of an old man, which Sir William Wilde diagnosed as resembling "in a most extraordinary manner those skulls of the so-called Celtic aborigines of North-Western Europe." According to effigy and epitaph it pertained to a Dean of the Cathedral, who there had eventually sought rest for bone and oblivion for heart. The passing stranger might read further and feel surprised that a Minister of the Sanctuary and a Professor of Christian retirement and benevolence should leave arresting and racking words upon a tomb:—

"UBI SÆVA INDIGNATIO ULTERIUS COR LACERARE
NEQUIT."

Why this savage indignation and what lacerations? Surely from ordained and established priests of settled conviction and settled income this was a hard saying and disturbing words to carve in black marble. Surely the lives of Christian Deans, protected from the cares, which afflict poor curates, and the responsibilities, which depress Bishops, should be the glorified impersonation of peace and good will upon earth. But this was a Dean, who sought beyond the grave a place where

the savagery of his indignation should no longer
lacerate his heart. This was a Dean, who was no
gentle shepherd even to his sheep; and, dividing
humanity into wolves and sheep, it would have
been difficult to say whether the cords of his tongue
fell fiercest on flock or foe. This was a Dean, who
finding no rest himself, was unwilling to allow rest
to others. This was a Dean, who was fretted by
the ungodly. This was one, who left no record for
theology when he lived, and who emptied no episcopal throne when he died. This was the writer
whom mortals called Jonathan Swift but whom the
gods, should he have traveled into their far country, must call Lemuel Gulliver, for, though his
bones were fashioned after the manner of mortal
bones, his mind befitted the godlike, full of anger
and power, and raining fury upon the righteous
and unrighteous alike, fiercely pitiful and con-
descendingly faithful unto those whom he loved,
but loving them as the gods love, and bringing
those who loved him to their death. His was a
mind not without vain ambitions, which he allowed to destroy themselves, not without desires,
which he compelled to die within. A mind not
without many affections and affectations, but a
mind, which pierced and broke the glass of illusions
and tore the imagery and rent the clothing which
swathed the minds of those about him. A

thwarted, frenzied and disappointed mind, which might have disappeared into the void like a bitter fume, had it not been tempered with the rare gift of irony. Men that are mortal and born of women write and utter themselves in satire. The gods are ironical in silence. This Dean had brought the irony of the gods with him to earth and used it to the dread and diversion of his fellow-men. Before he died, the irony had entered his soul also, and he asked only to suffer no further laceration by the acts of unwise men or by his own wounding thoughts.

The skull of Dean Swift was brought to the Phrenologists, who were camped at that time in the middle ground between Science and Fashion. This Phrenological Art enabled them to decipher "amativeness large and wit small" between the sutures of his dead brain. With this sapient finding let Phrenology at least rest content. The "Prince Posterity," to whom the Dean offered the most remarkable of his works, might be amused or puzzled by the attribution of "amativeness large and wit small" to a Dean, whose flashing wit was only small in comparison to the thunder-clouds of wrath from which it was derived; and whose amativeness was only the dancing shadow of passions as terrible as his hate. "Amativeness" is insufficient to describe that passion by which the

gods destroy those whom they cause to love themselves. Otherwise the Post-Mortem exposition of
this skull was unrevealing. The great gifts had
passed with the ghost. The Phrenologists were
condemned to conduct the autopsy of the hen which
laid the golden eggs. "Amativeness large and wit
small"!—and with that verdict both skulls were
returned to sepulchral peace.

II

A SURVEY IN PREFACE

(1667-1745)

THE Life of Dean Jonathan Swift will never be written. Many biographies have been attempted, and the best begun, that of John Forster, was never completed. What Lord Orrery flashed in envious caricature, Dr. Delany brought within the pious framework of a Chapter-House portrait. Between them they contributed the chiaroscuro, the thunder-storm and the sunshine of the Swiftian landscape. They were contemporary, however much they disagreed, and contemporary also was the derided Mrs. Lætitia Pilkington, dubbed "adventuress," lying gossip or notorious liar. Her *Memoirs* embalm a partial but faithful reflection of the Dean's declining grandeur. The "adventuress" realized at least the privilege of adventuring into his orbit. What the eighteenth century essayed the nineteenth could not perfect. The grumbling denigration of Dr. Johnson was only over-painted in blacker pitch by Macaulay and Thackeray.

6

The contemporary record could only have been corrected by Swift himself, but beyond a fragment of Autobiography and some personal poems he wrote no past of himself nor did he envisage biography by an alien pen in the future. What he had written to "Prince Posterity," he had written. As a result certain passages in his life remain contradictory, while others have passed into insoluble problemage. We know that Shakespeare was married. We do not know and never shall whether Swift married Stella or not. On other somewhat leading questions there has been disagreement among the Swiftians. We know that Shakespeare was not an Irishman. Whether Swift was one or not, the controversy has been loud. We know that Shakespeare was divinely sane. We are left in doubt whether Swift was really mad in his final phase, or whether he was an ecclesiastical Hamlet all his life. It is curious that we know more about Shakespeare than about Swift on such points. We can judge Shakespeare's religion as that of a Renaissance Agnostic drifting between congenital Catholicism and nominal Protestantism. Shakespeare was anti-Roman but not anti-Catholic. Swift was so violently anti-Catholic that he could be claimed by the anti-Christian. Whenever his mind lurched outside orthodoxy, it was not content with any gentle disbelief. It passed straight into the

annihilating scorn of his poem on "The Day of
Judgment," meet gift for Chesterfield to send long
after the Dean's death to Voltaire. In this poem
the Dean took upon himself to address both sheep
and goats as their Eternal Judge. 'Twixt Dean
and God Swift felt somewhat indistinct. To the
orthodox he stated distinctly enough:

> "You who, through frailty stepp'd aside;
> And you, who never fell—from pride:
> You who in different sects were shamm'd,
> And come to see each other damn'd;
> (So some folk told you, but they knew
> No more of Jove's designs than you!)"

In other words the righteous, whose conceit kept
them righteous are due to be disappointed at the
Dies Irae, for the Great God only pronounces them
sold:

> "The world's mad business now is o'er,
> And I resent these pranks no more.
> I to such blockheads set my wit!
> I damn such fools! Go, go, you're bit."

He did not believe men were damned in another
world but still less that they could be reformed in
this. Skeptics are as welcome to such lines as the
orthodox to his apologetics, if religious apologia
can be gleaned from his sly cantankerous attacks

on Infidels. By allegory and by satire he made the best case possible for the Church of England, in which he proved a model functionary and punctilious monger of rites, but he left a considerable and natural doubt whether he believed in worlds hereafter or in any Deity save the Aristophanic Jove of his own verses. Mysticism, Enthusiasm and Catholicism he tossed sky-high, for he would accept nothing except what lay before him. The State Church was a visible reality as well as his chosen profession. He was too meticulous to be mystic. He counted seconds and half-pence. He counted his friends and a servant's faults and the mathematical correctness of *Gulliver's Travels*. He oozed realism more than religion. Yet he was so far from being a hypocrite that St. John Bolingbroke, who as a free thinker was an impartial judge, called the Dean "a hypocrite reversed." It is simpler to deal with his ecclesiastical career on the supposition that Swift had no soul. Most creatures being too low to be possessed thereof, it is possible in the infinite vagaries and combinations of minds, bodies and souls that some human beings may be sufficiently exalted above good and evil to need or possess no soul. It explains much of Swift's inconsistencies and conundrums. It will be the only hypothesis we will venture to propose, although the problem whether Swift had a soul or not abuts

on more insoluble matter. We know that Swift
left a mortal skull. It is difficult to believe that an
immortal soul ever quitted that inverted bowl of
bone. The presumption that Swift with all his
gifts possessed no soul resolves an enigma, which
might prove as difficult to the Divinity on Judgment Day as it was to fellow divines and mortal
critics during his lifetime. His immortality is of
this world and is based upon prose writings, some
of which give the illusion of being written outside
planetary conditions. Of all his poetry not one line
was drawn from the higher heights. No poetry
was so soulless. If poetry and religion to any extent coalesce, Swift was to that extent unpossessed
of either. Lord Jeffrey, who found evil in Swift's
better side, found some "glow of poetical anima-
tion" however among the lines which included the
couplet about

". . . infants dropp'd, the spurious pledges
Of gipsies litter'd under hedges."

His writings, prose or verse, were streaked with
the earth earthy, and the further problem of Swift's
coarseness is best faced in the survey of a book,
from which any cited example is deleted. All that
need be said is that he often wrote more coarsely
than even his age. There are passages in the *Tale
of a Tub,* which shocked Queen Anne, lost him

his Bishopric and proved that if a writer was too impure to be a Bishop in England, he might become resplendent as a Dean in Ireland. There are passages in the unexpurgated *Travels of Gulliver,* which would make a sea-captain guffaw. And there are poems on:

"The Lady's Dressing Room"

"Strephon and Chloe" or

"A Beautiful Young Nymph going to bed"— which though hastily labeled by editors a disgrace to the English language remain too strong in their sickening unsickenedness to be called immoral or licentious. Utterly lacking in beauty or decency, they indulge only that part of the Dean's complex which became obsessed by loathing of the female form divine. Relentlessly he described the details of the nymphal or matrimonial chamber. This type of poem was the key to his moral character and unlocks the hidden room, in which the dead bodies of Varina and Stella and Vanessa swing mournfully in the sight of posterity.

Whatever Swift's mental or physical composition, it is equally loose-spoken and unproved to describe him as depraved of mind or impotent in his body. Whatever were his experiences as a young man, it is not proved that his mind or his body was diseased. In a letter offering to baptize the daughter of Archdeacon Walls he referred to

himself as an honest gentleman without the archi-
diaconal "faculty of increasing the Queen's subjects." Was this the reason that he delivered
himself on every occasion of a howling hatred and
most venomous vomit at any mention of the means
whereby the benevolent Creator has designed the
continuance of the human race? That the human
race had better burn than marry or even come to a
total end rather than fornicate was the form taken
by his Pauline complex. Meanwhile his poems
were as little provocative of romance or encouraging of matrimony as St. Paul's Epistles. If his object was to sicken youth of the charms of beauty,
analyzed or caught unawares, he succeeded abun-
dantly in showing that—

> "To him that looks behind the scene,
> Statira's but some pocky quean."

Better, he thought, the most humiliating scenes his
pen could describe

> "Than from experience find too late
> Your goddess grown a filthy mate."

To read these poems can not be immoral, for
they will cause the rudest and most desirous lover
to shrink within the confines of modesty abashed.
To make the contrast without straying outside the
poetical flights of Deans, compare the Dean of St.

Patrick's poem on a nymph going bedward with
the celebrated and beautiful verses which Dr.
Donne, the Dean of St. Paul's, inscribed to his
mistress undressing. The latter was an addition to
the literature of the Cytherean goddess. The
former only preserved some pungent anti-Aphro-
disiacs in rhyme. Of his prose vulgarities, in-
elegancies or indecencies, whatever they may be
termed, Swift's judicious critic will distinguish
passages from the Kingdoms of Lilliput and Brobdingnag, which only intensify the author's moral,
while passages from his *Directions to Servants,*
appear to be as pointless as dirt itself. Of the
Oriental setting to love, of the romantic, of the
charming Swift had no conception. To erotics he
frankly preferred emetics, because he thought them
more salutary. The run of virile indecency is constant in his writing until it dwindles away in the
pseudo-cipher letters to Dr. Sheridan at his last
stage. That he was not unconscious of criticism
appears in the subtle apology he attributed to
Gulliver, who like Swift himself "thought it necessary to justify my character in point of cleanliness
to the world, which I am told some of my maligners
have been pleased to call in question." Well—it
has been called in question and accounts for much
that is unpalatable in Swift to-day, for which ex-
planation is easier than apology.

Swift, who was described as the "hypocrite reversed," was also the lover or gallant reversed. An introspective hatred of women permeates his whole work from such acid etching as that in the *Journal to Stella* of a great lady, whom he visited after her confinement: "pale, dead, old and yellow for want of her paint, she has turned my stomach but she will soon be painted and a beauty again," to his picture of the ladies of Brobdingnag, who "were very far from being a tempting sight or from giving me any other emotions than those of horror and disgust"; and moreover "made me reflect upon the fair skins of our English ladies, who appear so beautiful to us only because they are of our own size." Obviously the grossest conduct in Canaries is lovely compared to the lightest amours of Elephants.

He stands then as a moralist, equaled only in the anti-feminist passages of the Sixth Satire of Juvenal. In private life he demanded a strict respect for his cloth and postulated against "those odious topics of immodesty and indecencies with which the rudeness of our northern genius is so apt to fall." The filth of "Strephon and Chloe" tails into wholesome matrimonial advice—

"On sense and wit your passion found,
By decency cemented round."

Spices from his "Letter to a Young Lady Marrying," might still be profitably distributed among
the hymeneal-elect. "You have but very few years
to be young and handsome in the eyes of the world
and as few months to be so in the eyes of a husband," could be slipped into every bride's trous-
seau. Prudence not passion he made the base of
marriage. Only the cultivated mind will hold a
man, "who soon grows weary of acting the lover."
Amorous fondness in company exhibits hypocrisy
or what the Dean thought unmentionable. The
wives, who clutter most over handsome husbands,
would pay most for the news they had broken their
necks. Wives should make men not women their
friends, for "I never yet knew a tolerable woman to
be fond of her own sex." But women he placed a
little above the monkey, "who has more diverting
tricks than any of you!" So far then the not irrec-
oncilable contradictions of Swift on the score of
Decency or Indecency. Swift was not afraid to call
a spade a spade and even a *Spado* a *Spado,* but his
poetry showed him overfond of calling Spades as
his perpetual suit. He remains the mightiest moralist in printed English, although a mocking and
malignant one. But in the private affairs of the
heart, in his combined relations with Varina,
Vanessa and Stella his problem remains insoluble.
Those charming ladies have certainly pained,

puzzled, pleased and divided the minds of his biographers.

Lord Orrery, Swift's posthumously candid friend, opened the floodgates upon the memories of Stella and Vanessa, out of whom biographers have woven so much fiction and writers of fiction have acquired some little truth. Orrery let his pen carry him away when he said that Swift "in painting Yahoos becomes one himself." Against another passage of Orrery, Macaulay wrote the curt counter-criticism "really this book makes one ashamed of being a human being." Of the vain and romantic Vanessa, Orrery wrote, "thus perished under all the agonies of despair, a miserable example of an ill-spent life, fantastic wit, visionary schemes and female weakness." Stella even more fantastically he alluded to as "the concealed but undoubted wife of Dr. Swift . . . married to Dr. Swift in the year 1716 by Dr. Ashe, then Bishop of Clogher." When Dr. Delany wrote to modify Lord Orrery, he not only accepted the marriage as true but claimed by second hand from Stella herself that Swift "offered to own the marriage too late!" With the rolling years more gossamer of evidence for the marriage was spun. The Bishop of Clogher, we are told, told Bishop Berkeley, who told Mrs. Berkeley, who told Mr. Monck Berkeley. Stella herself told Dr. Sheridan, who told Dr. Madden, who told Dr.

Johnson. But no telltale document or legal proof
was ever heard of.

Then the son of Swift's crony, Dr. Sheridan,
wrote a Life, summing Orrery's summary of
Vanessa as "rancorous malignity." But Sheridan
gave a full account of a marriage, which Swift
underwent in a garden to save Stella from present
sickness and future scandal, but only upon strict
conditions that the ceremony was kept secret from
Dame Nature and the damned public. Sheridan
added that the dying Stella had appealed to Swift
that he might "let her have the satisfaction of dying
though she had not lived his acknowledged wife,"
but that Swift without a word quitted her for ever
and that consequently she altered her Will to
charity. Sheridan, who scarcely believed Swift to
be tainted with original sin, only saw in this alleged
but magnificent gesture Swift's power to resist
avarice and an instance of "the same disinterested
spirit," with which he had previously broken off
relations with Vanessa, and lost her fortune as well!
As a matter of truth Swift was not cut out from
Stella's Will, for she left him her all-important
papers. Vanessa had left away her papers to
plague him after her death. It is clear that the
legends of these two ladies became mixed, for the
story of the Dean stalking in silent fury from the
death-bed of Stella was also told of Vanessa, who

caused his divine displeasure and her own mortal dissolution by addressing direct inquiry to Stella on the great unproved fact in Swift's life. Nevertheless, the evidence is accepted by a great modern biographer, Sir Henry Craik, who naively mentions that "it was never contradicted either by Swift or Stella." Who but Vanessa would have dared challenge contradiction from either?

When Walter Scott came to write the classic Life of Swift, he gathered up every version of the marriage like the fragments of a Border Ballad, the secret ceremony under an old oak in the garden, and the final scenes with Vanessa and Stella. Finally he combined Sheridan's with Delany's story and recorded under the authority of Mr. Theophilus Swift, that the Dean did not quit the dying Stella, but observed, "Well, my dear, if you wish it, it shall be owned," to which Stella sighed, "Too late." Scott included the stranger tale that shortly after the marriage in 1716, the Dean was seen by Delany to rush distractedly from the presence of the Archbishop of Dublin, who uttered the mysterious words, "You have just met the most unhappy man on earth, but on the subject of his wretchedness you must never ask a question." The authority for this tale was an "obliging friend of Mrs. Delany." The wretchedness alleged might have been marriage with Stella, but obliging critics

have attributed it variously to a possible impotence
on the part of Swift or to an impossible relationship
with Stella.   Scott mentioned as a famous relic
(which has not survived), a shorn tress of Stella
with an envelope for shrine and for legend in
Swift's handwriting, "only a woman's hair"!   No
more can be added except that, if the marriage took
place, it has remained the mystery that Swift would
have intended.   Of proof, proved or even probable,
no vestige remains.   His only statement occurs in
a letter of 1730: "those who have been married may
form juster ideas of that estate than I can pretend
to do," but of course he may have married without
entering into the state.

Scott feelingly describes the passage of Stella
"to that land, where they neither marry, nor are
given in marriage," but it is, of course, possible that
the lovers had simply forestalled heavenly conditions.

Their relations have certainly been "the despair
of judicious biographers."   In life they were their
own despairs.   Vanessa died of passion, and Stella
died of pathos.   Never was Stella alone with Swift
without some third person, and Orrery gives them
credit for never trespassing "beyond the limit of
Platonic love."   The meetings with Vanessa were
secret and solitary.

Wide spaces of sea and time separated the Dean

from Stella during the writing of the famous
Journal, which contained the nearest Swift ever
wrote to letters of love.   Letters they were as
private as private could be, which Swift never
dreamed would be delivered in "Prince Posterity's"
jumble-bag.   When he scribbled "faith, my letters
are too good to be lost," he was thinking of the
storms and privateers on the Irish sea.   He would
rather a thousand times have lost them than see
them glazed in the British Museum, but it is by
those letters to Stella that Swift's love and lovabil-
ity must be judged.   Stella's own letters, Swift
fondled under his pillow, and the world will never
read them.   Vanessa's, the world would never have
read, had they not been published from the rough
or foul copies, which she carefully disposed at
death.

Litera scripta manet.   Enough remains in poem
and letter to embarrass a husband of Stella in a
Divorce Court—or a lover of Vanessa in a Breach
of Promise Suit.

Vanessa was burned by the slow fires of his distant touch.   Stella *intacta* perished in a union that
was consumingly inconsummate.

Swift has been fiercely arraigned for his amours,
more fiercely than evidence will allow.   His story
must unravel what Vanessa owed to him, and what
he owed to Stella.   Walter Scott's tolerant and

romantic Life, became the signal for a violent turn
in the critical tide.   Monck Mason in his *History of
St. Patrick's* elaborately dissolved the marriage
with Stella as a myth.   Monck Mason then coolly
and impartially combed the tissues and tangles out
of Scott, and set the verses and letters touching
Vanessa in a less lenient light.   A fiercer critic of
Swift appeared in Lord Jeffrey, who took a sinister
view of the letters to Vanessa.

Horace Walpole had written privately of Swift
as "a wild beast who worried and baited all mankind," but public writers now haled him to the
pillory, and Jeffrey attacked the low brutality of
Swift, comparing him again to his own Yahoos.
He accused him of the "poisoned dagger" and the
"envenomed breath."

Macaulay decrying him as "an apostate politician, a ribald priest, a perjured lover," darkened
history with a Swift "to whom neither genius nor
virtue was sacred."   But Macaulay did not
realize that to impartial history even vice is sacred.
Thackeray joined in the "Hue and Cry after
Doctor Swift," to quote the title of an old lampoon.
Dr. Johnson had written of Swift as though he
had mistaken him for a Scotchman, but Thackeray
wrote as though he mistook him for one of his Irishmen, and the most revolting Yahoo of their combined imagination.   Thackeray's tirade in his

English Humourists is an effort to out-Herod
Jeffrey and Orrery. Thackeray was simply ludicrous even to point of fact. For instance he says
Swift "married Stella, and buried Vanessa." Swift
shrank from performing either act of corporal
mercy. Thackeray accused Swift of watching in
a sewer to strike his coward's blow with a dirty
bludgeon. Even the moral of Gulliver he slighted
as "horrible, shameful, unmanly, blasphemous,"
and Thackeray called for honest British hoots
against this Irish ogre. Thackeray invented the
"Gloomy Dean" in the words: "We have other
great names to mention. None I think, however,
so great or so gloomy." And the greatness of his
horror and his hate he compared to "an empire falling." Thackeray's Essay was not Swift nor was it
even Thackeray, who showed in *Esmond,* how exquisitely he could paint the times and people of
Queen Anne. *Esmond* himself "always thought of
Swift and Marlborough as the two greatest men
of that age." And Dr. Johnson coupled them in
their last slow miseries:

"From Marlborough's eyes the streams of
        dotage flow
And Swift expires a driveller and a show."

But Swift was not left to his detractors. The
last word in literature lies always with the patient

ones, who know how to wait and work better than
how to write.   Thackeray and Macaulay left only
the explosive impression of submarine volcanoes,
whereas the microscopic toil of a Forster or a Craik
raised monuments similar to islands created by the
tardy industry of coral insects.

The most industrious achievement of this kind is
the six-volume edition of *Swift's Correspondences*
by Elrington Ball, to which Archbishop Bernard in
a rare preface says what can be said in favor of believing Swift a believer or a married man.   Sane
and unsentimental is Leslie Stephen's crystal study
which took the place of John Morley's advertised
but miscarried volume in the series of *English Men
of Letters.*   He takes the marriage with Stella as
"not proved nor disproven," and remarks what no
other biographer seems to see, that even were it an
occurrence, it was only ceremony, no marriage, only
a nullity, dissoluble in all courts of the world.

Churton Collins, the latest English writer on the
Swiftian shelf, rejects the marriage and sets forth
to rehabilitate the Dean, but like a Balaam reversed, tumbles him unblissfully in the end.   However he draws a comparison between Swift and
Napoleon, which had not occurred to Scott, although he wrote the lives of both.   "Egoists,
despots, and cynics, each owned no equal, each had
no real confidant," wrote Churton Collins.   "Swift

at Dublin recalls Napoleon at Elba," wrote Leslie
Stephen. St. Helena rather. Finally Dr. Emile
Pons has published the first volume of a work so
accurately and closely wrought that every student
of Swift will send his vows to the University of
Strasbourg for its speedy completion and transla-
tion.

Swift is claimed alternatively as an Irishman or
an Englishman. Perhaps now it hardly seems to
matter. He would never reckon himself among
the old Anglo-Irish, for he insisted that "The family of Swift are ancient in Yorkshire" (which the
great herald Guilliam bears out), and that he was
born in Ireland by an accident. As Swift remarked of an English parson settled in Ireland,
"His children will be all Irish, while a thief trans-
ported to Jamaica and married to a battered Drury
Lane hackney jade shall produce true Britons."
Swift then was a Yorkshire man—a Tyke not a
Teague.

Macaulay said that Swift "no more considered
himself as an Irishman than an Englishman born
at Calcutta considers himself a Hindoo"; and
Thackeray catching the same thought, said, "he was
no more an Irishman than a man born of English
parents at Calcutta is a Hindoo." The parallel is
not correct, for numbers of English stock born on
the Liffey have violently asserted their Irishry, and

enrolled their banner in that struggle for Irish Nationalism, which the Dean of St. Patrick raised to
the wars of nations from the level of Battles of
Books. Swift was at one and the same time an
Irish Dean teaching Church of England, and
an English politician stirring the cause of Irish
liberty. The same pen laid the seed of High
Church and Nationalism, though no one hated
Anglican Bishops and Irish natives more.

Adepts of English style and doctrinaire cham-
pions of Irish freedom had preceded Swift, but he
left English letters and Irish politics fundamen-
tally bitten by the fierceness of his genius. One
sentence, "I should rejoice to see an English stay-
lace thought scandalous," carries the seed of Sinn
Fein. Swift's style attained periods of perfection,
which neither he nor others afterward reached,
paragraphs which would not shame the Recording
Angel. Dr. Garnett called him "Grand Master of the Order of Plain Speech." Chateaubriand
said that Rabelais began his language while Swift
finished his. "Rabelais in an easy chair," "a dry
Rabelais" have been the truisms of Swift's critics.
There was a gulf between them. Rabelais was
hugely unmoral whereas Swift was minutely a
moralist. Swift made metaphor out of a Tub
which would have only served Rabelais as a mether
of ale. Rabelais laughed. Swift sneered. "Swift's

wit was the wit of sense, Rabelais' the wit of nonsense," said Hazlitt.   Swift found himself in
La Rochefoucauld.   Hudibras he knew by heart.
"Milton," he wrote, "engages me in actions of the
highest importance."   Bishop Berkeley he found
"too speculative."   Rabelais he took for form but
in La Rochefoucauld he discovered symptoms of
self.   His style was judged by Hume to contain
"no harmony, no eloquence, no ornament and not
much correctness," but Mackintosh found it
"proper, pure, precise, perspicuous, significant,
nervous."   Into whatever molds he channeled his
fiery materials, the lava has cooled into an inde-
structible stratum in English literature.   At his
best his thought and his words were as consolidate
as the color and durability of gold, but for modern
readers the vast mass of his writing lies unreadable
and unread.   The *Tale of a Tub* has been made his
coffin.   *Gulliver's Travels* have been expurgated
of their quicklime.   A few dried specimens of his
minor humor must also be instanced in a survey.

Swift bequeathed to English not a mode of writing but the whole gentle or savage manner of Irony,
which lies at the base of good social satire or any
effective moral teaching.   His delicious manner
may be traced from less known squibs and skits
such as his *Meditation on a Broomstick,* against
sermonizing, the *True Narrative on the Prophecy-*

ing of the End of the World, against his Society, or the ferocious *Mechanical Operation of the Spirit* against Dissenters until the magnificent malignance of Gulliver was launched against the whole human race. His irony could seem two-edged at home but over-blunt abroad. A French writer gravely censured his *Modest Proposal* to convert Irish children into human food and the Inquisition of Portugal burnt his tract parodying the prophecy-mongers as a piece of dangerous Astrology.

Halley's Comet, which left its trace in Gulliver, occasioned the pure humor of the scenes presumable in his account of any sudden ending of the world. By noon on the day of the Comet, Swift stated that one hundred twenty-three clergymen had been ferried to Lambeth to petition a short form of prayer for the occasion. Fire officers were called to keep an eye on the Bank of England. One great politician began but feared to put his secret transactions to paper. Another handed half-a-crown to a starving creditor. Three Maids of Honor burned their novels and invested in Jeremy Taylor's *Holy Living and Dying.* An elderly dame was shocked at the idea that mankind would shortly appear naked. The Army took no notice, in fact the officers swore all the more to show their contempt for Damnation. Nobody showed joy save criminals condemned to hang. Guilty ladies confessed bastards to their husbands, and gentlemen solemnly transformed their mistresses into guiltless wives. Actors and ladies of pleasure became Catholics; and the Irish in town, foreseeing a general conflagration, hired almost every boat on the river. Each sect assumed the others would be damned and wisely declined common prayer. It was a delicious specimen of the Swiftian humor at its lightest.

A savager tone marks the *Operation of the Spirit,* in which he chastised whatever he imagined could be sacred to Presbyterians, whom he condemned to accompany Mahomet to Heaven upon asses since they declined fiery chariots or "celestial sedans"—a phrase which only Beardsley could illustrate.

As for the preachers of Dissent, he asked: "who that sees a little paltry mortal droning and dreaming and drivelling to a multitude even think it agreeable to good sense that either Heaven or Hell should be put to the trouble of influence or inspection from what he is about?" Swift had made the State Church his creed, because its policy was visible and its ethic could be enforced. He had no use for an imaginary Devil with "huge claws and saucer eyes" except to animate his poetical satires. He looked upon himself as a policeman in the pulpit, a surpliced sheriff. He had little use for modern Pentecosts or medieval Demons, making at

their combined expense one of his epigrams about
"cloven tongues and cloven feet."   Nasal prayer,
Enthusiasm and Republicanism he heaped together. Snuffling, he insisted, "first appeared upon
the decay and discouragement of bagpipes, which
fell with monarchy." One of his many shots at
Scotchmen.

Swift's satire reached perfection in *Gulliver's
Travels,* the clearest and also one of the most
elusive of the English classics. It is so clear that a
child may read, but so veiled with personal and
political allusions that the late Sir Norman Moore
used to say that no man lived who could edit Gulliver and unravel the wealth of references, of which
only the outstanding catch the search-light of
History. Even these saliences Swift was careful
to cover by crossing his own tracks. Gulliver must
be read as his own Autobiography. It contained
not only the style, which makes the man, but the
Life which made the style.

Gulliver's Travels is the most original book in
the English language, although commentators
have caught the plague of collecting plagiary. Let
it be granted that Swift had read deeply of
Rabelais, Lucian and Cyrano de Bergerac.
Rabelais' ridiculous Professors, Lucian's Dialogues
of the Dead, and Cyrano's fantastic Voyages had
sunk so deeply into Swift's mind that he could

digest and remold their matter to suit his own
Gargantuan stomach.   Like Shakespeare, whatever Swift borrowed, he adorned.   Of the many
critics who have dissected and decried Swift's
originality, let the German Borkowsky be pilloried
as a perfect type of the same pedantry which Swift
ridiculed in the *Tale of a Tub*.   Almost every
myth or theme employed by Swift can be labo-
riously traced or paralleled somewhere in the im-
mense floating sea of fiction. Swift's genius adapted
them perfectly to the parody and satire of his times.
A painter might be criticized for borrowing from
the pictures of all time such commonplace colors
as red and blue.   Galland's *Arabian Nights* were
translated into English in 1725 and there no doubt
Swift read of Sinbad being carried by the roc in
time to transport Gulliver by the beak of a gigantic
eagle.   Likewise the minute amour of Gulliver with
the huge Maids of Honor reflects the tale of
Hassan, turned over to the giant Princess as a pet.
All literatures have dealt with pygmies and giants,
but none so well as Swift, whose treatment remains
at once magian, magistral and magnificent.   Swift
was happily conscious of his achievement, remark-
ing that, "Gulliver will last as long as our
language."   Gulliver has fairly survived centuries
of Deans and Discoveries, but what impishness led
him to include Japan and California in that fantas-

tic world and how many American readers know
that Gulliver mentions "the Cataract of Niagara"?

With a merry scorn Swift entered upon a
Voyage outside the bounds not only of Space but
Time, although the unknown world was still wide.
Captain Cook and "Doctor Cook" were still behind
the horizon, and the unknown was open to adven-
turers without rivalry. Swift retiring to Ireland a
beaten and disappointed man, took imaginative
journeys to escape from a dirty and dreary Dublin.
He had desired power behind the political scenes
once and a Miter on the world's stage. He had lost
the former and been defrauded of the latter. To
finish life as an Irish Dean was his idea of Hell,
or, as he prettily put it, dying like a poisoned rat
in a hole. It was not enough for this gibing giant
to play with Vanessa or to ply Stella. One had
died and the other was dying upon him, when he
gathered up his life's libretto and transmuted it
into the merry sunshine and cantankerous thunder,
into the shrill fairy pipings and the Jovian organ
notes which make the Grand Opera of Gulliver.
The contemporary Episcopate, into which Swift
once desired so ardently to be numbered, has
dwindled into dust. The whole marvelous society
of Queen Anne's writers and politicians has attained the dead immortality of libraries. Pope was
a better versifier and Addison a purer stylist than

Swift, but Gulliver is a living immortality. Only one contemporary fame has kept pace with Swift. Robinson Crusoe and Lemuel Gulliver remain the literary myths, the Castor and Pollux of a greatly daring, greatly adventuring, stolidly suffering, humorless maritime race. Gulliver inspired Coleridge's definition of humor: "The little is made great, and the great little, in order to destroy both; because all is equal in contrast with the infinite."

Swift's Gulliver seems to have had the reverse history of *Alice in Wonderland.* Lewis Carroll's tale, which began as a story for children, has been used a hundred times to satirize politicians. Gulliver, issued as a satire on English politics, has become the most verdant of children's tales.

That children can pick their way between patches as coarse as primitive Saga and passages of almost uncanny prevision into modern problems shows the gamut of this extraordinary work. Is Jonathan also among the Prophets? We may ask. Perhaps, but without knowing it himself. In his terrible satire upon the Yahoos he unconsciously painted the much discussed Missing Link between humanity and the lower animals. Although he preferred to place a horse at the head of rational creation, Gulliver's previous adventure with the Monkey, which took him "for a young one of his own species" seemed to foretell the most contentious dream of

Darwin. Swift's peculiar view of Evolution was
expressed in the lines:

> "that now and then
> Beasts may degenerate into men"—

which give the hint that, if men are not glorified
apes, monkeys may be escaped men.

Gulliver's return from Brobdingnag to Europe
conveys that curiously modern feeling, which
travelers from New York feel on first landing at
Liverpool: "observing the littleness of the houses I
began to think myself in Lilliput." Gulliver foretold the enlargement of the star-map and the
discovery of the Moons of Mars with almost mathematical precision. The modern waves of Spiritualism and Eugenics, those desperate twin efforts
of mankind to control Birth and Death, the spirit
that has passed and the body which is unborn, are
treated in the Gospel according to Gulliver. The
ghosts of Glubbdubdrib reduce communion with
spirits to ridicule but not without opening the imaginative vista, which alone can make Spiritualism a
practical power. The civilized rational Houyhn-
hums limit their offspring, and the same serious
proposals are made to extirpate the race of Yahoos
by which Eugenists propose to sterilize the modern
negro or extinguish criminals. Most remarkable of
all was Gulliver's prophecy that the Law of Gravi-

tation would in time he superseded. That it was not a meditated vision of Einstein so much as personal pique with Newton on the part of the Dean illustrates the curiously roundabout working of his mind.

No jury is competent to return a verdict on that mind or even to assure posterity whether Swift was properly mad or not. Doubtless he was legally mad and the literary tradition embalms his lunacy, but Time's post-mortem leaves the question open. Water upon the brain and labyrinthine vertigo approximate cerebral malady. Although Swift followed Cyrano de Bergerac on his Journey to the Moon, yet he was never a Lunatic. But even on details there is blank contradiction. Faulkner, his Dublin printer, said he died "in great agony with strong convulsive fits." Lord Orrery said without a pang. His plaster cast seemed to Scott "maniacal" but to Wilde "remarkably placid." But whether he was married or unmarried, or the coarsest or most delicate of mortals, or an innocent skeptic or a most dangerous Christian remains paradox. Hazlitt pointed out that he was the most sensible of poets and one of the most nonsensical. In a famous phrase Lord Bathurst told Swift he had "set kingdoms in a flame" by his pen but Lecky described him as "the pacificator of Europe." Further, whether he was Irish or English, or loved

or hated Ireland most in his life, we have not
ventured to decide. But whether he had a heart?
—Oh yes.—A soul?—Nay.

Of soul and heart, two distinct but often confounded functions, one was entirely lacking; while
of the other, exquisite evidences were buried in the
lumber of Swift's remains. The Limbo, which
awaits the soulless, was his on earth. The tortures
of his mind were not the sufferings of the serene
martyr. His short times of happiness were gleaned
from the hurricane. He could not enjoy peace and
he could only rest in storms. The peace of old age
and achievement brought not beatitude but fatuity.
The peace of contemplation was impossible to a
spirit which was worn rather than rusted out.
There was no soul to take the place and set the
poise of his mind at the last. His entire writings
show no aspiration, no sentence even, marking a
soul's flight. All that produces the idealistic, the
credulous, the poetical, the enthusiastic and fanatical in man was lacking. When he wrote his Utopia,
mankind turned away with a shudder of horror or a
laughing shriek. Severely practical and avaricious
of this world's ways and means, he achieved what
was economically and professionally the best
possible for him. But the *beau geste,* the chival-
rous gesture, the bright and shining example was
as unknown to Swift as the power of taking

Pindaric flight above or a Dantaean voyage below. His flame was a burning hate. His weapons were assiduous criticism, revolted wrath, and acid satire. Scorn, contempt and pride shafted his pen. His Muse ascended from the Pit. Apollyon the Destroyer was his master and not Apollo.

Perverseness warped his nature; but his fate and circumstance were equally perverse. He was fated to be the curse of those who loved him, the champion of a Church, whose Bishops he hated, the idol of a country he detested and whose people he despised. To Swift Providence in any personal sense must have seemed a queer kind of Providence. Professionally he became a cleric, because neither he nor Heaven seemed able to prevent it. Perhaps the Divine sense of humor permitted. But he was preferably the Devil's Advocate rather than the priest of God. Once only he reversed his rôle and with unwitting pen canonized "one of the Saints of English literature." But the downward character of his writing, if not aslant like that of the Lilliputians, tended in a sense other than Gulliver's to be "from up to down like the Chinese not from down to up like the Cascagians." His writings invite no confidence in the Divinity. Certainly they destroy all in Humanity. He was appalled by what he found in created man and he made himself appalling to Man and appalling (who shall deny it?) to

his own Creator. Much that he wrote seems too
terrible to be true, but it was often too true to be
terrible. Terror comes from the unknown and
undreamed. When Swift went furthest in the
dreams of his imagination, he wrote the truest truth.
Truth breeds not terror but horror, and no English
writer has achieved the horrible more successfully
than Swift. That he had religious standards without soul left him only prejudices, and he was religious in the sense that no one was more sincerely
prejudiced against the prejudices of others.
Reasoning powers without soul reduced him to
Logic's logomachy and flung him finally into the
Pit of Pessimism.

Swift has been compared to Prometheus chained
by jealous gods and devoured of a vulture in moun-
tains trackless to men, because he brought them fire
from Heaven in a reed. If irony was the perquisite
of the gods, Swift surely brought it to men in his
inky quill, but he was condemned to torturing
chains and to laceration by that very vulture, which
was his own genius. Goldsmith attributed his fame
to the boldness rather than the greatness of his
genius, which John Morley classed as "savage
and unholy." The Life of Swift must be of
the nature of filming the Vulture. Without the
regality of soul proper to the Eagle, the vulture
plays his earthly part by scenting the carrion and

swooping upon the carcass at our feet, but we do not look to him for direction heavenward. Swift's flight was always set steadily downward and downward he carries all who care for him. Swift had no wiser or gentler friend in modern times than Sir Norman Moore, but Sir Norman could only say that Swift "had arrived at a conclusion, unaffected, horrible but to him irresistible, to hate mankind not out of mere inhumanity but as a result of long observation, a conclusion that made him wretched till he reached the place *'ubi sæva indignatio ulterius cor lacerare nequit.'* " It is this wretchedness, intrinsic rather than acquired, which makes it charity as well as criticism to relieve Swift of possession of a soul then or after.

III

SIR WILLIAM TEMPLE

(1685-1693)

THE master of Moor Park in Surrey opened the door leading into his bowling green and garden. He walked upon a heavy gold-headed cane through the tonsured yew trees, which lined his favorite paths like the sentinels of silence. Every day he touched and tampered with a few papers in his library before strolling among his shrubs and plants and sitting in a shady seat beside a sundial, upon which the hours could pass chimeless and dustless. Silence and silent places he loved. There was charm in a clock without noise. His time in Court and in cities had been full of din. He accounted himself happy to have left the sound of cities for ever and the street cries in the air and the coach-thunder upon the cobbles. His household was a quiet one and his servants were trained as though to minister to melancholy. His secretary was particularly silent, whether from love of his

master or from dislike of the world which chatters
and is given to chattering.

Sir William Temple was a short, richly dressed
man, well-balanced in head and heart. A diplomatist retired from the world's diplomacies like a wise
gambler, who, chancing and winning a hazard or
two, leaves the table to watch other players win,
or more often lose, greater sums. In the game of
human hazard Sir William had never made a mistake, though he had seen his gains snatched from
him. He had seldom been fooled in his survey of
Courts or Courtiers, States or Statesmen. He had
made no promises to himself or others and he had
avoided responsibility as easily as fame. He had
watched for conjunctions on the horizons of states,
and only taken decision and action when the
political firmament was clear. He had served his
country when it was most convenient to both.
Failure, scandal, poverty and disgrace, those
unnecessary camp-followers of the daring, had
been excluded from his journey. If his fellow-
countrymen were grateful to him for the Alliance
he had brought them with the Dutch and the
Swedes, their gratitude was not displeasing. If he
was envied by the Courtiers his share in uniting
their present Majesties the Prince of Orange and
the Princess Mary, that happy prelude of the
glorious Revolution was sufficient reward. He

had prepared and presaged the change, while studiously avoiding the actual disagreements and anxieties of the blow. If the Prince, now King William, was friendly and grateful to him, he wished the King long life and power as long as he himself was left in his Dutch garden. The crowd he neither valued nor feared. He considered them unworthy to dictate or advise any sentiment of religion or policy of State. It happened that the London mob had fallen in with the Revolution made by their betters, but he knew them as mobile as their name. He remembered poor De Witt, the Dutch minister, with whom he had compassed so much important business. His fickle following had torn him to pieces. What an ill-deserved fate! And he imagined in his darkest moments a crowd of the commons from London trampling down his garden. . . .

Sir William stood high in the world which he despised and disliked. Men feared him not but they respected him. He was considered a great Whig, but Tories were not prone to tremble before the decisions of his intellect. He took marvelous care not to bring troubles upon others or upon himself. He was remembered for the impartial respect he had given King James and King William at a time when there was clearly only one throne between two Kings. Sir William had been careful to welcome the coming and to speed the parting ruler. He had as a precaution given his word to King James not to assist his rival until all was over. He then let it be understood that he was a hearty partisan of the conqueror. But he avoided any prospect of reward or promotion by withdrawing to his country retreat. In vain King William wished him for Secretary of State. He had refused, but even there Fate had tempted him to his hurt.

He had allowed his son John Temple, young, keen-witted, ambitious and full of regards for conscience, to be advanced to the place of Secretary of War. Sir William could not teach him the emptiness and surfeit which came out of men's politics and settled into his soul. He must discover by his own trial and learn for himself that public life flowed between the bank of vanity on one side and of flattery upon the other. John Temple had stepped without armor into high office and paid with his naked soul for his lack of subtle steel. Called to advise the King on Irish matters, he essayed some callow counsel, but John Temple need not have taken a misjudgment of his head so deeply to heart, for he wrote wishing the King all happiness and abler servants than John Temple— and in a moment of despair, the despair which older men of politics tread under foot in the knowledge that if Hope is a myth, Despair is a lying prophet, John Temple slew himself. He had thrown himself into the rushing Thames and drowned in the eddy which lay under London Bridge. Sir William had since shrunk even from friends. His second-hand ambition was dead with all the vicarious hopes he had allowed his heart to breed upon this boy. A greater shadow had come over his shy and shadowed life.

With three broken-hearted women he had retired from his son's house at Sheen to Moor Park in Surrey. His heart contained the barest haven for himself. Dorothy Osborne, his wife, must comfort herself. Theirs had been a great romance. He had wooed and won her against the will of families and the clash of parties. She was of Royalist stock now called Tory while he had been cradled a Whig. All her relations and connections were Royalist and among them the fanatical but loyal family, the Swifts, who had recently supplied Sir William with a young and brooding secretary, who in halting verses had tried to drape the tragedy—

"such ghastly fear
Late I beheld on every face appear;
Mild Dorothea, peaceful, wise, and great,
Trembling beheld the doubtful hand of fate."

The Swifts were desperately loyal and poor, and young Swift's mother had been no exception. She

had used the Osborne connection to make a place
in the world for her gaunt, ungainly boy. Lady
Temple had very kindly persuaded Sir William to
receive him under his roof as a scrivener and copier
of sorts. Should he be of no service with the pen,
he could clean and dust the book-covers in the
library. He might even become a superior servant, while his degree from the Dublin University
prevented him sinking into scullery or servitude.
So Dorothea's impoverished and awkward relation
had been brought to Moor Park. His name was
Jonathan.

For Jonathan it was a Paradise garnished and
gardened after his mother's lodgings in Leicester.
There he sat and studied, a subdued, subterranean-
minded-looking object. Without being very
gracious, he was grateful to the Temples. Life
had impressed him with the value of a haven,
should he not be able to sit like a book on the shelf
of some learned and comfortable profession. Here
he sat sheepish among the sheepskins and grew
melancholic in the great library where he observed
that "the best author is as much squeezed and as
obscure as a porter at a coronation." For Jonathan was of an original turn of mind or remembered King William's recent crowning.

His memories were moody enough, but Moor
Park after his wretched scramble for education in

Ireland was like Parnassus and a palace of plenty
and leisure compared to his poor mother's house.
He had watched her, a gentlewoman born and
endowed with wit and spirit, scrubbing and sewing
to maintain the precarious respectability demanded
in Leicester. To share her poverty was to increase
it and to stay with her was to sink her in that boor-
ish and Bœotian tide. He had fallen into sulky
distraction and reverie, happily to be roused by her
clear counsel to take advantage of their connection
with the great and the good Sir William Temple.

At one time Jonathan had meditated taking any
position in Ireland. He had dreamed of becoming
a Fellow of his old College of Trinity. He had
glimpsed the world of the great in Dublin,
Provosts and Archbishops, Earls and Lords Lieutenant. He had envied their independence and
sensed the pleasant influences that accrue to position and flow from the power of causing veneration
or fear in the minds of others.

Jonathan's thought had been read by his mother.
The wolflike look in his eye was not lost upon her,
though it was a mother's burning love that drove
him from her door. Across England he had made
his way on foot. He had taken a curious pleasure
in staying in country inns, where often he was
lodged for a penny a night, and in preferring
wagons to coaches. Ambitious to be heard by the

great, he enjoyed listening to the talk of pedlers and postboys. Coarse speech amused him when it was direct and exactly covered the speaker's point. He liked to hear the vulgar words of Chaucer or Shakespeare rising to English lips. Sometimes he had pricked ears and stored a phrase like a dirty diamond in his mind. It had amused him to contrast this fresh and rough talk with the sophisticated jargon of College, where the fly-blown Fellows span the spider's web of Philosophy and the Collegians aped the Fellows. Jonathan's hungry mind had made lively contrasts and already he divided speech-dividing mortals into those who used metaphor and those who did not. Where the learned used a pretty circumlocution he noted that the common herd dropped the actual word, ugly though it might sound. But Jonathan was never affrighted nor disgusted. He was interested when the uneducated were able to make a point quicker and more strongly than the learned and gentle.

Foot-sore and weary but over-bubbling in his brain pan, Jonathan had been admitted for the first time into the presence of his patron, when to be out of the march of the armies Sir William had moved into his son's residence at Sheen. Jonathan had advised him of his approach and had turned over a number of rhythmic sentences in his mind, as he walked across England, preparatory to

Sir William Temple, 1628–1699

After a portrait by Lely

an Ode to Sir William Temple. He never forgot
his ushering into that family, when with palpi-
tating heart he was presented to Lady Temple clad
in the deepest of mourning and to Lady Martha
Giffard, Sir William's sister. Sir William had
looked at Jonathan with the half-hungry, half-
agonized look of a father who had lost his son.
Nothing could have replaced the pride and praise
of his house. Jonathan could fulfil none of his
hopes, but he could not cause another tragedy. All
that the world could write in Sir William's worn
and creased old visage had been blotted with
tears. Whatever iron Fate had had to discharge
into his soul, had entered there.

Civil toward Jonathan and courteous even, he
had shown no warmth beyond immediately adopt-
ing him as his secretary. To Old Age it is agreeable to find Youth within call and obedience. With
the passage of days he had softened toward the
lonely youth at the lower end of his board. Under
the rough features and coarse clothes he recognized
a sensitive being, easily touched by the bludgeons
and blunderbusses of a world which was insen-
sately divided by opposing creeds and factions,
theories and nations. Sir William had found
himself incurably sensitive and had withdrawn
from the world in consequence. It did not seem
likely that Jonathan would ever enter such mighty

lists or consort with Cabinets or have the arrange-
ment of Treaties, but Sir William was pleased to
instruct him against the guile and guilt, which
the protagonists of such had impressed upon his
memory.

Sir William had been surprised and pleased to
note how quickly Jonathan answered the least
slight or rebuke, and that he could control his secretary by looks easier than by words.   Both
watched and studied each other.   Sir William felt
a faint humor in watching the younger man prepare himself to meet the world (for Jonathan had
let fall sundry hints indicative of ambition) by
studying the Orations of Demosthenes or prac-
tising Pindaric poems in the English tongue.   He
had known occasions great and small, when the
eloquence of Demosthenes would fail, and Pindaric verse he considered more suited to crown than
to create the events of humankind.   The hedgehog rather than the nightingale seemed to him
fitter to meet the world.   But he was pleased to
shelter this young man, who had obviously suffered and was likely to suffer even more, should he
return weaponless to a world, which even Sir
William with all his powers had been content to
escape scatheless.   Jonathan, though busy prac-
tising the nightingale, betrayed external symptoms of the hedgehog—happily for himself.

The days had set themselves into a happy flow. Sir William was a stiff but serene mentor, a stern but not censorious master, seldom inclined to the trouble of rebuke but at the same time never moved to praise. To Jonathan the least reproof, though veiled in a senior's advice or under guise of a statesman's anecdote, fell like a lash upon the most willing horse. When Sir William offered his amanuensis a crumb of knowledge or experience, it dropped like ambrosia upon that young and unclogged palate.

Sir William soon taught his secretary the remarkable use of the truth, whether to further an end or to provide a defense. In a profession which involved a limited use of the truth he had always employed it as a shield or a rapier with excellent diplomatic results. Though Governments and Churches, accommodations with God or man, were presumably built upon truth, truth was generally and purposely obscured. Words in moderate numbers might reveal the truth, but their excessive deployment acted as truth's concealment. Sir William treated the betrayal of truth with contempt and even pity. He imposed on Jonathan a respect for truth for truthfulness' sake alone, apart from consequences or innuendoes. However, favored and recognized the use of metaphor had become in literature, metaphor was a descent from

the higher steps of the Temple into the lower
evasions and fabrications of Thought involving
Fact. Jonathan came to consider even an excuse
as a "guarded lie." In the art of letters Sir William
noticed a possible permanency and standard for
verities. The verities of his life in retirement he
placed in Gardening and good Health. His keen-
est pleasure lay in transmitting an innocent Epi-
cureanism into literary forms. He once nobly
declared that "a good plum is better than an ill
peach." Into search for quotations and passages,
in the engrossing of fair copies of Sir William's
Memoirs Jonathan entered with unswerving industry.

In the presence of this rugged old oak he was
glad to bend his sapling spirit. Pride no longer
stiffened him. He had been thwarted of his desire
to company with the great on equal terms and to
share the movement of great events, but he had
become the trusted servant of one, who had once
been great and who allowed him a keener insight
into the great than if he had known them himself.
He learned to respect Sir William's fastidious pride
and to admire his intelligent virtue.

The Odes he had intended for his patron took
slow shape. The Pindaric steep is long and poets
are short-winded. Jonathan stumbled often
enough. His first broken verses were to "prim-

itive Sancroft" the deprived Archbishop of Canterbury. When his stanzas seemed flawed or failed,
he burned them quietly and sharpened his pen
again. He desired that he might excel publicly as
a poet. There were plenty of patrons for academical versifiers. Noblemen and Statesmen bequeathed their names to posterity upon the
dedication pages of great authors. The Poet
Laureateship hung upon the tree of State like a
prize for the free-lance. Jonathan's cousin, Mr.
John Dryden, had possessed it on poetical merits
but had been deprived on political ground. Jonathan wrote not merely to flatter Sir William but
hopefully to amaze the glorious John. Of his own
pleasure there could be no doubt. "When I write
what pleases me, I am Cowley to myself and can
read it a hundred times over." To Sir William
he sang:

> "Let not old Rome boast Fabius' fate;
> He sav'd his country by delays,
> But you by peace.
> You bought it at a cheaper rate;"—

which only shows that "peace" was pronounced by
Swift with an Irish accent. Other lines show that
Sir William had made him a fierce Pacifist, for the
Peacemaker's was the only Beatitude Jonathan
was ever to deserve.

In Jonathan's eyes Sir William assumed god-
head, for he hardly admitted in his poem that a
spirit so rare had been cast into human mold.

"About the head crown'd with these bays
Like lambent fire the lightning plays."

Watching the grim old diplomat passing down
the flowery paths Jonathan conceived the feeling
that, as mankind had come to grief in Adam's
garden, they might be led to glimpse, if not to
recover, bliss through the vistas of Sir William's.

"You strove to cultivate a barren court in vain,
Your garden's better worth your nobler pain,
Here mankind fell, and hence must rise again."

But to Jonathan himself had befallen a curious
lapse among the fruit-trees, to which he was often
to refer in future years. In an orchard he experienced a carnal fall to the extent of eating a hundred
pippins, to which he attributed the lifelong pains
of giddiness, which had begun to seize him while
reading or listening to his patron. Sometimes he
hardly felt he was himself and experienced the dis-
embodied sensation of watching himself and his
master and pitying the little schemes and desires of
both. Sir William's childish love for yew hedges
and flower-beds and his careful pride in all his scrip

seemed petty and pitiful enough. Something in
Jonathan peeped out and laughed. Perchance it
was some demon within himself. Nor did his un-
quiet, unkind spirit spare him either.

"Malignant goddess! bane to my repose
Thou universal cause of all my woes."

It laughed to see himself at an age, when he
might have gone a-Maying, settled down to work
in the library sometimes for eight hours of the day.
He had learned how little the attainment of a University degree had carried him toward true
education, and he struggled to garnish the gaps
amid—"stale memorandums of the schools."
Very slowly had Jonathan grown confident with
Sir William. At moments only he had felt suited
to offer and receive opinions. But at one gloomy
look from Sir William he shrank back quickly into
his own shell, while an angry gesture troubled his
very sleep. For Lady Temple he felt gentle respect
and coined her name to "Dorinda" in his verse as
though she, who might be called Dorothy by men,
required more classical synonym upon the speech
of the gods, among whom Sir William, in spite of
the rheumatics he had brought from the Hague,
was also reckoned. It was his jealous sister Martha,
not the delicate Dorinda, who ruled the roost, and

as a humble cockerel Jonathan learned his place.
He dreaded a little the fierce fuss which he came to
associate with Martha's regular and noble features,
the massive nose, the heavy-lidded black eyes and
small mouth, which Sir Peter Lely had picked out
with his brush and tricked into the oil painting
hanging among the Vandykes and Titians upon the
wall. Martha Giffard was a little fond of treating
Jonathan like a lackey to be sent or called at will.
Jonathan would obey, but the giant within his brain
signaled an intense displeasure. Jonathan's growing dislike of the sex was barely tempered by "aunt
Gifford's" puddings in which "suet and plums were
three-fourths of the ingredients."

There was perhaps an exception. At the end of
the Park in a little cottage lived Sir William's old
housekeeper, Mrs. Johnson, with her tiny daughter Hetty and Rebecca Dingley, her companion.
Hetty was the secret queen of the house. Ever
welcome at Sir William's side she moved like a
sunbeam through Jonathan's obscure studies.
When he found how much it pleased Sir William
to please her, he told her stories out of the voyage
books, which he had collected to one shelf of the
library. Even Martha Giffard's black eyebrows
relaxed when Hetty passed. Further to please
his patron, Jonathan exerted all his powers of
mimicry and persuasion to train her tiny talent

to read and write. He guided her little white fingers until she wrote his same undeviating and
beautiful characters. He was glad to find his
handwriting a worthy model to so sweet a pupil.
All the graciousness and breeding, not to speak of
the dark eyes and hair of Sir William, seemed
reflected in her, but that perhaps was only noticed
by Sir William himself. Days passed and Jonathan had quaint and curious thoughts but he had
begun to play with phrases and allusions. When
Hetty showed Sir William her first clean written
pages, it was observable that the writing was
Hetty's but that the hand was Jonathan's. Did
Jonathan wonder if in return she would ever give
him hers?

IV

(1693)

FORWARD and then backward let break the span
of Time!

Forward for a time and back for a time. The old
statesman is sitting among his figured yew trees,
beguiling his spirit with their thick foliage all
curiously cramped and clipped, not a bough nor a
twig and hardly a leaf out of line. They made the
model of his prose writing. The hill ran back to the
house, whose breadth was marked by a gravel terrace, from which the garden path threaded the
laurel standards. Flights of stone steps led into
flower-beds encircled with stone cloisters, covered
with roses and set with a pair of summer-houses.
Beyond a grotto embellished with rocks and shells
and water-works lay the fruit orchard like a wilder-
ness of trees. In the Orangery mused the antique
and rain-stained heads of Mark Antony and
Theocritus.

The old man calls to the house, "Jonathan,
Jonathan!" and his dark-haired, beetle-browed
secretary runs with active hare-leaps down path
and steps. He is leanly but prodigiously grown
since his first arrival and his long legs have been
activated upon the hills and roads. He has become
his master's reverse, scarcely able to slake his quick
body or slacken his eager mind, while Sir William
is more than ever given up to Quietism and Apathy
and all manner of Indisturbance. Jonathan's
shoulders are squarer and he has disposed the drop
in his back. His black hair is longer and his eyes
glare like sunken loadstones from their occiput.
He approaches more courageously to his master
and necessarily, for the spleen of melancholy crops
into the older man's face. He has been distempered
by something more than rheumatic memories of the
mists at the Hague. Something had risen to stir
his old political disappointments. Jonathan is
wondering whether Sir William wishes to convey
a velvety rebuke or an ungracious favor.

"Jonathan, I would that you would take an
errand of mine to the town with this letter. You
may ride whichever horse pleases you."

Jonathan bowed. It was some matter of those
higher politics, which Sir William had made believe
were left behind for ever. But they have followed
him and discovered him in his rural retreat.

"More, Jonathan. I wish you to plead a good case and to offer some better advice. My advice, but you are now the fitter of us to find and press the argument."

The young secretary of twenty-five pricked his ugly ears. A look of pleasurable curiosity warmed his eyes. He bowed as though he felt sufficient to fight any cause his patron laid upon him. For the first time Sir William showed open satisfaction in his acquirements at Moor Park that he should wish to entrust him with his business in the town. "To whom, Sir," he asked, "do you wish me to ride?"

Sir William handed him a sealed letter of introduction addressed to His Majesty.

"The King?" gasped the eager youth.

"Yes, sirrah!" replied the other. "I do not forget how well you distinguished yourself in conversation when His Majesty honored us by a visit to Sheen."

Jonathan was fain to acquiesce, though he did not believe the King had taken the fullest measure of him during that ever-to-be-remembered visit.

"His Majesty was so agreeably inclined that he taught you the manner in which the Dutch nation cut and eat their asparagus?"

Jonathan bowed again but not without a contemptuous flush as though he detected some dry humor at his own expense.

"And I believe that His Majesty condescended
to offer you some position yourself?"

"A Captain's commission in his Horse," confessed Jonathan testily, but added, "I am a
tolerable rider." He stood waiting to be dismissed.

Sir William knew very well that the ambition,
lurking behind that ugly boy's mask, aimed at more
than a broidered saddle to his horse's back or a
silken scarf to his sword. But he enjoyed rallying
him, for he suspected it was a white lawn sleeve
and not a red and gold coat that Jonathan cherished
at heart. His humor did not rankle maliciously,
for it was to set Jonathan on his way to preferment
that he had summoned him to take his letter to the
King. He continued:

"His Majesty, Jonathan, has been much troubled
whether to give his assent to this Bill for Triennial
Parliaments. His Majesty still finds Dutch Burgh-
ers honester than English Peers and is uncertain
how to act, fearing the precedent from the time of
the late King Charles, whose memory remains like
a sword of Damocles suspended upon the English
monarchy. The Earl of Portland has been sent
with the royal view to Sir William Temple, who
is desirous to send his view to the King by Mr.
Jonathan Swift. In our opinion the King need
have no fear to give assent to a Bill of entirely
different nature to that which caused the ruin of

King Charles. I leave you to furnish the King with the arguments both from history and, when your memory fails, from your own solid wit."

On the next day Jonathan rode to London with his head high and his patron's best horse under him. As he covered the slow miles, a cast of satisfaction settled in his gaunt features. He was riding toward great occasion, great people, great opportunity. He approached a parting of the ways. If he persuaded the King, he would not only have pleased his first patron, but possibly won the last he would ever need. From the King flowed curatives of greater evils than the King's Evil; positive allayment for the sores of poverty, the anguish of ambition and the vulgar plague of obscurity. From Kensington stretched the clerical Pilgrim's Way to Canterbury.

Within a few hours Jonathan might place his foot upon the ladder of preferment. Time seemed to stand still during the pleasant advance toward London and his mind became sufficiently released from present bondages to recall his life. Indignantly he reconsidered the knowledge of his birth in Ireland. It was an accident that he had been born an Irishman, an accident that might occur in the most English of families, for it might be the fate of the son to a Lord Lieutenant himself. He recalled not the squalid Court behind the broken

Alley in Dublin, nor the dust-curtained windows peering through moldering sashes out of the ruinous four-storied house; all of which he hated as the spot of his nativity, and had never passed without shuddering.

He remembered his old nurse, who had carried him away from Ireland to the North of England and he remembered the long hours she spent teaching him to read her Bible. The long chapters and the long sonorous words still flowed and ebbed through his memory. They were so soothing to recite and so incomprehensible to understand. His mother had fathered him. As an orphan, he had never seen his father and he nourished a strange feeling that his mind was more fatherless than his person, that it was not begotten or related to kindred minds upon earth. He had always found himself solitary, always meditating alone.

He thought upon school-days under the shadow of the Duke of Ormonde's Castle at Kilkenny. The uncle, who had used him so sparsely in those years, had had some connection with those mighty Ormondes, with the consequence that Jonathan had found himself imbibing Latin and Greek in Saint Canice's city, though eight years had dwindled in memory to eight weeks, eight days almost. He remembered old Master Ridler and the ferule, under which he and his companions had nosed and

grubbed their inky portions of Grammar. Those
had been hard and dull years leaving little mark
with him and he chiefly remembered the care with
which he had carved his name upon the bench, feeling a less terror of the ferule than of the oblivion
which menaced even his schoolboy days. He
remembered satisfaction at seeing the big letters
cut permanently in the wood and wondering
whether those who followed him would read his
name and wonder what manner of boy great or
small had left this vestige in his tracks. He always
felt treated like a dog and that his uncle thrust him
into any kennel. He remembered feeling so
slavish himself that he had once bought with his
savings a mangy horse, which he saw being led out
of the town to the slaughter, in order to enjoy the
feeling of possessing an animal himself. After he
had ridden through the Kilkenny streets to the
envy of his companions, he had seen the sorrowful
jade lie down and expire. The memory made
pleasant contrast to the rider of so fine a horse as
Sir William's that morning on the highroad to
the King's Palace at Kensington. . . .

His thoughts still brought him back to Dublin,
to his entry as a pensioner at the University and to
the first tastes of liberty; liberty to range the
streets and dive into the byways and blind coffee-
houses of Dublin; liberty to seethe his brain in

The House Where Swift Was Born

the recesses of Trinity with his first debauches in
History and Poetry. He recalled the crazy old
Fellows of Trinity powdered with snuff and stained
with claret, bachelor-hermits living their scornful,
enviable lives unapproachably, unassailably. He
had set his soul immediately then to become Fellow
of Trinity like his tutor St. George Ashe, who was
lost to the world upon remote paths of mathematics,
but could come to earth to bandy his flashing wit
with fellow-creatures of earth likewise soaked with
College port and reeking of tobacco. Jonathan
had liked Ashe, though, when Ashe tried to cramp
his restless mind to the study of Logic, he could
not help asking the wherefore and had been told
that Logic would teach him to reason. He had
replied that he could reason rather well without it.
How he had hated the philosopher and formulist!
How contemptuously he had thrown away the
Works of the great Kechermann and the Logic of
the good Smeglicius! Their names and their learning had not overawed him. He had merely sub-
stituted a more native and natural philosopher in
their place, to wit Jonathan Swift.

He looked back with a taste of misery mounting
into his mouth from years of dependence and
charity upon his relations. He had felt a beggar,
and his uncle had kept him begging and horribly
restrained. He knew what it was to lack penny.

He had confined himself to fellow-students as poor
and restive as himself. Together they had prowled
the windy, rain-racked alleys, and guttering drink-
shops of the Dublin night. Again and again they
had fallen foul of the College, breaking away from
the bleak discipline of Class and Chapel. Often
they had failed to appear seated neatly arow in
their surplices under the nose of some mumbling
Fellow, who was a Deist when sober and more
orthodox under liquor. Jonathan had kept few
friends and few whom he wished to meet again,
except his tutor, Ashe, and Congreve, his junior,
who had followed him to Dublin from Kilkenny.
Out of the memory of the soaking rain and the
chilly dark nights, and the damp stinking folios,
and the snuffling candles, and the coarse foods, and
College brews, and Dublin brawls, there arose the
faces of these two friends ever cherishable: Ashe,
the devout Mathematician, and Congreve, the beautiful Comedian—Congreve since lifted into Fame
and Ashe only lifted upon those wings which are
called by prophets, the wings of Seraphim, and by
astronomers, the *Calculus in Differentiis*. In those
days there had been a movement like a breath of
the spirit through the dry bones of Science. Men
had been stirred to examine the Celestial Mechan-
ism, and to speculate upon fixities of stars and
visitations of comets and orbits of planets, and to

weigh the weights of the Universe after the manner
of Him who weigheth both the stars in the
firmament, and the hearts within men.

Riding along, Jonathan bethought his veneration
for the metaphysical Ashe, and love for Congreve,
who cared only for boon companionship and the
comedy of life, and already was being noised as a
writer for *Stage and Spectacle*. Ashe and Congreve were kindred spirits to his own, but both had
found absorbing occupations. Each in his own
world had touched a tolerable fame, and Jonathan
grimly contrasted his twenty pounds a year as Sir
William's secretary. Moor Park must be only a
retreat, a refuge, a preparation and a spring board.
He had already made and buried a fruitless effort
to reach into the world when Sir William had given
him a testimonial to the Irish Secretary. He remembered angrily that nothing had come of that
journeying to Dublin, and cursed the fate which
always turned toward Ireland as remorselessly as
the needle of the compass to the north.

He felt that he had attained more than merely
the character of an honest and diligent servant, with
a knowledge of Latin and Greek and French. The
career of civil life seemed choked, but he had decided
in heart to try the ecclesiastical, which duly entered
with proper excuse could combine a handling of
politics and frequentation of the famous. Unless

he could secure such interests, his spirit would set him wandering about the world, and seeking whatsoever Misery or Mischief placed in the way. In Dublin he had been told that he was a conjured and enchanted spirit, and he had felt the Demon within him. He remembered how he had taken his Dublin Degree by a Special Grace, but he had studied well into subjects which pleased him. He was indifferent to the *"negligenter,"* which the posing examiners had affixed to his theological theme and to the *"male,"* which branded his dislike for Philosophy. His classics had upheld his repute for scholarship, and he had since been able to attain a Degree from Oxford. It was necessary, since an Irish Degree did not appear more helpful in England than an Irish accent or that Irish Nativity of which he would so heartily have disrobed his origin.

But the star of his nativity seemed anchored over Dublin and he never felt well rid of the uncomfortable Irish magnet dragging him back across the Irish Sea. A prebend at Windsor or Canterbury was the only antidote, and he gloried that his horse's hoofs pointed toward a King who was actually seated at Windsor, and over Canterbury could presumably cast his shoe.

Thanks to Sir William's influence, Jonathan had taken his degree at Hart Hall, after a few convivial

weeks of smoking and drinking at Oxford. His
own University had done nothing for him, and he
had been more obliged in seven weeks to strangers
at Oxford, than in all his years in Dublin. Oxford
had been very attentive to Sir William's request,
as Academies always are unto Statesmen who have
held and may hold secular power again. The
civilities of Oxford had cushioned Jonathan's
rasped mind. But Dublin be confounded, and he
began strumming:

"From leaving fair England, that goodly old
    seat,
And coming to Ireland to serve for our meat
In hopes of us all being all of us made very
    great;
            Libera nos Domine.
"From staying at Dublin until we have spent
Our last ready coin in following the scent
Of what we could never secure, Preferment—
            Libera nos Domine.
"From turning Tory or highwayman,
And leaving our bones near Stephen's Green
Now let us all say, I pray God Amen.
            Libera nos Domine."

The day came when Jonathan bitterly realized
that an Irish Miter came easier to a highwayman
than to a Tory. Meantime, like a black-touseled
raven alighting among ocular peacocks, Jonathan
rode into Kensington, and dismounted among the
crowd of haughty courtiers and flashing officers.

Sir William's letter brought him immediate admission to Lord Portland, a Dutch nobleman, to whom Jonathan poured a ready discourse on the importance of the Triennial Bill; since, forsooth, it was owing to the passing of another Bill entirely that King Charles of holy memory had come to ruin, in that he had let it escape his power to dissolve the Parliament without the consent of the House. Thereby and therefore he had prepared the ax which eventually fell upon his neck. And with much more precedent and precision Jonathan broidered and brayed and broiled his case, which he finally served in writing, until the Earl of Portland yawned and advised him to keep his best arguments, and also his briefest for His Majesty, who was pleased to receive him that hour.

"The King!" Shuffling, scraping and silence, and the curtains were thrown back, Jonathan bowed stiffly as from the saddle. Between two gentlemen ushers, advanced the diminutive figure of the renowned Prince of Orange, thanks to the folly of the Stuarts, ambition of King Louis, self-denial of his own Dutch, and foresight of Sir William Temple, King of Great Britain and Ireland, which latter country had at least seen his only victory in the field, and occasioned Jonathan's poetry:

"Amazed, thy action at the Boyne we see!
When Schomberg started at the vast design:
The boundless glory all redounds to thee,
The impulse, the fight, th' event, were wholly
    thine."

A look of sickened weariness filled the lean face
of this dull demigod of the English Whigs, whose
wishes in the matter of the Triennial Bill Jonathan
began to urge.

Quickly he rehearsed precedent and preamble,
and bowed again. The King bowed neither to
reason, nor in reply. Jonathan's say was finished,
but not by a hair's cast did the King's features
alter. The piercing eyes peered past Jonathan out
of their anemic mold of flesh. The aquiline nose
vaguely scented distant battle. Was this the
celebrated Dutchman, who had sacrificed all to
resist the French ambition? Morose and industrious, he ceased not calculating the detail of war
and peace in the everlasting struggle between
Europe and the strongest Prince in Europe. The
roar of battle, to speak not of a bellyful of recent
reverses at Landen and Steinkirk, had surfeited
him of fanaticism. Symbolically Prince of the
Reform and god of the Protestant nations, he had
learned the tolerations of diplomacy and the indif-
ference necessary to success in the world. Cradled
a Dutch Calvinist to the marrow, he had become

Defender of the English Faith. It was all a weary
farce, save that Holland must be at all cost protected. England, Ireland and the Churches of
England and Ireland were only pawns against the
raging, devouring, Lys-spangled Louis. Even the
Holy Roman Emperor had taught him that
Catholics were acceptable when not in the colors of
the King of France, and the Pope's Holy Self had
been so fearsome of the Gallican claimancies of
King Louis that he had underwritten the assurance
of the Emperor, Roman and Holy, that Holland
would not be invaded while William was out-
maneuvering King Louis in the barbarous bogs of
Ireland.

Mistrusting his disliking courtiers, William held
England as an outpost against the French King.
Sick of body and grim of soul, he listened to the
pupil of his old friend and adviser, but Jonathan
could see he had made no way by his advice. He
bowed a last time, and the King passing to another
subject inquired whether he was still unwilling to
take a Commission in the Horse. Jonathan assured
him with all humility that he preferred a black coat,
and that his studies led Churchward. The King
advised him to wait and take Orders as soon as a
prebend offered itself. That was all. But a
Prince's word was worth more than an ordinary
man's promise. The King gave him his hand to

kiss, and, making some signal for dismissal, turned
to some papers, which his next entreatant was
blandishing or brandishing his way. The feeble
figure of the King disappeared behind the bustling
courtiers and Jonathan sighting no objective for
further protestation or prostration turned on his
miry heels.

Before he left the Palace, he was bidden by Lord
Portland to inform Sir William that the King was
deeply indebted to his loyal prudence and proffer
of advice, but was nevertheless determined to use
the Royal Veto, which had been entrusted to him
at his coronation. A pang of anger passed through
Jonathan's heart. All his learning and trouble had
been in vain. Had he ridden hopefully across
Surrey in order to become the medium of the royal
refusal to Sir William's wisdom? He felt secret
rage, which he could not and would not control,
overcome him, rage against Lord Portland, rage
against Sir William, and rage against King William; hypocrites both, save that one was cold
and the other warm and mellowed. And Jonathan,
buried in memory that cold-eyed King of royal and
frigid singularity; that unwilling deliverer of his
unwinsome subjects, over whom he was condemned
for the rest of his life to reign in contemptuous
sovereignty of their suspicious factions; that silent
watcher of a censorious watchful Court with but

one aim in life, but one vice to keep him human, and
but one victory enrolled on his silent standards; a
victory, that, being gained in an Irish river and not
upon the battle-board of the Low Countries, was
lessened of value in the eyes of any professional
commander. A black mark collected under Jonathan's skull to reform itself years later in inky com-
ments on Burnet's *History*. To Burnet's famous
attribution of one vice only to the King—Jonathan
scrawled "two" and Portland he dipped in the
King's "infamous pleasures."

But Jonathan's gall retreated at the promise of
a prebend and he still trusted mildly in princes
and his wrath returned rather to his patron. He
could not guess that this journey was a device not
in favor of Triennial Bills but for throwing
Jonathan Swift into royal notice. He would have
been wise to give Sir William credit for wishing to
do the best for him. Nevertheless he felt too serv-
iceable to Sir William for Sir William to wish to be
over-serviceable in return. His desire to break
away from Moor Park began to fester within and
he was determined by many a mile, before he
reached home and reported his ill success, that at
the first opportunity he would take Orders, Holy
or unholy, and enter upon a path of independent
preferment.

Jonathan returned to Moor Park with the sense

of savagery suppressed in his heart. The hope, which ambition hallowed, had risen that morning like a red sun upon the horizon, and it had set, as Jonathan's suns all set, into total darkness. There was no gentle shade or twilight in his mind. All was stark and he was again left to swelter obscurely in a country library. Making ten hours of work a day his voluntary portion, he choked without contenting his hungry spirit. Sir William encouraged him to translate Virgil, which stuck plaguily on his hands. Nevertheless he knew that a few lines of Virgil deftly applied made the difference between the gentle and the vulgar in England. Every day he crushed his heavy thought through the Pindaric mill. He had noticed that soaring Odes brought fame and patronage. Day by day he patched and burned and copied his lines. Day by day he struggled in the coils of inspiration until he could peel and boil his poems to sensible and sonorous form.

He still ambitioned to try their melody on his cousin, Dryden. Though shorn of his laurels, Dryden maintained his power over the Wits. Jonathan envied that independence which could mock the slights of politics, or changes of dynasties. He determined to make way among the Wits even by eccentric manners, if he could not astonish them by the Pindaric splendor. Somewhere beyond the

heaths and coach-runneled roads lay that world
where men of State fawned upon the men of
letters; where men were ranked by the titles of
their books, where mind cut mind, wit sharpened
wit, and the devil took the dullest. Some day he
determined to surprise the glorious John in his
chosen coffee-house, and to throw him his own
rhymes like a challenge.

Heavy with allegory and gravid with apostrophe,
Jonathan completed an *Ode to the Athenian
Society.* He really had little of rhyme or reason
to offer mankind except for his philosophical discovery that mankind was chiefly wind, which leaked
through lines like:

> "Who, by that, vainly talks of baffling death;
> And hopes to lengthen life by a transfusion
>   of breath,
> Which yet whoever examines right will find
> To be an art as vain as bottling up of wind!"

Already his mind was working out a Theory of
Wind as the basis of all speech and much religion.

The next time he came to London on business, he
waited in the Rose coffee-house with a bundle of
manuscript. Congreve and Dryden were sitting
there, in the careless insolence of achievement.
Upon Dryden rested the fame of years, and upon
Congreve the fame of youth. Unfamed, the poor
secretary of Sir William Temple saluted them
both. With Congreve he quickly engaged in com-

mon memories of Kilkenny School, of the games and classes, of the frowning old Ormonde keep, of old Ridler and his smarting ferule. In Congreve's honor Jonathan had a poem prepared. He realized the light of fame, the nimbus of divinity upon his fellow: "Godlike the force of my young Congreve's bays." And when he had read him his poem, "My Congreve," he whispered, "some day I will make sin and folly bleed."

But the glorious John was reading his other Ode with acrid eyes. Anxiously Jonathan awaited the verdict. Then spoke Dryden, but whether as a cousin or a poet, Jonathan could not conceive, whether as a friend to poetry or as a friend to Jonathan, though perhaps truly as a friend to both. "Cousin, you will never be a poet," quoth the Prince of Poets. And Jonathan went into his dwelling and hated him unto the hour of his death.

Jonathan knew now within his brooding self that only the Church remained. His visit to the King at Kensington had burned his vanity to ashes, but John Dryden had scattered even the ashes at a breath. There was only the Church, and his chance lay with the Supreme Head thereof, upon whom he had so recently failed to impress his historical knowledge. The scene and consequences continued to come back to him. A Whig King should not veto a measure so dear to Whigs and to the noblest of Whigs, the inhabitant and owner of Moor Park.

To assuage the Whigs, the King would be bound to pacify them with power, and with the advent of Whiggery what would befall the principles of the Tory High Church, to which Jonathan perceived he must be driven to ally his fortunes? The past must bury the past.

The King had already become a distorted vision in Jonathan's mind. Some demonial faculty transmogrified the characters whom he met so solemnly and seriously in real life. He dreamed of King William's doleful face ironed by fate, the eyes wandering slowly to right and to left but forbidding their owner to lay his trust either way; the small embittered man, who wore the Crown not for love of England, but from hate of France. . . . Jonathan was dreaming of snatching a Bishopric at the King's right and a Canonry at his left, but their prospect grew smaller and smaller, and the King himself, so far from strengthening or assisting him, seemed shrinking and shrinking. Was this Demigod of the Whigs and Savior of Liberty but a pigmy after all, like a tiny fairy creature upon the edge of that great grasping ink-stained hand, which Jonathan stretched so eagerly into the future? . . . When Jonathan woke from his phantasmagoria, his horse was standing still upon the terrace at Moor Park. He must go in and finish Sir William's *Memoirs* before he played with memories of his own.

V

(1693-1696)

JONATHAN had set his mind upon the Church. It remained for him to work until the Church would turn her mind to him. Of a soul or a soul's conversion he was unconscious. Nor could he assure himself of a celestial organ, subject to divine visitations, but he perceived a verŷ solid Church buttressing the society of his country. The Church of his England was the Church of his Royalist ancestors, the Church of Sir William Temple, the Church of King William, the Church of Irish Whigs and English Tories. The first act of a Christian Englishman was the decision between Whig and Tory, but between the Church of England and her rivals there could be no doubt. The Whigs had saved the State and brought the glorious Revolution. Under Sir William's roof, Whig he must remain, though Whiggery tended to monstrous Dissent, to Deists, Socinians, Muggletonians, Presbyterians and the like. He needed a Bishopric, the Church needed a Champion. To be a Church-Champion, he must hold Tory principle, but sufficient unto the day the Whiggery thereof, and he knew how to abide his time. If he could not love Fellow-Churchmen, he could at least hate and hammer Dissenters. When he came out of his tent or vestry, they would know upon which side was Jonathan. Absurd and pedantic were the niceties of theology, "the lumber of the Schools," but there was an Establishment of which Statesmen and men of the world were kindly to take notice, and, if they did not, it was for Jonathan to teach them!

Jonathan had discovered or suspected that the two most important things in life were sex and religion; the mother Church of a man's soul, and the would-be mother of a man's progeny. He had already cleared his mind on both points. He was not unready with his decisions when either crossed his career. A parson-uncle called John Kendall had recently heard of his improved prospect with Sir William and, recalling a light-of-love of Jonathan's in Leicester, had written warning against precipitate marriage. But Jonathan had taken measure of man's angelic helpmate, and by close observations chased matrimonial visions from his mind.

It is not necessary to believe that he was inno-

cent or made no trial of those adolescent adventures which are happily sunk in marriage. His
own correspondence shows traces which he would
have wished buried. In 1729, a generation later,
he asked a friend to inquire about the daughter of
Betty Jones, an old Leicester flame.

> "My prudent mother was afraid I should be
> in love with her; but when I went to London,
> she married an inn-keeper in Loughborough,
> in that county, by whom she had several
> children. This woman, my mistress with a
> pox, left one daughter, Anne by name. This
> Anne, for it must be she, about seven years ago
> writ to me from London, to tell me she was
> daughter of Betty Jones, for that was my mis-
> tress's name."

And in 1733 he told his printer of a rascal in
possession of letters he had written to a Mrs. Davys
and her husband. If there was a hint of blackmail,
he forestalled the celebrated answer of a Duke to
"publish and be damned," for he wrote:

> "I believe I writ to her four or five after she
> was a widow and at Cambridge and generally
> some present was mentioned. Pray desire him
> to restore them to you to burn them and, if he
> will not, let him do what he pleases, being only
> the common amusements of young people."

To Uncle Kendall he replied with the cold calculation of a demon preparing to take Holy Orders

that he was so hard to please he would put off
marriage to the other world. As for playing with
love:

> "I could remember twenty women in my life
> to whom I behaved myself just the same way;
> and I profess without any other design than
> that of entertaining myself when I am very
> idle, or when something goes amiss in my
> affairs. This I always have done as a man of
> the world, when I had no design for any thing
> grave in it, and what I thought at worst a
> harmless impertinence. But, whenever I be-
> gin to take sober resolutions, or, as now, to
> think of entering into the Church, I never
> found it would be hard to put off this kind of
> folly at the porch."

Twenty women were an easier weight to drop at
the Church porch than one. Their mixed memory
would not trouble his single-hearted dream of preferment. Sir William would prove harder to
drop. Writing Sir William's *Memoirs* was like
writing a play in which the actors were dead and
the plot long spun. He asked Sir William frankly
of his prospects, and Sir William, being little
inclined to present so useful a servitor to so useless
an institution as the Church, delayed him, and
delayed. But to make some show of generosity he
offered him office in Ireland under the Master of
the Rolls, a sinecure of a hundred and twenty
pounds a year.

Sir William was relying on Jonathan's hatred of life in Ireland, but Jonathan, coolly repressing his sullen fury, snatched at the entangling net as though it were a life-rope and declared: "Since I am offered now the opportunity of living without being driven into the Church, I am resolved to go to Ireland and to take Holy Orders."

Sir William's face mantled with the peculiar rage of the aged when thwarted by the young. He expressed anger that Jonathan should slip a second time from his shelter, when he had no further use for a port out of storm. But Jonathan's timidity had preceded his own departure and he felt mighty and tyrannical powers moving him. For the first time in his life he answered his old patron word for word, wrath for wrath, an eye for an eye and much the fiercer was Jonathan's.

The next day a young gentleman, though a spoiled one, in Jonathan's own opinion, set forth on his travels in search of a religious position which he could support spiritually and which would support him with temporalities in return.

At Leicester he called his first halt to stay with his mother. There he found a letter from a cousin in trade with Portugal telling of life in Lisbon, of religious processions and witch-burning. Jonathan felt no aversion to processions, as he answered:

"But your burning the old woman, unless
she were a duenna, I shall never be reconciled
to; though it is easily observed that nations
which have most gallantry to the young, are
ever the severest upon the old."

For the moment he desired to travel abroad and
craved the chaplaincy in his cousin's factory, once
he could persuade some Irish Bishop to confer
celestial powers upon him. To Ireland (it was
always Ireland in his life) and to Ireland's bleak
shore he struggled back like an orphan to his step-
mother. This was in June, but October found him
with diminished funds and hopes paying court to
the Irish Bishops, who asked less return of his
home learning than an account of his conduct
abroad. To the Archbishop of Dublin, the vener-
able Dr. Narcissus March, he appealed for Ordination before he was flung friendless and penniless
on those hateful streets. His Grace contemplated
this eager, half-handsome, heavy-faced youth, and,
unable to penetrate the mask, asked frankly for a
certificate from the hand of Sir William Temple.
Jonathan read the thought and blushed angrily.
The Archbishop seemed as doubtful of Jonathan's
behavior as Uncle Kendall. Jonathan withdrew,
knowing that he had no chance for Ordination
except by writing Sir William the abject letter of
a runaway servant-maid requiring a character

from her old mistress. And he had hoped to be rid of the Temples for ever. He had sickened of writing Odes on his patron's sicknesses and recoveries. Nevertheless he sat down to write like a dog requesting to be whipped:

"I entreat that your Honour will consider this, and will please to send me some certificate of my behaviour during almost three years in your family; wherein I shall stand in need of all your goodness to excuse my many weaknesses and follies and oversights, much more to say any thing to my advantage. The particulars expected of me are what relate to morals and learning, and the reasons of quitting your Honour's family, that is, whether the last was occasioned by any ill actions. They are all entirely left to your Honour's mercy."

Jonathan's letter caused considerable interest at Moor Park. So the fledged hawklet had struck his wild head against invisible glass! Martha Giffard read it with pleasurable scorn and exultation. She was pleased by so penitential a document. But her brother was moved with pity for his impetuous scribe. So softly-worded a letter turned aside whatever rested from the wrath of parting. He had had time to reconsider their relations and in spite of their quarrel he no longer blamed Jonathan. He missed him too much. He realized that his own life of leisure, retirement and tradition could not satisfy a fierce younger spirit, desirous to make sin and folly bleed. If there was little sin, there was no folly at Moor Park, and the young satirist had had to go abroad to seek the predestined subjects for his bludgeon. For Sir William with both feet planted in the past and Jonathan with one stretching into the future, there was little common ground except the narrow ever-perishing strip of sand, which horologers call the present. Sir William missed his rough-grained amanuensis and in secret cried out for Jonathan. The letter touched him to act.

Sir William did not hesitate to use all his influence with Bishops and to write with that Essayist's skill of which he was so proud. The effect upon Jonathan's fortunes was immediate. Before the month of October Jonathan was ordained a Deacon. It was now but a question of taking a step at a time. In January he was raised to the Orders of a Priest and pushed northward into a little curacy at Kilroot. Independence was won at every cost, even of exile. Jonathan found himself on the bleak and dreary shores of Belfast Lough, so called from the miserable little fishing village and post-town lying on the mud-delta of the Lagan. Dreary and bleak as was Nature, it was rendered even more so by an infusion of black-faced Scotch Pres-

byterian sheep, who in spite of the vigorous
admonitions and hammerings of Bishops Leslie
and King had declined to enter Episcopal folds.
At Jonathan's cassock they immediately sniffed
askance and he returned the sniveling suspicions
of Dissent with the thorough detestation of an
established Curate.

In this surrounding he took refuge with gentry
representing the elegant orthodox.   There was
Squire Dobbs, from whom he could borrow books,
and the Mayor of Carrickfergus and My Lord and
Lady Donegal, who had settled in their Castle on
the Lough.   In and out of this brilliant society he
flashed, whenever he could ride away from his
miserable parish.   Whenever leaving such company, he commemorated in a note-book the most
memorable jest or stupidity to cross his delicate
drums. He still practised Letters. In his leisure he
turned over and corrected a singular manuscript he
had brought from Moor Park, entitled *The Tale
of a Tub* after the pretty conceit that mariners
would throw a tub into the waves to make play for
a pursuing whale.   This tale was a religious
allegory and Jonathan took occasion to draw and
insert a Presbyterian caricature from Irish models.
Behind the roar of the winds and the plash of the
soft rains and the cries of the sea-mews; he struggled to recreate and refurbish his book until a

desolation of loneliness seemed to descend and drown him with his books and his parish and his ambitions. Moor Park seemed lost Paradise.

He was fain for company to ride into Belfast to talk with an old College friend, Waring. He clung to his comforting friendship and, when Miss Jane Waring appeared as hostess on the scene, his conjured spirit swallowed her enchantments. Day after day he rode through dust or mud, in rain-time or sun-time, to tempt her with a share in his hundred-pound living or in the yet unmeasured talents of his mind. Against the wild and somber scenery the questing intellect of Jonathan sought a field for domestic romance. Miss Jane Waring he proceeded to idealize, idolize and even to Latinize. In his fancy she became the goddess Varina. His intellect became harnessed to his heart. Prospect and preferment melted into the mists of Belfast Bay. Irish rains rusted his ambition's keen edge. Liberty of heart and head he laid at Varina's scornful feet.

Weeks passed into weeks, but Varina trod or danced upon any immediate happiness. Jonathan prepared to suffer. Varina's fortune was small, but he hoped they might subsist on combined revenues and enjoy the usufruct of bliss into the bargain. But he soon found he had a rival, dunce enough to be endowed with five thousand a

year. With keen agony he realized early that holy
truth, which is engravable in bronze over every
temple, in which marriages are registered or celebrated, that "any man had better have a poor angel
to rival than the devil himself, if he were rich."

Months passed into months, and Varina became
as chilly as the Antrim mists. Jonathan writhed
on his own anvil, awaiting the hammer of fate. He
longed to bring matters to decision and crisis. The
matrimony even of the clergy he knew was not a
concern of Providence. Heaven might be expected to provide his daily bread but not his
nightly companion. Heaven assigned Bishops
their Sees but left them to choose their wives. The
idealized Varina floated rainbow-wise through his
lonely vision, but when he visualized the squalor
and squabble of married life, he found a power
great enough to check his fancy. "Matrimony has
many children," he recorded, "Repentance, Dis-
cord, Spleen, Loathing." Nevertheless he desired
Varina and awaited the sign or design of fate.

The sign came from England, like a bolt from
the *Deus ex Machina,* cutting his wedding knot
before it was tied. His old god, Sir William, invited him to return to Moor Park, offering to find
him a better living in England. Meantime there
were papers and legacies awaiting Jonathan if he
cared to resume work in the library.

Demonial vigor stirred Jonathan. He would
capture Varina or return captive himself to Moor
Park. If he could not nest with Varina on these
northern shores, he would fly back to his comfortable book-lined bower in Surrey. He dispatched
a sudden ultimatum, such as commanders dispatch
to beleaguered cities, to inform her that renewal of
his ancient acquaintanceship with the great had
been offered him. In a fortnight he would leave
Ireland never to return, even as Lord Deputy, unless Varina surrendered to his passion. With
fierce strokes of his pen he challenged her pretense
of love:

> "The love of Varina is of more tragical con-
> sequence than her cruelty. Would to God you
> had treated and scorned me from the begin-
> ning. It was your pity opened the first way
> to my misfortune; and now your love is finish-
> ing my ruin. . . .
> . . . Is it possible you cannot be yet insen-
> sible to the prospect of a rapture and delight so
> innocent and so exalted? Trust me, Varina,
> Heaven has given us nothing else worth the
> loss of a thought. Ambition, high appear-
> ance, friends, and fortune, are all tasteless and
> insipid when they come in competition; yet
> millions of such glorious minutes we are per-
> petually losing, for ever losing, irrecoverably
> losing, to gratify empty forms and wrong
> notions."

With torch alight in hand Jonathan rode for a
fall and, before Varina had time to realize his burning onslaught, he had quenched his fire and escaped
to England. He had offered her all and been
refused all. He was free to turn his thoughts elsewhere and Varina was left thinking and thinking
beside the shores of Belfast.

His prebend he had no difficulty in shouldering
upon a poorer friend with a family. He returned
to England so quickly that his surplus books and
papers fell to his successor Mr. Winder, to whom
he sent word to return at least to Mr. Dobbs a
"piece of fustian virtuoso rubbish" and, as a friend
to one befriending, and a cleric to a brother, he
requested the destruction of a certain packet of
love-letters left behind. "I remember those letters
to Eliza. They were writ in my youth. Please
burn them."

To Moor Park he came once again, but not as a
servant or hired scrivener. The Reverend Jonathan could preen himself a Chaplain and behave
as an invited guest and accepted friend of the old
Statesman. The social magic of Holy Orders had
begun to work. Winder apprised him of Varina's
affairs and with a light heart Jonathan sang back:
"You mention a dangerous rival for an absent
lover; but I must take my fortune."

VI

THE BATTLE OF THE BOOKS

(1697)

FORTUNE may not be forced. Even while Jonathan was resigning his Irish preferment to rejoin Sir William Temple, Temple's friend Sutherland fell from office and with him fell Sir William's influence and Jonathan's hopes. It was the return of a chastened and sullen Angel to Paradise. Once again Jonathan found himself in the only home that was ever his. Sir William was there happy to welcome him, and Lady Giffard's garrulous parrot, Laura, and the raucous rooks in the windy trees and little Hetty, now full-sprung to girlhood, joined in the chorus. Jonathan strolled delightedly round the house and upon an elm-tree he cut a Latin inscription commending the tree to Sir William's successors—FACTURA NEPOTIBUS UMBRAM.

Thanks to the black coat and white bands which he wore punctiliously, Jonathan was treated to the honors of the cloth without duties additional to his

90

labors in the library. Sir William was quiet enough in his conscience not to need professional ministry. He practised a reverent unbelief in matters metaphysical. He was willing to be told that Heaven was a Garden, the Deity a Gardener who sowed stars like seed and the Angels not only reapers but good weeders. Perchance the soul, if soul existed, was like a Dutch bulb. Perchance Paradisal flowers would crown the dullest buried life. Sir William's use for a parson was at the card table, where evening after evening Jonathan sat with Hetty and Lady Giffard, while the retired diplomatist threw pennies on the table to encourage the laughing gamblers. Jonathan's formal duties were slight. He read prayers to the servants, especially one which Sir William had ironically framed to include the views of all sects and dissidents in his household. And Hetty was not yet ready for Confirmation.

Nevertheless Jonathan felt she was not unready for the laying on of Curate's hands. When he glimpsed her on his return, his breath had bounded in his throat. Her beauty had become extreme. Her features were clean-cut and white, crowned with raven black hair. Her fifteen-year-old purity absorbed his turgid and swollen thoughts like sediment run through a fresh spring. She had become more than a pupil and less than a sister. She was

a companion ready to exchange dalliance of speech
or to meet and parry his rising powers of masculine
mockery.

His mind was no longer virginal. Varina had
plowed her furrow sharp and short, but it was
Hetty who scattered the tiny seeds, and to Hetty
he inwardly promised the harvest somewhere in the
future, when the *Battle of Books* had been fought
and his last preferment gained. He enjoyed his
easy dominance of her grace. To his care and
nurture she promised all the return that mind could
make. He was not afraid to let his imagination
move in her company. He showed her glimpses
sometimes of original thoughts, which he concealed
from Sir William. If they were not understood,
they were never misunderstood. Sometimes he
seemed to affright her a little but never to disgust
her. Almost he seemed to be guiding that little
marble-white hand up the ladder of his brain, so
quickly she responded and followed and left him
behind. Almost he felt her little feet ascending the
spirals of a mind whose summit he had never
reached himself. High as he reached, she always
flitted above and beyond like some pale Evening
Star, the Stella before which the garish sunset of
Varina sank rapidly in the west.

Jonathan found his patron in the throes of the
literary storm, which had been gathering since Sir

William had published his celebrated Essay esteem-
ing Ancient above Modern writers. This was the
theme which had rent France even more than the
wars of Louis. In every country the Moderns and
the Ancients found parties and partisans, since
Learning was international. Jonathan had been
well acquainted with Sir William's theory that
Moderns lived on borrowing and plagiary, while
the Ancients sat impassible and unsurpassable on
Parnassian heights. Sir William had gravely
carried his theory to all limits possible. The music
of Orpheus, which had charmed birds and rocks,
was obviously superior to modern music, which
charmed neither man nor beast. As for modern
astronomy, the Greeks had predicted eclipses, and
had Harvey surpassed Hippocrates in Medicine?
As for authors, the most ancient were the best as
shown in the Fables of Æsop or the surpassing
genius of the Letters of Phalaris. Sir William's
challenge to pedants had remained so unanswerable
that the scholars of Oxford felt they could safely
rally the rival University of Cambridge from behind his sure shield of erudition. The young and
noble Mr. Boyle, the pupil of Dean Atterbury of
Christ Church, constructed an edition of Phalaris
and threw not only Sir William by name into the
medley but cleverly piqued the **Cambridge**
champion of Modernism, **Dr. Bentley.**

Behind this preposterous Doctor had arisen the precocious Mr. Wotton, who poured scorn upon Sir William's Essay and divined the new experimental sciences, upon which the Moderns were rising sky-high above the dusty past. Not only were Sir William's theories trampled with juvenile scorn but the Phalarian Epistles were proved stupid forgeries, a fraudulent fiction confounding Ode with Elegy and employing Attic instead of Dorian Greek. It was a mortifying blow for Sir William Temple, but Knights Templar were coming to his defense.

Jonathan did not know whether his patron was wrong or right. He had doubts about Phalaris himself. Modern Medicine and Astronomy were formidable in their claims, blood circulating, fixed stars moving! Newton and Harvey were upon the horizon, but the old Classics were impregnable and he felt that he could defend Virgil and Sir William with the same blow. Boyle and Bentley were exchanging monumental wrangles. Oxford and Cambridge were in inky arms. Jonathan raced through the contending literature. A French account of a battle between Ancients and Moderns gave him ideas. Jonathan looked for the most foolish to make bleed the deepest. Then he leaped into the lists. Let Oxford save the cause of Phalaris! He would at least prick the bloated

Dean Swift's Cradle

Preserved at Brede Church in Sussex. It came from the sale of the Honorable W. Hastings at Stratford House, Worcestershire, and was bought in 1884, by the grandfather of the present Rector of Brede, the Reverend C. Frewer

insolence of Cambridge. Taking broader ground
than that of combatant, he would bring the antago-
nists of the whole combat to book. He would be the
Homer of this battle and incidentally save Sir William's fame from perilous collapse. If Pelion was
piled upon Ossa and the knowledge of Oxford upon
the ignorance of Cambridge, it would be no harm
for a stripling scholar to add a few pebbles from
his sling.

While he sat with his skull abubbling and dreaming in the old library, the very books came to life
in spite of their lifeless contents. Like the tomb-
stones depicted quaking under the Last Trumpet,
the covers of books arose under summons of Criticism and their pages fluttered with long imprisoned
thoughts. The theological among them thundered
anathemas, the epical chanted, the lyrical sang and
the polemical went verily to war in that day when
shelf was upraised against shelf, when Folios
fought Folios and Folly fell upon Folly. Jonathan took Sir William for his protecting god and
entered battle with visor closed as firmly as his
patron to the great Esquires of Science, to Newton
and to Locke, who were ranging silently with Bentley. Bentley the irreproachable had fallen heavily
already upon the irrepressible Boyle, while against
the irresistible Wotton gaily charged Jonathan the
irresponsible.

Fierce was that carnage of covers and well-contested were the individual passages between pages, cut being surely given for cut, while many a proud tome sank to the bookworms. Over the dust of battle Jonathan laughed aloud, describing the critics of Sir William in grotesque array. Wotton he likened to some child of the horrible goddess Criticism, who lived in Nova Zembla's snows devouring books. Pride and Ignorance were her parents and her brood included Impudence and Dullness, Vanity and Pedantry. Wotton was naturally enlisted with Sir William's special bugbear and bookbane, Bentley, at whose patchwork armor and rusty helm and crooked leg and hump, the Moderns could not forbear to laugh Homerically. Then Homer and Virgil like Horsemen of Apocalypse rode down the paltry Moderns. In a momentous moment did Virgil meet his own translator Dryden, and Jonathan laughed aloud to contemn his old contemner. In armor too capacious and over-helmeted Dryden appeared "like the lady in a lobster or like a mouse under a canopy of state or like a shriveled beau from within the penthouse of a modern periwig." Faster waxed the fight and fun in Jonathan's skull, as he played like some giant with marionettes, who in their day had conceived their stature so great. Paralyzed by his own Allegory, Jonathan allowed his rushing

spate of imagery to carry him where it listed.
Against Bacon Aristotle drew bow, but his arrow
only pierced the pasteboard of Descartes "till death
like a star of superior influence, drew him into his
own vortex." Cunningly Jonathan mixed mocking satire of contemporaries with high Homerical
phrases. Came Davenant and Denham the modern
poets; Davenant as his own "Gondibert" with intent to spoil Homer, who slew them both, but from
Denham "Apollo took the celestial part and made
it a star but the terrestrial lay wallowing upon the
ground." Then Dryden and Virgil met and agreed
to exchange horses, but at the trial Dryden feared
to mount. Still the battle raged and Homer's
horse with a kick slew the insufferable Wesley and
all his ten books of ridiculous heroics. And Pindar
slew Mrs. Afra Benn the Amazon, while Cowley
with his mock Pindarics only averted Pindar's
spear upon the shield given to him by Venus, for
the sake of his love poetry to his Mistress.

But with his sword Pindar clove Cowley in twain
and one half of him Venus washed in ambrosia and
touched with amaranth, so that "the leather grew
round and soft and the leaves turned into feathers
and being gilded before continued gilded still, so it
became a dove and she harnessed it to her chariot."

Gathering all his wit and memory, Jonathan
brought the battle to comical climax. Bentley ad-

vanced with "vizard of brass which tainted by his breath, corrupted into copperas nor wanted gall from the same fountain." His lips distilled an atramentous quality and he grasped a flail in his right and worse in his left. But this brutal railing Bentley, who became as dangerous to his own leaders as a wounded elephant, was somewhat of the ideal that Jonathan fancied for himself in future battles upon fields broader than libraries and among contestants more living than books.

Collecting his beloved Wotton, Bentley essayed to spoil the armor of Æsop and Phalaris while they slept. So Bentley went, "in his van Confusion and Amaze while Horror and Afright brought up the rear." Wotton meantime found Temple himself at the Parnassian spring, but feared to meet one that "fights like a god," for "Pallas or Apollo are ever at his elbow." Wotton grazed Temple with his lance, and Apollo, assuming the shape of Dean Atterbury, descended to urge Boyle toward the fight. Boyle pursued Wotton into the arms of Bentley, laden with the arms of Phalaris which Boyle had lately with his own hands new-polished and gilded. At one thrust he pierced them both.

"As when a skilful cook has trussed a brace of woodcocks, he, with iron skewer pierces the tender sides of each, both their legs and wings close pinioned to their ribs, so was this pair of friends transfixed till down they fell, joined in their lives, joined in their deaths; so closely joined that Charon will mistake them both for one and waft them over Styx for half the fare." Thus Jonathan filled with Homeric grandiloquence and pseudo-mockery and scintillating scorn closed the measures of his Epic. "Farewell, beloved pair," he concluded in mockery, "immortal shall you be, if all my wit and eloquence can make you."

As Jonathan read over his work to Sir William and watched the smiles which relieved that pale and mortified visage, he knew that his work was good and that unto his pen was given Rhadamanthine and Amaranthine powers: to judge or to immortalize.

VII

THE TALE OF A TUB

(1697-1699)

Sir William never felt the same toward Jonathan after he had read his *Battle of Books*. He had no doubt now of his genius and sometimes he gave a wondering glance at the black beetling-browed young cleric writing Hetty her French verbs, when he thought that the same quill had transfixed modern Pedantry alive. He admired the way in which Jonathan had taken and transmitted into myth and metaphor the very thoughts and fancies of his own mind.

Nothing delighted Sir William more than the Fable of the Spider and the Bee, into which Jonathan spun the very pith and spice of Sir William's Essay. The Spider he made a Modern type, an academical mathematician sucking dirt and poison from its many victims to produce a little flybane and venom, whereas the Classical Bee preferred to range fields of antiquity and furnish mankind with "the two noblest of things, which are sweetness and light."

Jonathan was content to wait. He was immensely soothed by his patron's pleasure. He was beginning to feel his wings spread and his claws sharpen. He felt wider powers of satire growing under him. He began to rewrite and rearrange his first manuscript. He was still content to copy and clear Sir William's *Memoirs* from their uncorrected originals. Sir William wished Jonathan's name to accompany his own as the best way to present his name to the world of letters. He did not feel that the words Jonathan Swift would cause to quicken or quiver that public, to whom the unknown or the magnificent made appeal. Sir William Temple's name carried a certain magnificence. He himself would wait in the unknown.

He had reached powers of body and mind that knew not tiredness. Sentence by sentence he read aloud Sir William's *Memoirs* like a schoolboy. Like a master he slipped in correction by correction. Seldom he ventured to make a suggestion, but a passage about Sunderland he entreated Sir William to allow him to omit and the old man took his advice. To the omission of other passages he did not consent, but Jonathan bore the trouble to come for them. Ten hours a day Jonathan spent in the library reading and studying. At the end of

every two hours he stopped his labors and ran to
the top of a small hill in the neighborhood and
back. It only took six or ten minutes of his
precious time, but sent the blood tearing through
veins which otherwise bookworms might have
sucked a little dry. And the days passed de-
liciously for Jonathan.

His gathering powers of ridicule and scorn had
no direct targets, but they were made content with
accumulating toil and varied by voyages and
adventures into books. For human company he
lived his life between Sir William and the maiden
Hetty; all that was amiable and experienced in one
sex and all that was inexperienced and even more
amiable in the other.

When Sir William took Hetty to town to have
a glimpse of the Czar of Muscovy, Jonathan felt
quite lonely, though he enjoyed being left in charge
and ordering himself a dish of pigeons from Sir
William's cook and scribbling chaff to London.
He pretended that the Czar was in love with Hetty
and bade her get muffs and sable tippets suitable
for that icy clime. Nothing more exciting had
occurred at Moor Park except a gale among the
elms, and Jonathan reported that "Æolus has made
a strange revolution on the rooks' nests." Wind
had blown into Jonathan's skull lately and he was
playing with the theme that man was mostly wind

and that the religious, certainly Enthusiasts and Dissenters, were of the wind windy.

Meantime he had passed afield into the universe of books. He began with the lugubrious Fathers of the Church, with Cyprian and Irenæus. He attended the Council of Trent with Sarpi. Argument about sin and synod, about dogma and catechism with their cat-and-dog scuffling was not lost upon a mind with a predilection for punning. He came more gladly to true history. The recorded follies and failings of men interested him more than the idealized and idolized emotions of a Deity like Æolus—the King of the Winds himself.

He came back with pleasure to the Classics. To Virgil and Homer he lay anchored. Thrice he read the Epic of the serene and religious destroyer of deity and universal constructor of atoms, Lucretius. French he learned from Sir William to read like a Gallic native, though he wrote it in the style of a hedge parson. He could read Montaigne, that delicate Essayist, who seemed at Moor Park to be a French counterpart of Sir William himself. Father Rabelais Sir William read but not aloud, though Jonathan expanded both his lung and his style reciting passages from that mighty animal Gospel written unto all stout and hearty habitants of the earth earthy. Fontenelle's *Dialogues of the Dead* was a rare treat and Galland's *Arabian*

Nights in French revealed new worlds of tale-
telling. Forsooth if ever he was allowed to preach,
Jonathan felt his sermons would be patched with
strange and rich stuffs.

The more he read of History and reality, the
more he detested Theology. The more he traveled
into fancy, the less he wished to stay at home in
the narrow ruts of sermonizing. Sermons were
like gruel with a little brimstone, insufficient to
make sin or folly bleat or bleed!

From the shelf of the Historians he passed to the
Geographers and the makers of Voyages. Far
more wonderful than Burnet's *History of the
Reformation* and the *Memoirs* of the Prince of
Orange were Bernier's *History of the Kingdom of
the Great Mogul* and the Jesuit Tachard's *Journey
into Siam*. He read all and noted all. The Voyages caught him imaginatively and enabled him to
sail away from Moor Park, Surrey, England and
Europe even. He liked to stand clear outside the
narrow latitudes into which he had been cast. The
cant talk about sin and repentance enraged him.
He could not somehow believe in the perfections of
European religion, English law, Jacobite politics
or even Whigs!

He felt detestation for whatsoever things are
petty, morose, sentimental, metaphysical or stupid.
Concrete instances of all hung like stalactites or

grew like mushrooms about him. Jacobites were clinging to a divine right of a line of Kings. It was all wrong and the Non-jurors, who would not swear to King William, were as stupid and sentimental as the Catholics, who clung to the divine right of the Bishops in Rome. It was all pretense and Pretenderdom. He wished and aimed to be a Bishop himself, but an enlightened Bishop at one with men of Letters and men of the State without the shield of a consecrated periwig. It was good common sense for the English State to select her King and choose her Bishops; but it was enlightening to learn from Sir William what manner of mankind the State accepted for Churchmen and Statesmen. In making riddance of religious and political cant, Jonathan felt no drag nor prick upon his conscience. Conscience he felt to be an organ of which the sensible intellect had no need. As for the controversies of religion between the Catholics and the Calvinists or against both, it was the warfare of windmills milling against windmills.

One sermon out of thousands had often taken his fancy in Sir William's library and he amused himself embroidering the theme into his *Tale of a Tub*. It was the famous sermon preached by Doctor Sharp against Popery, for which poor old King James had ordered Sharp's suspension. It had made Sharp a Protestant hero and set him climbing

the ladder of English Bishoprics as high as York.
Sharp's idea of Christendom as an estate left by
Testament to several sons, one of whom arrogantly
claimed the whole patrimony, appealed to Jonathan immensely. According to the allegory the
sole claimant termed his brothers bastards or schis-
matics for basing their lawsuit or controversy upon
the text of their Father's Will. The idea grew in
Jonathan's brain and he stole Sharp's pulpit-
thumping to make some solider thunder of his own.

He divided his satire between modern pedants
and ancient superstitions. He personified the
Catholic Church by Peter, the English by Martin
and the Calvinist by Jack, all sons of One Heavenly
Father. For seven years like the primitive Christians they had respected their Father's Will, which
left them each a plain and sober suit of clothes,
until they conceived the universe itself as only a
suit and took to lace and colored vesture, making
religion as flashy as modern learning.   Church
history, the dullest dry dust in the world, became
a fairy-tale under Jonathan's pen. The brethren
tampered with the Will to find excuses for wearing
shoulder knots, and, like the theologians who
deduced Purgatory from Apocrypha, Jonathan
described the brothers embroidering a Codicil,
which allowed them "a pretty sort of flame-
colored satin for linings." This was easier reading

than the Council of Trent, and as for the Reformation, he sketched how Peter turned out his
brethren and began to live like a Lord and to "take
three old high-crowned hats three-story high with
a huge bunch of keys at his girdle and an angling
rod in his hands," until things went from worse to
worse and caused "that great and famous rupture
which was never afterward made up."

When the ousted brethren obtained a copy of
the Will, they trimmed their raiment to their
former sobriety, but Jack went further than Martin and ripped Peter's livery from his coat, "so that
he looked like a drunken beau, half-rifled by bullies
or like a fresh tenant of Newgate when he has
refused the payment of garnish or like a discovered
shop-lifter left to the mercy of Exchange women
or like a bawd in her old velvet petticoat resigned
into the secular hands of the *mobile*."

Chucklingly Jonathan drove each simile like a
pricking pin into the gaunt Belfast Presbyterians,
who had worried his little episcopal pasture at Kilroot; described how Jack took a windy and
over-literal sense of his Father's Will, in which he
found "the philosopher's stone and the universal
medicine," to be used as a nightcap or an umbrella,
excluding everything but "the phrase of the Will"
and insisting "that a wise man was his own
lanthorn." Refusing outside guidance, Jack ex-

uded by way of preaching "a soporiferous medicine to be conveyed in at the ears. It was a compound of sulphur and Balm of Gilead with a little pilgrim's salve."

The result of likeness between rags and finery was that Jack and Peter were mistaken for each other. Catholic and Calvinist were equally convicted and pilloried in Jonathan's screed. He sent both trundling and toiling as it were up the hill carrying pails of Boyne and Holy Water and tumbling down the hill between them.

It was not only other people's Religion, which earned his scorn but other people's Learning, and he continued to fight the *Battle of the Books* in his Digressions to the Tub. What is Wisdom? he asked as though Solomon had risen from the grave in the glory of an Irish Curate. Jonathan's penshaft swarmed with answers:

"Wisdom is a fox who after long hunting will at last cost you the pains to dig out.

"It is a cheese, which by how much the richer has the thicker, the homelier, the coarser coat and whereof to a judicious palate the maggots are best.

"It is a sack-posset wherein the deeper you go you will find it the sweeter.

"Wisdom is a hen whose cackling we must value and consider if it is attended with an egg.

"But then lastly it is a nut, which unless you chose with judgment may cost you a tooth and pay you with nothing but a worm."

Squires and farmers around Moor Park would understand Jonathan explaining Wisdom. Between chapters he renewed his onslaught upon the Moderns, poking perpetual fun at the gaunt periwigged Doctor Bentley and at Cousin Dryden, who, as he remarked, "has often said to me in confidence that the world would never have suspected him to be so great a poet if he had not assured them so frequently. . . ."

Jonathan let himself go laughing secretly at all things in Heaven and earth. The Universe after all was but a suit of clothes and the Deity a scarecrow. Besides "what is land but a fine coat faced with green or the sea but a waistcoat of watertabby"? Even the foliage of the trees followed fashions, for "among the vegetable beaux, observe how sparkish a periwig adorns the head of a beech and what a fine doublet of white satin is worn by the birch." Men wore clothes over body and soul. "Is not religion a cloak, honesty a pair of shoes worn out in the dirt, self-love a surtout, vanity a shirt and conscience a pair of breeches?" And the quick ensuing thought was irresistible, however devastating. "If certain ermines and furs be placed in a certain position, we style them a Judge

and so an apt conjunction of lawn and black satin
we entitle a Bishop." It was a daring shot. Perhaps Jonathan felt that a physician should apply
the hot iron to himself and that a satirist should not
hesitate to brand his own profession, if Bishop he
was to be. But Jonathan was not thinking of
readers as he worked over his work and over and
over again. He added an Introduction beginning:
"Whoever has an ambition to be heard in a crowd
must press and squeeze and thrust and climb . . .
it being as hard to get quit of Number as of Hell."
Though he seemed to associate the majority in
numbers to Hell, no ideas of Hell or of Number
held a clear place in his uncobwebbed mind. He
pointed out how fostering and finding attention
was best gained by taking a mystical number in
every part of nature and among the rest the profound number THREE is that "which has most
employed my sublimest speculations." Attention
from the crowd could be commanded by several
Oratorical Machines such as the Pulpit, the Ladder
and the Stage. Pulpits were best made of Scotch
fir, and the closer their resemblance to the Pillory,
the mightier their influence upon human ears. The
Pillory pointed to the Gallows, from whose ladders
condemned men were wont to utter "the choicest
treasury of our British eloquence."

From life Jonathan felt something savage and

bitter fill his gall and he looked round for an occasional word or idea as coarse and cruel as anything in life itself.   He resumed his sartorial theme and pressed it to nakedness and beyond.   Not content with ripping away the clothes, in which men's souls and bodies shivered, he tore the very human flesh and ironically remarked to show how preferable the outward in all matters was to the inner: "Last week I saw a woman flayed and you will hardly believe how much it altered her person for the worse!"   Almost he sensed a future reader of words wince or some lover of women grow sick.

Nor did he spare analysis to his own mind, which, given spur and bridle, "doth never stop but naturally sallies out into both extremes of high and low, of good and evil," and passed to the most perfect before falling into the lowest depth, "like one who travels the East into the West or like a straight line drawn by its own length into a circle." His own Fancy he pictured falling like a dead Bird of Paradise to the ground and traced that "tincture of malice in our natures, which makes us fond of furnishing every bright idea with its reverse." After climbing to God we imagine the Devil. "They have seldom forgot to provide their fears with certain ghastly notions, which instead of better have served them pretty tolerably for a Devil," as though the Beatific Vision was more enjoyable when "equally terrified with the dismal prospect of the precipice below."

Away Jonathan soared and swung through the void, and, whether he sighted Satan or his own ambitions threading space like a dead Bird of Paradise, he certainly came to enjoy "the dismal prospect" after his manner.

The *Tale of a Tub* included a stretch of Universal Sea, as well as the original barrel, by which the author sought to make play with the Leviathans of Pedantry. The rush of waves corresponded to the churning sentences and ideas eddying from Jonathan's brain. When he contemplated his own saline and brilliant bubbling in the sea of his own creative mind, he modestly mentioned "the author of this miraculous treatise" and concluded: "I shall here pause awhile, till I find by feeling the world's pulse and my own that it will be of absolute necessity for us both to resume my pen."

Sir William's quick sense of style was touched by this unexpected product of his own library, which was almost the begotten child of his own mind. His keen and experienced sight into the frauds and fooleries of men was pricked by the recited manuscript. Often he recognized more than his own table talk; his secret thought reflected like color caught upon a glass and held by

the glazier's art. He sometimes suggested a modification but of radical alteration he was unwilling.
He was only worried foreseeing the public effect
of the profane touches mingled with so much salt.
Divines and Bishops could not fail to smart under
so much logic and coarse common sense. That
believers were simpletons Divine Writ and human
opinion agreed. Reason could be as fatally applied
in defense of religion as against. This, Jonathan
had achieved. Sir William smiled and sighed and
then he smiled again.

Jonathan only smiled, for he felt the transport of
genius rising out of its egg and, much as he
hankered to preen his fresh-hatched feathers in the
gilding rays of fame and success, he consented to
wait in deference to the goddess called Preferment.

Sir William hardly tired, listening to a *Tale*
which crystallized or delivered so many of his ideas
into winged words. But he was worldly shrewd
enough to see that Jonathan had only assailed two
Churches to the momentary advantage of the third,
which was really as much undermined as Christianity as a whole. Jonathan's Church of England
claimed to trim her sails to the wind of private
judgment, which wafted Dissenting craft, and yet
to furbish her hull with selected timbers from the
Bark of Peter. To sink Peter was to endanger the
Anglican Martin and, to ridicule the winds of

Inspiration, was to exclude the Spirit that bloweth where it listeth. To rend the independence of Presbyterian Jack was to endanger the claims of the half-way house, which, being built neither upon the Rock nor upon the sands, appeared to occupy a golden mean. Then Jonathan had made a dangerous allusion to the number THREE, sacred in Trinitarian theology. There was a good deal, also, which might have been written by Turk or Atheist and might provide sly amusement to Jews. Jonathan's chances of preferment in the Church were in peril. It was advisable to leave the *Tale* unprinted until Jonathan's death. After that interesting event, it was not likely to hinder his promotions. Jonathan realized that it would be wise never to put name to his *Tale,* but the love of fame lingered and he inserted a melancholy passage:

"I have a strong inclination before I leave the world, to taste a blessing which we mysterious writers can seldom reach till we have gotten into our graves, whether it be that Fame, being a fruit grafted on the body, can hardly grow and much less ripen till the stock is in the earth; or whether she be a bird of prey and is lured among the rest to pursue after the scent of a carcase, or whether she conceives her trumpet sounds best and farthest when she stands on a tomb, by the advantage of a rising ground and the echo of a hollow vault."

Death he envisaged as one step in his fame, if
fame was to come, but that he had written one of
the most poised and pathetic sentences in English
scarcely crossed his mind. It was a passage which
must have struck the failing Sir William, whose
herbs could avail him no longer, though he medi-
cined himself with sage and saffron and powdered
centipedes in fresh butter for his throat. He could
no longer correct or dictate to an amanuensis with
pinions grown Mercurialwise to his scornful heels.
Sir William lay at peace and was little troubled by
thoughts of one world or another. But as one who
had made a famous Peace among nations of men,
he did not expect conflicts in Heaven. Whatever
awaited him on the other shore, he could be diplomatic. He was a man of peace and he looked
forward to a peaceable death-bed. He had once
written in accents of quiet beauty that "when all is
done, human life is, at the greatest and the best,
but like a froward child, that must be played with
and humored a little to keep it quiet, till it falls
asleep and then the care is over."

And one night in January of that year Lady
Giffard called to Jonathan that Sir William's care
at least was over. Diplomacy herself was dead.
Throwing on his black gown, Jonathan ascended
the old stairs and beheld his master lying on his
bed, as restfully as one who had been as little tor-

mented by those triune tormentors of men, Faith and Hope, and Love, as any man of his intellect and time.

Jonathan was sincerely moved, and, when he returned to his own room, he wrote "that Sir William Temple died at one o'clock this morning the 27th of January 1699 and with him all that was good and amiable among men."

VIII

(1699-1710)

DAYS followed of infinite sadness, heavy with the peace of life just ended and ambitions long abandoned. Sir William's body was carried to Westminster to be laid with other shells and shards disused from England's pageant. His heart was buried under the sun-dial of his own Dutch garden, digged into the earth like a bulb from his beloved Hague and left to flower in the mind of one faithful henchman.

Sir William's last Will and Testament fell into the hands of Lady Giffard, who briefly told Jonathan that he was left a hundred pounds and the profits of publishing Sir William's *Memoirs,* but that he must use only faithful copies. Lady Giffard, like all relations, resented any sum bequeathed to a stranger: even the lands left in Ireland to little Hetty. Death is always accompanied by the disagreeable and the ludicrous, as it were undertakers.

117

The ludicrous in this case came with the sermon preached over Sir William by a parson of the High Church, which filled Jonathan and Hetty with uncontrollable laughter. The suitability of laughter to Christian burial has never been sufficiently exposed by any Divine, or that uncomforted tears and haggard lament should be appropriated to the unbeliever's funeral and the atheist's plumeless hearse. Sir William would not have quarreled with the amusement which his rural obsequies afforded to the two nearest to his dead and buried heart.

Jonathan allowed the dead to bury the dead. Then he took the manuscript of the *Memoirs* and cleaned and cleared those disordered papers into the likeness of a book, which could properly and profitably be dedicated to the King, for the King had been Sir William's friend and the King had promised Sir William's secretary a prebend, whether of Windsor or of Canterbury.

Before leaving Moor Park for ever, Jonathan set down in writing his experience of the elderly:

"WHEN I GROW TO BE OLD—1699
Not to marry a young woman.
Not to be fond of children or let them come near me hardly."

But the last few words he erased, as though he feared to give his liberty or affection to one, who at that moment not only approached between a young woman and a child but between his ambition and his heart. He continued his scrip;

"Not to tell the same story over and over to
the same people [poor old Sir William!]
Not to keep young company unless they really
desire it. [Perhaps poor Jonathan!]
Not to be over severe with young people but
give allowance for their youthful follies
and weaknesses.
Not to boast of my former beauty or strength
or favour with ladies.
Not to hearken to flatteries nor conceive I can
be beloved by a young woman."

It was a good page to add to any matured man's prayer-book, for no man, young or old, had ever dared write as much. And he added in Latin, for fear of prying eyes, a memento to hate and avoid legacy-hunters. Was this a hint of Lady Giffard's behavior? Whatever the Temple family thought, Jonathan had not hunted legacies and his spoil was small pay for all his hours of labor on Sir William's papers. He was glad Hetty had received so solid a gift to leave her independent. Their smiles and tears had mingled lately, and though the old life and company of Moor Park was broken for ever, they seemed left together. Sir William, without writing the words in his Will, had left Hetty to Jonathan. To have disposed her formally to his

care would have been to acknowledge greater interest and possession in her than was allowable.
Whether Hetty had ever been his, she became Jonathan's. The Evening Star of his life became
auroral light to the younger. Jonathan knew himself her master, but he had resolved that he would
never make her any kind of a mistress now or ever.

Jonathan left for London, where he endeavored
to petition the King for his preferment through the
acquaintance of a Lord, but noble honor proved as
elusive as regal memory. Receiving no word by
June, Jonathan snatched an offer to accompany
Lord Berkeley as chaplain and secretary to Ireland. The fatal land and the accursed city again!

Destiny seemed to be working, for on arrival
another secured the secretaryship, and Jonathan
was left to curse to himself and read prayers to
Lady Berkeley. Nevertheless life at Dublin Castle
was pleasant and important. The young ladies
Mary and Betty delighted him. The family took
his jesting powers seriously and he took their un-
feigned piety lightly. The Lady Berkeley took
religion from her chaplain like drugs from her
doctor or a posset from an apothecary. Jonathan
was required to read every evening from the dull
and decorous Meditations of the devout but Honorable Mr. Boyle. At last enduring the task no
longer, he secretly composed a *Meditation upon a*

Broomstick, which he solemnly read to the Countess
and her household saying among many witty
things:

> "Surely man is a broomstick! Nature sent
> him into the world strong and lusty wearing
> his own hair on his head, the proper branches
> of this reasoning vegetable, until the axe of
> intemperance has lopped off his green boughs
> and left him a withered trunk."

And the powdered periwigs assumed by men,
Jonathan parodied by the false twigs of birch
proper to broomsticks, whose last days resemble
men's in being spent in slavery to women.

The parable was successfully imparted and
seriously imbibed, for folly disguised as wisdom or
wisdom as folly are equally appetizing to brighter
spirits. Jonathan had no mood to be chaplain to
any man, not even to a Lord Lieutenant. His
genius would have made better business of a
Deanery in Hell than of a Curacy of pious ladies
in Heaven. But at this moment ecclesiastical
watchers from the Birmingham Tower of Dublin
Castle perceived that the Deanery of Derry lacked
a Dean. The first preferment had been promised
to Jonathan and he might have become the
youngest Dean in Christendom, had not the same
usurping secretary accepted a thousand-pound fee
to bestow the Deanery elsewhere. Jonathan's fury

burst and, though he left his blessing with the ladies
of the Castle, he cursed Lord Berkeley and his
secretary for scoundrels and departed after writing a few ordurous verses on his noble employer.

Jonathan's attitude struck the Berkeley family.
The daughters missed the rhymes in which the
chaplain enshrined the humors of their servants'
hall. Lady Berkeley had enjoyed her *Broomstick*
and Lord Berkeley felt he had unwisely disappointed one whose nature could not brook hope
deferred. The new Dean of Derry was made to
disgorge his living at Laracor and the angry Jonathan was thrown sufficient sop to induce his return
to the Castle. The sweets of Simony being beyond
reach of his purse, he was content to accept this
quiet living, when Varina, scenting a restoration to
revenue, commenced to pester him over his former
affection. Now that his foot was planted on the
ladder and his ways were among the great, Varina
reproached him with change of style and love.

A different Jonathan awaited her advances. He
had not forgotten her scorn or forgiven her cruelty.
Of scorn and cruelty he could show himself now a
master, not a pupil or a slave. He realized that love
was a malady, and that men resorted to women to
heal them in their fever. Relief of the malady is
proved by the abatement of sighs and groans following. Marriage for love resembles the sick man

who takes a doctor into his household and can never
be rid of his healer, in sickness or in health, for
better or worse!

Jonathan accordingly dealt shortly with Varina.
Rival love he denied on the word of a Christian and
a gentleman. Attendance upon the Irish Government prevented him going to Belfast, and, as for
marriage, his education had been otherwise than
the company kept by Varina. However, he offered
her a few unengaging conditions:

> "Have you such an inclination to my person
> and humour, as to comply with my desires and
> way of living, and endeavour to make us both
> as happy as you can? Will you be ready to
> engage in those methods I shall direct for the
> improvement of your mind, so as to make us
> entertaining company for each other, without
> being miserable when we are neither visiting
> nor visited? Can you bend your love and
> esteem and indifference to others the same way
> as I do mine? Have you so much good-nature
> as to endeavour by soft words to smooth any
> rugged humour occasioned by the cross ac-
> cidents of life? Shall the place wherever your
> husband is thrown be more welcome than
> courts or cities without him?"

If he offered her the name of wife, he enforced
terms proper to a drudge, but how many unhappy
marriages might have been averted by courageous
repetition of his words!

Jonathan had considered matrimony and the wifely impediment. In later years the thought took rhyme when he

"Computes that half a parish dues
Will hardly find his wife in shoes."

To carry Varina round his neck would not assist him to climb ladders. He might afford a wife when he was a Bishop. Not to Varina alone but to all the marrying sisterhood he wrote his Pauline letter. A woman must please bend her intellect, and inclinations, passions and pastimes. She must be content to give him mental companionship without troubling for a share of bed and board. Any fool could beget children and most of them did, to judge by the numbers of humanity. He considered the frusty, old-fangled wives of the clergy and the impoverished estate of the clergy. The thought of honeymoon was sickening to his gall. He had no desire to beget children. His children would be the progeny of his genius, the brats of his brain. Ambition for freedom and fame overcame desires for Varina and one lust happily exterminated another. "Ladies make nets not cages" he once wrote. From the net of Varina his soul escaped like the bird from the fowler.

Varina had not proposed to hold him with silver shackles even. A will power, which he had trained

by fixed hours of study and exercise, came to his
assistance. He crushed bodily wishes. Not that
he was no man and could not feel like a man, but
he yearned to live life different from other men
and preferred to be a giant solitary and unmated
in the midst of a world of dwarves who marry and
give in marriage. Such a state was not irrecon-
cilable with those mysterious Scriptures which he
was expected to search rather more thoroughly than
other folk, and he recalled a strait and stark text,
bidding men make themselves celibate for the
Kingdom of Heaven's sake. Giving the text a
grim twist he preferred to be celibate at least for the
sake of his chances in this world. Varina could go
drown in Belfast Lough!

Meanwhile the old Narcissus by God's Grace,
Archbishop of Dublin, advanced him to a prebend
in St. Patrick's Cathedral, which left him free to
serve Laracor by curate or by occasional visitation
of his occasional flock. Jonathan set to work to
convert his cabin to a gentleman's residence, to
repair the low broken-shaped church and to lay out
a garden and to plant willows along the stream.
Entry into the Dublin Chapter enabled him to
claim a Doctorate of Divinity, but he was aching
for more human fields, and, when Lord Berkeley
returned to England, he accompanied him in
search of pastures new.

Restlessly Jonathan reentered the English scene.
His old mother was at Leicester still and in lodgings at Farnham he found Hetty and Mrs. Dingley
become inseparables. He advised them to emigrate
to Ireland and to live on the remarkable margin
between the price of provisions and the prevailing
interest upon money. They accepted the adventure and, though it looked like a frolic, gossip
was quelled by perfect behavior in a city whose
censure will melt the chastest ice. Jonathan, having provided a self-supporting companion for
himself in Ireland instead of a wife draining his
resources, turned his attention to politics in England. The Tories were impeaching the Whig
Lords, and Jonathan sent secretly to the Press a
parallel drawn from classical times and skipped
back to Ireland. The dedication of the Temple
Memoirs brought him a last quarrel with Lady
Giffard and a final interview with King William.
Jonathan took occasion to tell His Majesty that the
highest Tories in Ireland would make tolerable
Whigs in England.

The delicate and emaciated King was readier for
Epitaph than Epigram, and for a Kingdom where
there would be neither Whig nor Tory. The brown
was grayed in his hair and the sparkle of battle
dimmed in his eye. Asthma and smallpox had left
their wizening. Indifferent to Churches, he kept a

dry appreciation of the God who had checked, if
not sufficiently chastised the power of France. He
had not found speech silver nor silence golden.
From behind reserves of reserve he looked with
equal coldness upon favorite or opponent, upon the
flatterer or the sermonizer, on foolish servants or
knavish ministers. Men were much the same to him
unless they were Dutchmen. The King stared a
little queerly into this queer Irish clergyman, who
did not appear to be entirely usual. But he had
little to say to him and less to prefer him to. To
England he left the cloud of war and to the succeeding Princess Anne he bequeathed the successful Marlborough. He had few weeks to live. All
the emotions had been blotted out of his face—love,
fear, trust, hope. Perhaps his last hope like Sir
William's was that Paradise was a Dutch
Garden. . . .

When Jonathan returned the next year, a Queen
ruled England. The weary worn-out King had died
and with him promises to many including Jonathan. His dust was deposited in the country
which cared for him so little, and his deified legend
passed into the mythology of a country for which
he cared less. It would not have been within the
limits of expectation that that black-browed push-
ing Curate, whose disagreeableness won a certain
approval in William's disagreeable sight, would ac-

company King William one day into Ireland's
mixed Valhalla.

Meantime Jonathan's arrowy squib drawn and
disposed at a venture had stuck in Tory harness and
he found the Whig Lords Somers and Halifax as
anxious for his society as the Bishop of Salisbury,
the brilliant buzzing Burnet, to whom Jonathan's
shaft had been actually attributed. Lord Somers
was destined to great office, and Jonathan, pulling
out his old *Tale of a Tub,* inscribed his name in a
dedication of flattering comicality. Many became
liberal in promises, but Jonathan kept ground between Whigs, who seemed lethal to the Church, and
Tories, who were fatal to the State.

These were days when it was necessary to keep
one foot in each party and to live in two countries.
For the tenth time Jonathan journeyed between
England and Ireland. He could not yet say in
what party or what country he might be compelled
to settle. There was a Tory Queen and, since the
French King's recognition of the Pretender, there
was a Whig war abroad. In England Whigs were
becoming Tories to reach the Queen and in Ireland
Tories were Whigs to keep out a King. Jonathan
himself was a Whig among Tory churchmen but
among Whig Statesmen he felt Tory. He stepped
delicately.

Hetty and Mrs. Dingley were left to warm his

lodging in Dublin or his glebe at Laracor. Hetty's repute was safeguarded by Jonathan's rule never allowing himself sleep under the same roof or consortation without the presence of a third during the day. Neither in present nor in future did he envisage her as wife or mistress, and the way seemed open to swains. An impudent parson, William Tisdall, began to tamper with Hetty, who, perhaps with some secret motive, let him go far enough to ask her protector for the hand she had reserved for Jonathan. It was a hard pass for Jonathan, who could not prevent or refuse her marriage with another, since he proposed only to philander with her himself, but he wrote Tisdall good wishes and commended Tisdall's advantages to Hetty's mother:

> "Since it is held so necessary and convenient a thing for ladies to marry; and that time takes off from the lustre of virgins in all other eyes but mine."

He might have added that his opinion was shared, according to the theologians, by God.

This year of 1704 was full of chance and event for Jonathan. It was in April that he chanced the loss of Hetty. A month later he gathered courage and flung the nameless manuscript of the *Tub* to the printers. Ambition urged trial of his powers to

make women and books subservient to him. Into
the same volume he threw the *Battle of the Books*
together with a scurrilous curse upon Dissenters.
His pen was the lance of Whiggery, long-desired
but free. He had made the Whigs no promises.
The promises had all been on their side, and he
scarcely awaited their fulfilment. His course was
clear, whether they betrayed him or not. If they
did, his betrayal would be an enjoyable excuse for
betraying them. He enjoyed doubling his tracks
like a wild Irish hare. In June he doubled back
to Dublin. He was content to wait at Laracor
and plant sallies and cherries and watch trouts and
pickerels in the stream, the Tories and Whigs of
the fish world. In August came great tidings, dire
to the French and the Tories, amazing to the English Army and the Whigs. Marlborough had won
the battle of Blenheim and henceforth his giant
shadow darkened Jonathan's horizon. Jonathan
hurried to England to take stock of the new events.
The Whigs and the War would obviously continue.
The young Secretary of State, Harley, was gathering the moderate Tories into the camp of the
Whigs. Harley allowed both parties to expect his
leadership. It was Jonathan's ambition to be
caressed by both before he signally championed one,
but which one Time and Harley would show to him.
He left the lead to Harley.

Meantime low lay Jonathan, haunting taverns, and consorting with Wits, like Addison and Steele and Prior, striving to outwrite them and generally outtalking them. He found acceptance of his authorship of the *Tale of a Tub* general and generous, though his accursed parson-cousin had claimed it. He kept incredibly close eye upon the affairs of State. He watched the rift between the Lord Godolphin sagging Whigward and Mr. Harley rising Tory and listened for the buzz of the Queen Bee, *Anna Regina* herself. The Tory Queen was filling Bishoprics with High Churchmen, and Jonathan felt Harley would take the Tory line higher and higher. He sent excited word to Archbishop King of Dublin, telling how Harley was intriguing with Mrs. Masham, one of the Queen's dressers, and nearly removing Godolphin, "the greatest piece of Court-skill that has been acted these many years." So it was, but it miscarried through a clerk of Harley's being found in treason with the French. Harley was thrust into that Limbo, where unhorsed politicians and expectant ecclesiastics wander and meet. Jonathan felt his spirit approaching to-day's sunken but the morrow's possibly risen sun—Mr. Harley.

The stage was now set. Marlborough was adding laurel to laurel, Oudenarde to Ramilies, at enormous expense of blood and treasure. More

and more unpopular became war and Whigs and
even Marlborough. The harassed Queen trembled
between his insulting Duchess and the insinuating
Mrs. Masham, who played and plied the Queen for
Harley. But Harley, little as he knew it, had a
greater champion and more lasting friend waiting
in the wings. Years later he wrote to Jonathan, "I
believe in the mass of souls ours were placed near
each other." Meantime both could feel the cold.
The Whigs sent Lord Wharton to succeed Jonathan's friend Pembroke in Dublin, and he learned
that he would no longer be needed as chaplain at the Castle. To Archbishop King's
sympathy Jonathan hinted the working of Low
Church Bishops in England, chiefly "the dullest
good-for-nothing man," Archbishop Tenison. And
though he did not mention it to his Diocesan, he had
learned that the *Tale of a Tub* was raising more
than one enemy in a black gown.

Without his two feminine curates at Laracor
Irish life would have been insupportable. Jonathan was sure now of Hetty's life-love and he began
to love her and Mrs. Dingley as one person. If
Destiny thrust him into the wilds and bogs of
Meath, he could take his star with him. Otherwise
his was a dismal prospect among an Irishry
prostrate under the penal effects of religious felony
and Jacobite attainder. "It has not been known

in the memory of man that an Irish tenant ever
once spoke truth to his landlord," he wrote to Jack
Temple and remembering Moor Park, he was filled
with home-sickness: "No time will make me forget and love less. If I love Ireland better than I
did, it is because we are nearer related for I am
deeply allied to its poverty." He found that only
the defects of England were exported to Ireland.
All Irish friendships were spoiled by English politics. Whigs had made ingratitude synonymous
with Whiggery, and Irish Tories were only Whigs.
It made an unpromising syllogism in Jonathan's
mind, which noted: "About seven years ago frogs
were imported here and thrive very well; and three
years after, a certain great man brought over Whig
and Tory."

However much Jonathan sank into Irish life, he
kept one eye upon England. The smallness of his
Irish flock and their peccadilloes were covered by
occasional winks from his other eye. He had
realized that promotion cometh neither from the
North nor from the South nor yet from the West,
as long as London's latitude lay East. He was
grateful when Archbishop King used his questing
spirit as his agent in London. He was fain to
plunge into that world of industry, insinuation and
innuendo upon excuse of Church business. Queen
Anne of her historical Bounty had remitted the

First Fruits upon the revenues of Church in England, and Jonathan was sent to induce a similar remission for the Irish clergy. Laden with figures and reports he sought, if not the Queen, at least the Ministers of the Lady Bountiful. Lord Treasurer Godolphin received his petition and mentioned the ingratitude of English Clergy, unkindly adding that the Irish were Tories and disloyal, and must show more gratitude if any Bounty were remitted. But Godolphin spoke as a Whig, and Jonathan, who nourished his own opinions concerning the gratitude of Whigs, was fain to bow and save a black mark for Godolphin. Archbishop King continued to receive due word of Bounties and policies, of the promises of men and of the machinations of women and all that secret stir on back stairs, for which ears ecclesiastical itch. The Archbishop promised Jonathan the first good prebend, and, as Jonathan reported to a friend, "You know great men's promises never fail."

Meanwhile Jonathan's pen never tarried nor wearied. He used the advantage that the *Tale of a Tub* had given him among the Wits, to make mockery of the astrologers and to predict events, including the death of Partridge, the leading prophet of the time. When the time approached, he printed a circumspect account of the death of Partridge, who in consequence was unable to per-

suade his friends that he was not risen from the
dead or defrauding some honest coffin-dealer. By
a special touch Jonathan caused him to die in Dissent, in whose favor the Whigs were for repealing
the Test. The Test was the turning of the ways
sought by Jonathan. The Test of receiving Communion in the State Church was imposed upon all
who desired the offices of the State. Fanatics and
Infidels were naturally for repealing the Test.
They might be simple Deists and believe in a God
but not in a Church. On the other hand there were
High Tories who, without always believing in a
God, upheld very straitly the Church of the State.
Toward this group Jonathan approximated.

He decided that to be Whig or Tory entailed the
violence to his integrity or understanding of choos-
ing a place among fools or knaves. Whig or Tory,
knave or fool. But as the knavery of Whig was
directed against Jonathan's Church and the foolery
of Tories was in favor thereof, he was constrained
to lift his pen for the fools against the knaves; but
secretly and under no name lest he might offend
the still powerful Whigs. To conceal himself the
more effectively, he wrote a Tract for the Test,
mentioning his Archbishop and himself and in
criticizing his own work he wrote to Archbishop
King to say:

"Your Grace's character is justly set forth: for the rest, some parts are very well, and others puerile, and some facts, as I am informed, wrong represented. The author has gone out of his way to reflect on me as a person likely to write for repealing the Test, which I am sure is very unfair treatment. This is all I am likely to get by the company I keep. I am used like a sober man with a drunken face."

Surely this was cleverly done, for to slip his own person was as difficult as unraveling body from soul, if Jonathan had ever met a soul in the labyrinths of his brain. If he were ever a Bishop, he would no longer need subterfuge. And it came to pass that, while he was in London, the Bishopric at Waterford fell vacant and his Lordling friends pressed his name before the fussy pharisaical Queen. Lord Somers advised his promotion in particular but His Lordship's name unfortunately recalled the *Tale of a Tub* and, as Jonathan learned afterward from Lord Berkeley, the Queen had been shown marked passages by the Archbishop of York, the very Doctor Sharp from whom Jonathan had borrowed the original theme.

Was it the rifled author or the outraged moralist who was most indignant? And it would have been difficult to enmiter an author, who described Bacchus as "first inventor of the mitre, which he wore continually on his head to prevent vapours and headache after hard-drinking."

It was only an Irish Bishopric that Jonathan wished. Once free of obedience and financial care, he could live contentedly in his bog and throw thunderbolts under his sign and seal into English politics like a god from Olympus. Hetty and Mrs. Dingley could live under the shadow of his Cathedral, and he might even share his name with Hetty, provided she was unwilling to share nothing else except companionship. And Waterford would be a very pleasant spot for the invitation and entertainment of London Wits. What a dream! Waterford, Waterford! And then the new Bishop was proclaimed, an altogether dull and displeasing person. Jonathan crept to his lodging from Whitehall and one more dream oozed out of his splenetic skull. He scribbled, "I once had a glimpse that things would have gone otherwise. But now I must retire to my morals and pretend to be wholly without ambition." But not wholly, while Fever threatened Cork. He wrote to Halifax, whose coming to Ireland he compared to a Titian on a signpost or a Grecian statue acting scarecrow, "if you think this gentle winter will not carry off Doctor South, my Lord President may think on me for Cork if the incumbent dies of the spotted fever." Cork was duly widowed, and Jonathan strained himself in feverish suspense but in vain. Cork was rebishoped and Jonathan was no more Right Reverend but plainer Reverend than ever.

Puzzled and worried, Jonathan felt no temptation to cast his gown. He preferred to cast the
Whigs. He had taken a nominal side in politics as
in religion. Little good had either brought him.
Ill-temper had turned him to change politics, but
innate savagery kept him upon the side of orthodoxy. Diabolical pride would not allow him to
leave the side of God. He had no wish to become
a free-lance among the free-thinkers, a divine
among Deists, a god unto the Atheists. Perhaps it
was too easy. His mettle demanded difficulty. He
continued to attend Divine Service as punctiliously
as he had attended Whig Levees, when he
munched the dry hay of hope from the empty-
handed, empty-headed Whig Lords. Fifteen
months he passed in the warrens of London ferret-
ing for a phantom miter. At his farewell visit to
Lord Halifax, he could scarcely restrain the bitter-
ness of his bow. In suffering his Lordship to
present him with a small volume of Christian
poetry, he begged leave to mention it was the only
favor he had received from the Whig party.

Jonathan had decided to defend orthodoxy as it
had never been defended before. Denied access to
the pinnacles of the Church, he would try to bolster
her foundations. If he could not even prop Christianity, he would at least undermine her oppo-
nents. He scribbled a Tract to prove that the

abolishing of Christianity might be attended with inconveniences. He proposed to defend nominal and not real Christianity, which would be too wild a project. Something could be said for a nominal belief in clergy and laity, and incidentally for himself.

It was true that if religion were abolished, all the able-bodied clergy could be pressed into Army and Navy and their revenues taken to support two hundred Wits and fops. Well and good, but, as fops and elegants breed scrofulously, the clean-lived parsons were the nations' best stallions, and ten thousand of them already "reduced by the wise regulations of Henry the Eighth to the necessity of a low diet and moderate exercise, are the only great restorers of our breed."

Sunday could be abolished with religion, thus restoring one day in seven to business and pleasure, though where are there more appointments, queried Jonathan, where are there more dress and gallantry, more business meetings or conveniences to sleep than in Churches of a service time?

Granting England was staunchly free-thinking, there might still be found uses for a Supreme Being, "to keep children quiet when they grow peevish and providing topics of amusement on a tedious winter night." Above all, in view of the decline of wit, why abolish the chief target for

witticism? Finally the Abolition of Christianity
would reduce the bank-rate by at least one per
cent., which was a greater risk than had ever been
taken for its preservation!

As he moved his two-edged sword, Jonathan
felt his power to slash backward as well as to cut
forward. If Deists and Infidels fell before his forward stroke, he knew that a swathe of orthodox and
pompous hypocrites was wriggling to hindward.

Readers hardly knew what to think. So cheerful
a considering of the effects of abolishing Christianity pleased equally Wits among the believers
and unbelievers among the Wits. If the author had
turned his other cheek, he had kept a mocking
tongue therein. Jonathan watched his distant
butts without claiming his arrows. He had learned
to plume himself in secret. It became clear that he
must approach his Bishopric by a broad and open
flight of steps rather than by the most clever
winding staircase. Accordingly he wrote and
dedicated to Lady Berkeley a *Project for the
Advancement of Religion.*

He summoned the virtuous Queen (since
prudish she was to blush over his writings) to
enforce morals upon her own Court. He casti-
gated fellow-clerics (who were mishandling the
Tale of a Tub and secretly or publicly slandering
the author). Jonathan added to the national cor-

ruptions "the pert pragmatical demeanor of several young stagers in divinity to say nothing of scoundrels in gowns reeling home at midnight" as "a sight neither frequent nor miraculous," but presumably occasional.

Religion had become so nominal that Jonathan's simple suggestions rang like iron jesting or wooden Quixotry. Why should vice not be made unprofitable or virtue profitable? Why should religion not be necessary to favor and preferment? Of course it would entail hypocrisy, but quiet hypocrisy was better than open infidelity, since "it wears the livery of religion. It acknowledges her authority and is cautious of giving scandal." And what of hypocrisy? Jonathan argued, "I believe that it is often with religion as it is with love, which by much dissembling at last grows real."

This sounded like a laugh in the sleeve of his black gown, but if Jonathan were laughing at religion or love, it was nominal religion and nominal love that he mocked. It was best to accept hypocrisy without actually calling nominal religion the Established, or making matrimony a synonym for nominal love.

There were other reforms such as closing tavern and ale-house by midnight and censoring the stage, which since the reign of Charles the Second had glorified criminal intrigues. A committee should save worthy squires from marrying the cast wench or cracked chambermaid, good aldermen from becoming cuckolds and deluded virgins from debauchery at the hands of successful rakehells. Finally he called for new churches in London, where only one in six could at present hear service. The idea might employ the excellent Mr. Wren and also act like a branch of pleasant southernwood to the Queenly nose, which had so disrelished his previous writing.

Meantime he was reduced to playing picquet with his Curate and the Vicar of Trim. It was exile in the Parish of the World's End for one who loved the London coffee-house more than all the wooden temples and pulpits of the Lord and had liefer sit with Addison and the Wits than at the tables of Bishops.

The year 1710 brought some of the changes and chances he had awaited. In April he opened a letter to say that his mother had died in Leicester. He shuddered to think of the dull poverty and unrequited drudgery which had engulfed a spirit like his own. The flash of annihilation passed before his vision. "I have now lost my barrier between me and death," he wrote. She was dead before she saw him raised or honored. Private grief swelled his rancor against the Whigs. Still he could not believe he was utterly thrown aside and he clung

to Addison, writing: "If you will come over again
when you are at leisure we will raise an army and
make you King of Ireland." He prayed for a hint
to come to England and escape from Ireland. He
had been disappointed, hoping to go Chaplain to
Vienna or Bishop in Virginia. He begged Addison to find him the office of Historiographer, above
all for "early notice to procure an addition to my
fortunes." The dismissal of Godolphin and promotion of Harley rang the signal. It was August,
and, without waiting for Addison's answer, he set
out on business of his Archbishop, to apply to
Mr. Harley, "who formerly made some advances
towards me and unless he be altered will, I believe,
think himself in the right to use me well."

Mr. Harley's only alteration was that like Jonathan he was altered to Tory. Jonathan reached
London in September and on the ninth he wrote his
first letter to M. D.—"My Dears" *alias* Mrs. Hetty
Johnson and Mrs. Rebecca Dingley—letters to be
treasured as the *Journal to Stella.*

IX

(1710-1714)

SEPTEMBER saw Jonathan riding hard enough into Chester to take a fall, but fortunate in his horse understanding falls well enough to lie quietly till his rider got up. The Whigs did not understand the art of a graceful fall so well, for Jonathan found them in despair, "and ravished to see me and would lay hold on me as a twig while they are drowning," he wrote to the Ladies at Laracor. On the other hand, "the Tories dryly tell me I may make my fortune if I please but I do not understand them, or rather I do understand them."

He intended to enjoy a spectator's rôle between "the struggles of a cunning provoked discarded party and the triumphs of those in power." The excitement over Doctor Sacheverell's suspension from preaching was changing the Government.

Jonathan moved naturally and scornfully from one side to another. With Archbishop King and

Dean Stearne of St. Patrick's he corresponded
officially, but with an edge sharpened by his Irish
politics, about "great men every day resigning their
places; a resignation as sincere as of a usurer on his
deathbed." Godolphin gave him short and morose
reception, after a surly breaking of his stick of
office. Jonathan noted with one of his strange
Biblical allusions:

> "Here are some that fear being whipped
> because they have broken their rod and some
> that may be called to account because they
> could not cast one up. When a great Minister
> has lost his place, immediately virtue, honour
> and wit fly over to his successor with the other
> ensigns of his office."

Halifax was the only Whig left in Jonathan's
affections, and to his toast for their resurrection
Jonathan was fain to add their reformation.

From his lodgings every evening Jonathan
wrote his *Journal* to his eager worshipers at
Laracor. He composed a chronicle of his English
exploits and vented his sentimental love in sub-
script and postscript. He made love from one
country across seas to another and strained his
fantastic affection through the post. He felt
doubly safe living two lives, sometimes three. He
reverted to the old days at Moor Park, when Stella

was a child and he was still teaching her the paths
of literary innocence and not the ways of political
guile. He swaddled and sealed his long practical
screeds with the little children's language they had
used, when she could hardly lisp her words. Once
again he felt his grown mind play with her growing delight. Only Stella and Dingley could
understand his baby-talk. They were his "deelest
logues" or dearest rogues. His girls were "dal-
lars" and their conversations were "tonvelsasans."
Stella herself was PPT or Poppet or Poor Pretty
Thing, and Jonathan himself was Presto, thanks to
the inability of the Italian Duchess of Shrewsbury
to remember his name in any other language.

Jonathan set to work to sponge socially and to
lampoon anonymously; arts raising him consider-
ably in the London world. He was felt to be an
incipient power, all principle and no scruple. He
showed a legal power of close reasoning and an
almost Christian taste for defamation. As friend
or foe he was never dull. Swordmen of State
entering the arena looked for rapiers, so it was no
surprise when, "To-day I was brought privately to
Mr. Harley, who received me with the greatest
respect and kindness imaginable."

Jonathan was sick of the caresses of great men
out of place. Harley's were more acceptable and
each quickly estimated his man, making little mis-

take. Harley had no difficulty in bringing Jonathan to the Tories, since he was already there, and Jonathan had no trouble in persuading Harley to be friendly to the Wits, since wittiness was his ambition. Long afterward Jonathan recorded his friend and patron to fame for virtues commensurate with love of power.

It was a warming sensation to find himself nursed by this stranger, whose destiny saluted him as though they had long communed behind unseen curtains. Passionless and moderate in his grip of affairs, Harley only minded lest men of wit and learning were not upon his side. Scurrility and ignorance he left to his enemies. He was attracted to Jonathan by the rare mixture of wit and scurrility in his pen. Seldom mistaken in judgments for good or ill, he reserved his initial opinion within a mind that was already one of reserve. He foresaw Jonathan's effect upon the fortunes of the Tory Party, which Fate rather than choice was directing him to lead. Upon Jonathan's fortunes, Harley's effect was considerable, though not so complete as Jonathan hoped. Jonathan immediately qualified for Tory friendship by shooting his first shaft at the sulky and now shieldless Sidney Godolphin, entitled *Sid Hamet's Rod*. What delight it was to let Stella into the secret of his verses before Mr. Harley, who at dinner

"repeated part and then pulled them out. Lord
Peterborough would let nobody read them but
himself and Mr. Harley bobbed me at every
line to take notice of the beauties. Prior rallied
Lord Peterborough for author of them and
Lord Peterborough said he knew them to be
his; and Prior then turned it upon me and I on
him."

This was political as well as intellectual happiness and Jonathan's letter set two little old maids
twittering in Ireland. But Jonathan appreciated
Stella's independent criticism of the poem, delight-
ing in his own curious mind "that an enemy should
like it and a friend not." Jonathan always hankered for Irish opinion: "Do they know anything
in Ireland of my greatness among the Tories?" He
flung himself into the case for the Irish Church
and, though the Irish Bishops believed his influence had died with the Whigs, he secured them
their First Fruits. The hands of Bounty were the
hands of Queen Anne, but the voice was the voice
of Jonathan Swift, who had official leave to inform
the Irish Primates, "but they are to take no notice
till a letter is sent them by the Queen's order."
Meantime the pleasing Ormonde had succeeded the
displeasing Wharton as the new Lord Lieutenant
and the Irish Bishops adjusted themselves like
weathercocks. Incidentally they decided to relieve
Jonathan of being their solicitor. But while their

letter was speeding to Ormonde, Jonathan's crossed
with account of the thing done. "Pretty manage-
ment," he commented. As for reward,

> "Mr. Harley will think he has done me
> a favour. The Duke of Ormonde perhaps that
> I have put a neglect on him and the Bishops in
> Ireland that I have done nothing at all."

And Jonathan muttered to Laracor that "the baseness of those Bishops makes me love Ireland less
than I did." His better reward was work and
influence. His pen wrought incessantly. He tried
his hand at squib and poem, pun and broadside.
He wrote a poem on a *London Shower* with result
that "there was never such a shower since
Danae's," said his classical friends. It compared
vividly with "the rainiest day that ever dripped," in
Ireland.

In November he undertook to write the *Examiners* every week for the Ministry. When he was
not writing, he was among the writers. Steele had
lost his place as Gazetteer for aiming a *Tatler* at
Mr. Harley. Jonathan tried to save him and later
helped him to a good hint for one of his *Spectators*
"about an Indian supposed to write his travels into
England." He visited poor Congreve under gout
and cataracts, not ripe enough to couch, to assure
him of his place. "I have made a worthy man easy

and that is a good day's work." He passed his leisure in coffee-houses and blind taverns or threatened his way past pompous porters into the presence of the great. Great men used him as their better, which drew angry thoughts about "the puppies in Ireland hardly regarding me." He preferred to listen rather than talk, and loved "to be the worst of the company."

Richly he enjoyed wearing veil and vizor and hearing his own anonymous work bespoken in his company. "Here is a damned libellous pamphlet come out against Lord Wharton," he told Stella; "the character is very well but the facts indifferent," and since they were too far away for his laugh to be heard, "get the *Examiners*. The great men assure me they are all true!"

The *Character of Lord Wharton* has not lost libel with the centuries. It was as fierce and malevolent a specimen of shameless and shattering spite as History can pickle. Wharton was assailed for ruining England while he sunk his fortunes, and ruining Ireland while engaged in raising them. Wharton "goes constantly to prayers and will talk bawdy and blasphemy at the Chapel Door. He is a Presbyterian in politics and an atheist in religion," but with the gracious tolerance of the age he chose his mistress among the Papists! A caddish touch tells how his Epicurean Lordship

"bears the gallantries of his lady with the indiffer-
ence of a Stoic." Jonathan's political rant lacked
the philosophy of the *Tub* and the light sheen of the
Battle of the Books. They assumed the superficial
brilliance and bright brutality of the Period of
Queen Anne, when the exercises of a Laureate in
the practise of libel led to the offices of State. Three
ages of English literature have coincided with the
reigns of female sovereigns. Not the least splendid
was the Augustan period of *Anna Regina,* when
Love and War were clothed in ceremony and con-
ducted with equal gallantry; when Addison rose by
one poem on the Battle of Blenheim from obscurity
to a Secretaryship of State and espousals with a
Countess; when Congreve could claim office by his
Comedies and win the amours of a Duchess; when
Prior could pass through published poetry into
secret Diplomacy; when Harley could save Congreve his post by quoting Virgil to Halifax; when
Jonathan Swift could send one Minister into the
House to call out another to learn that Jonathan
would not dine late that day. In the antechamber
of Queen Anne, Jonathan attained his zenith of
intrigue and interest when seen soliciting an Earl
to ask a Duke to place a clergyman, stopping a Red
Bag on its way to the Queen and instructing a
young nobleman that the best poet in England was
Alexander Pope, whom he would not allow to pub-

lish his Homer until he had collected a thousand guineas.

His life became more and more wonderful. He would walk down to Chelsea with Harley by moonlight, but, when Harley wished him for chaplain, he protested: "I will be no man's chaplain alive." The Lord Keeper offered him a living "but I told him I would not take any from him." Angrier still was his protest when Mr. Harley sent him a note for fifty pounds which he returned: "I absolutely refuse to submit to his intended favour." But if his heart were as proud as Hell, it could reflect a heavenly gleam of pity. Sir Matthew Dudley dismissed a butler, who died in the street that night. Jonathan wept a tear as pure as the tear of God or Lesbia over the fall of a sparrow. "But what care you?" he wrote to Stella. "But then I knew the butler."

In summer he used to swim, going down to the river at Chelsea in nightgown and slippers, which his drunken rogue of a Patrick held for him, while his landlady brought him a napkin for bathing cap, which he lost diving. He had a real accident in a sedan-chair and made such a scolding that the chairman dared not grumble or charge him for broken glass. One day he was buying "hugeous battoons" from a toyman or paying three guineas for a new periwig on another. A further-reaching outlay of twenty-five shillings brought him a Strabo and an Aristophanes. Upon Strabo he could voyage into unknown latitudes. Aristophanes could enchant him with a country where birds were superior to human beings.

All the while he was clubbing and colloguing with real Ministers, who called him Jonathan, though he protested they would leave him Jonathan at the end. He was sure that Ministers did nothing for their boon companions. But his hope was set on Harley, when suddenly the French Spy Guiscard stabbed him. Jonathan felt his heart broken. "I am in mortal pain for him." It was the cry of the horse-trainer, whose favorite falls in the race, or the grimmer grief of a Warwick when king-making material cracks in hand. But it gave Harley his needed popularity and he recovered. Guiscard, who could not have done Harley a better turn, was cut down by St. John and died slowly. Jonathan was furious the Law would not allow his untried body to be hung in chains and was fain to gloat over "showing him pickled in a trough this fortnight for two-pence a-piece." He was equally ferocious over a man whom he hindered of his pardon for a rape.

"The Under-Secretary was willing to save him upon an old notion that a woman cannot be ravished; but I told the Secretary he could

not pardon him without a favourable report
from the Judge; besides he was a fiddler and
consequently a rogue."

Meantime he enjoyed pricking the fickle and
finnicky Archbishop King for an indiscreet quotation from Tacitus he was reported applying to
Harley. All the busybodies sent it from Dublin,
but Jonathan snuffed them out on the spot, leaving
his Archbishop to owe him a decidedly good turn.

The Archbishop always intended to do something
for Jonathan, but he only wrote to advise catching
preferment from his new friends or putting pen to
"some new subject in Divinity not handled by
others." "Hang him, hang him!" groaned Jonathan, "a rare speech this with a pox!" as he remitted
the First Fruits of ingratitude. He blazed with
fury against the Dublin world.

> " 'Tis a pity the world does not know my
> virtue. Pray talk occasionally on the subject
> and let me know what you hear. Do you know
> the greatness of my spirit that I value their
> thanks not a rush? The Duke of Ormonde
> had no more share than a cat. And so they
> may go whistle and I'll go to sleep."

Jonathan recorded how the world and his own
straight path swayed upon the smallest event, the
insolence of a Duchess or the smoothness of a serv-
ing-woman like Mrs. Masham. Harley's life had

fluctuated with his own, and here was Mister
Masham eagerly telling him in White's Chocolate
House that his wife had a boy, a most imprudent
and uncalled proceeding when the peace of Europe
depended on her influence. "God send her a good
time: her death would be a terrible thing," prayed
Jonathan with political devotion. One could not
be too careful with a Queen, who was always having
gout in her hand or stomach. The Whigs feared
that the gout reached her conscience. Jonathan
reached Windsor with his great acquaintances and
wrote Stella an account of the Queen hunting in a
chaise and driving a single horse furiously like
Jehu, as mighty a hunter as Nimrod. What a contrast between the gouty horse-lashing Queen and
the lovely Stella riding down Irish lanes. Jonathan was not forgetful of Stella's steed: "What
sell anything that Stella loves and may sometimes
ride?" In his London garret he would lie back of
a night and imagine her riding until he called out
directions in his letter home.

"How hasty we are. She must go a cock
horse, pray now. But the horses are not come
to the door; the fellow can't find the bridle;
your stirrup is broken. Where did you put the
whips, Dingley? so, so, a gallop! Sit fast,
sirrah, and don't ride hard upon the stones."

Stella made a prettier picture than the thought of

the Queen wearied with hunting receiving the
bowing courtiers in her bedroom with her fan to her
mouth, once a minute uttering three words to those
near her and at the word dinner rushing out and
leaving Jonathan at the bed-post.

Peace with France was the People's desire and
the Ministry's ambition.   Unfortunately, the
ambitions of Treasurer Harley and the treasured
Secretary St. John always conflicted and Jonathan
strove to enclose them with widening arms.   The
peace of Europe depended on a woman in waiting
and an Irish curate.   " 'Tis a plaguy ticklish piece
of work," reported the curate.   Day and night he
attended them, suffering their quarrels and their
whims and vices.

> "Saw the Secretary steal away from us in
> the Mall after some wench," he noted in a
> letter he never dreamed would survive and,
> "to-morrow he will be at the Cabinet with the
> Queen. So goes the world."

It had taken one Parson to bring the Tories in.
It would need another to keep them there. All
this year of 1711 there was rumor of peace. Harley sent an offer asking the French if they wished
peace. It was grasped like a cure by a dying man.
In April died the Emperor, and in May Mrs.
Masham's brother, to make a foil to Marlborough
from another hemisphere, led a disaster to Quebec.

In July Harley secretly sent the poet Prior to
France to mingle an olive branch among his bays.
Jonathan feigned ignorance until Prior was by mis-
chance held up by overzealous officers at Dover. In
his amusement Jonathan sent for a printer and
dictated a "formal grave lie" of the whole journey
to Paris. The jest succeeded mightily, for Jonathan dined with the Secretary at Prior's, who
rushed at him with the pamphlet crying, "here is
our English liberty!" Jonathan read it solemnly
and said,

> "I like it mightily and envy the rogue the
> thought. Had it come into my head, I would
> have done the like."

In September he was dining with the Secretary,
the poet and a priest from France, with two
Ministers.

> "They were good rational men. We have
> already settled all things with France and very
> much to the honour and advantage of Eng-
> land, and the Queen is in mighty good
> humour,"

ran the bulletin to Laracor.

Opposition pamphleteers were busy and Jonathan advised the Secretary, who was only amused
by reading libel, to make some examples. The
Protestant Postboy, which had reflected upon Jon-

athan, was given "a squeeze extraordinary." St. John committed fourteen booksellers and through the great breach in Grub Street Jonathan issued his famous pamphlet for Peace entitled the *Conduct of the Allies.*

Jonathan asked why a good Peace could not be drawn from ten years of successful war. The English were really paying the Allies for the privilege of fighting their battles to their own money-ruin and the setting up of National Debt. Civil War was better in that both sides circulated their money at home! Upstarts, Projectors and Undertakers had created a Monied Interest to vie with the Landed. It was the old story. Allies joined the war purely for the subsidies. The English had engaged as Principals in the war instead of Auxiliaries, and taken the burthen. The war was maintained by annually going into pawn. The only personal quarrel against the French King was his pretending the Pretender. For ten years the whole war had been kept where the enemy could best hold the Allies at bay. Ten glorious campaigns had left England like a sick man expiring with all sorts of good symptoms. When the English took a town in Flanders, the Dutch were put in possession and the event celebrated at home with bonfires. Wingless Victory only brought "a few rags hung up in Westminster Hall." What was it for unless to increase the fame and wealth of the great General?

Across Jonathan's paper stole the shadow of Marlborough, impassive and terrible like a Giant playing battles with armies of pigmies, himself invulnerable. Upon English Whig and Tory, upon soldier and statesman, upon Queen and subject, upon enemy and ally lay that tremendous shadow which darkened the windows of Jonathan's garret and the doorways of his counsel.

The darkness of his own mind mingled with the shadow of the Duke. Here was his enemy and rival in political power! Here was the sword to cross and criss-cross with his pen! The Ministry of his friends could only stand if Marlborough fell. Jonathan gathered his gall to his pen-tip and stabbed in the dark. He proved that the continuance of the war suited the accounts of the General and the Allies. In the background Money-changers feared the overthrow of their tables. Was it not for the perquisites of the General that fuel was squandered in bonfires, cities taken for the Dutch and blood poured in torrents? Was it to become King that a General during pleasure had sought to become a General for life? The Queen herself had fled from a Castle to a Cottage, following the advice of Solomon that it was better to dwell in a corner than with a brawling woman in a wide house. This

arrow at Duchess Sarah was the only one likely to
have touched the Duke. The great are seldom
wounded save by wounding of the woman they love.

Meantime the Pamphlet, inspired and corrected
by the Ministers, leaped from edition to edition.
Printers were working day and night and even of
a Sunday. But Jonathan could meet the charge
of dishonoring the Sabbath with the Beatitude
promised to Peace-makers. The Dutch envoy was
complaining. Prior and St. John were accused
of the writing. Jonathan wrote to Stella, "I suppose it will be printed in Ireland." Not that Jonathan cared. Ireland became a back thought.
"They say the cocks and dogs go to sleep at noon
and so do the people," he laughed. "They tell me
you in Ireland are furious against a Peace; and it
is a great jest to see people in Ireland furious for
or against anything."

It was in England that the stakes lay. The
Ministry could not command the Lords and were
uncertain of the Commons. The pamphlet was
running prodigiously, but it had not reached full
tide before the Queen handed her royal hand to the
Duke of Somerset, who was loud against peace.
Jonathan rushed to Mrs. Masham and told her that
she and the Queen had betrayed the Tories or else
the Queen had betrayed Mrs. Masham and Harley.

It was "a day that may produce great alterations

and hazard the ruin of England," Jonathan
scribbled to Stella, if he was not contemplating the
ruin of the Tories and of the author of the
Pamphlet. Five days later his printer was bound
over by a Chief Justice scenting the way of the
wind. "He would not have the impudence to do
this if he did not foresee what was coming at court."

Over soldier's battles no curtain is drawn save of
dissolving smoke, but the conflict between master-
spirits is held in darkness. Around the Queen's
chamber waged the campaign against Marlborough
with all the fierce obscurity which delighteth the
practisers of peace and bewildereth the men of war.
Against the Marlburian influences Jonathan could
scarcely hope friends to prevail. He watched the
blackening onset and confusion, wondering whether
he could even ride the storm. For the moment he
found himself a commander and a protagonist. But
his heart boded fall, and in his heart of hearts he
feared and admired the great Duke, whom he
summed up as "covetous as Hell and ambitious as
the Prince of it." Once he had questioned whether
any wise State could lay aside a General who had
been successful nine years together. After ten
years he appealed to the State to lay the Duke and
his wars and his Duchess aside for ever. In later
years he sketched some of their traits: how the
Duke's good understanding supplied his want of

letters, how his passions were melted in his love of avarice. But in the Duchess three Furies reigned—"a sordid avarice, disdainful pride, and ungovernable rage."

What strange star had lifted him into antagonism against so kindred a spirit? He dared not compare himself, but he could not miss the fact that their quality and their vices ran parallel. What the exaltation of the Army was to Marlborough, the High policy of the Church was unto Jonathan, and by their several wars each waxed famous. As the Duke desired Captaincy for life, Jonathan desired life interest in a Bishopric no less. If the Duke was covetous as Hell, Jonathan was as avaricious as a Church rat, and admired the Duke for it, writing years later, "I dare hold a wager that the Duke in all his campaigns was never known to lose his baggage." The lives of men meant as little to Marlborough as their reputations to Jonathan. Neither was over-burdened with the charitable magnanimities which spare weakness in the armor of most men. Wine, gallantry and gambling touched them not, nor women, save the objects of their single devotion, a Sarah and a Stella. The same singular affection dictated the scribble which the Duchess received from the battle-field of Blenheim, and the laborious *Journal*, which the Irish post carried to Laracor. By head and shoulder the two men,

covetous as Hell and as ambitious as its Princes,
towered among others. Finally both lacked what
their fellow-men would call a soul. They ordered
their thoughts and their ways outside the circles of
Bliss and Loss, which trouble and affect other men.
Either they belonged to some other planet, or their
species and country lay undiscovered in uncharted
oceans. To their contemporaries they were unpleasant necessities, to posterity specimens of
Genius.

For mastery their spirits and deputies fought in
their bodily absences around the weakling Queen,
of whose "confounded trimming" Jonathan
despaired. Fates and foibles were fighting.

Jonathan scribbled the *Windsor Prophecy*
charging the dangerous Duchess of Somerset with
red hands in the death of her second husband, Tom
Thynne, and worse with possessing red hair.

"And, dear England, if ought I understand,
Beware of *Carrots* from Northumberland.
Carrots soon *Thynne* a deep root may get,
If so be they are in *Somer set*."

With the passing of the year the blow fell. Mrs.
Masham foiled the Duchess of Somerset and Harley meshed the golden-mailed Duke. On the
twenty-ninth of December Jonathan opened one of
his own letters to add; "that we are all safe; the

Queen has made no less than twelve Lords to have a majority." The Lords were swept after the Commons and Marlborough dismissed.

"Nobody at Court," wrote Jonathan, the next month, "takes any notice of the Duke of Marlborough, who says there is nothing he now desires so much as to contrive some way how to soften Doctor Swift." They had a grim respect for each other. The Doctor was merciful and "sure, now he is down, I shall not trample on him. Although I love him not, I dislike his being out." Jonathan claimed "preventing five hundred hard things being said against him."

St. John sped to France while Harley arrayed the Tories in both Houses, and the Tories did nought but read Jonathan's pamphlet. From the Commons he could report "that those who spoke drew all their arguments from my book and their votes confirm all I writ: the Court had a majority of a hundred and fifty: all agree that it was my book that spirited them to these resolutions." In vain the Whigs read a treasonable passage to the Chief Justice, in which Jonathan hinted that Posterity might be driven by the Tyranny of Princes "to the fatal necessity of breaking in upon the excellent and happy settlement now in force." To invoke Whiggery against the Whigs was summoning Baal against Baal.

Cries of treason could not alter votes, resolutions
and majorities. The people cared not at heart for
High Church or for Low Countries. They required peace, and Jonathan's pamphlet forced
peace. Queen and Ministry accepted his reasoning. Like a shadow faded away the great Captain,
the Great Whig, the Great Miser. The building
of Blenheim Palace was suspended, and the
French Marshal was politely assured against attack. But the Duke was never assured against
Jonathan, who assailed "Midas" unto his grave for
his perquisites on food of man and beast. "Old hay
is equal to old gold," he screamed.

Jonathan heard that "Marlborough is growing
ill of his diabetes; which, if it be true, may soon
carry him off and then the Ministry will be something more at ease." Before the end of the year
the Duke crept away from England. In vain
Prince Eugene hurried to England on his behalf.
Jonathan dismissed him for "plaguy yellow and
literally ugly beside." The great Duke could not
brook defeat and passed into exile. The Dutch
properly treated him as a god, but among his own
people he lost honor until his death, when his tomb
and dwelling were piled into memorial of his
greatest victory. Believing in the ordering power
of Destiny, he had become the destiny of thousands,
whose mortal event one way or another he had

ordered with greater than the genius of man, something of the patience of deity. Such men are the
nearest to gods that mankind can ever know.

Peace claimed her victory and Peace was clothed
in the gown of an Irish Curate. All the pomps
of war had proved powerless against a parson's
pamphlet. The Duke's dark hour made Jonathan's splendor, though Jonathan wrote, "I serve
everybody but myself."

In January of the next year he told Stella that
the Duchess would join the Duke, and Jonathan
"bid a lady of his acquaintance and mine let him
know that I had hindered many a bitter thing
against him; not for his own sake but because I
thought it looked base. And I desired everything
should be left him except power." It was not a
sentence he would have enjoyed for himself. However, he was punished by a snubbing from the
Duke's daughter, Lady Godolphin, at cards wherefore, "she is a fool for her pains and I will pull her
down." Godolphin died in September and he
wrote; "the Whigs had lost a great support. It is
a great jest to hear the Ministers talk of him now
with humanity and pity because he is dead and can
do them no more hurt."

Jesting was close to Pity in Jonathan's mind and
closer to jesting was his indignation. When his dear
Lady Ashburnham died, he groaned that "to see so

many thousand wretches burdening the earth, while
such as her die, makes me think God did never
intend life for a blessing." When the Duke of
Hamilton, about to proceed as Ambassador to
France, was killed by Lord Mohun in a duel, Jonathan ran to comfort the widow. "She moved my
very soul."

Jonathan slipped from the arena of politics in
and out of Society, fluttering like a black, bushy-
eyed moth among the candles, though he let Stella
know that in the daylight of Windsor he had been
seen in light camlet faced with red velvet and silver
buttons. All social glory, which is reflected from
the greatness and familiarity of others, was Jonathan's. Laracor could hardly have known its Rector
handling the finest gold snuff-box in England, a
gift from Mrs. Masham's brother, for which the
Duchess of Hamilton made pockets, while Mrs.
Masham induced the Queen to send the privileged
snuffer some of her preserved ginger. Jonathan
had learned that, though he could do without
women in the home, he needed them in the world.

Of Elizabeth Villiers the left-hand relict of King
William, he reported, "Lady Orkney, the late
King's mistress, and I are grown mighty acquain-
tances. She is the wisest woman I ever saw, and
Lord Treasurer made great use of her advice in
the late change of affairs." Lady Orkney came of

that celebrated family which had provided romance both for Stuart and usurper of Stuart. Jonathan liked her. "I dined yesterday with Lady Orkney and we sat alone from 2 till 11 at night."

The tacit acceptance of Mistresses Royal has been one of the few indulgences that ecclesiastics permit themselves. Jonathan declined to dine with the husband of Arabella Churchill, mistress of King James, but Lady Orkney became his dear, squint and all, and he wrote:

"Lady Orkney is making me a writing table of her own contrivance and a bed-night-gown. She is perfectly kind like a mother. I think the devil was in it the other day that I should talk to her of an ugly, squinting cousin of hers, and the poor lady herself, you know, squints like a dragon."

So Jonathan confessed a type of social accident which may befall the politest. But Lady Orkney overlooked his mistake, for she gave him her picture by Sir Godfrey Kneller who "has favoured her squint admirably and you know I love a cast in the eye."

As for the writing table, he wrote her, "it is but giving a fiddle to a scraper, or a pestle and mortar to an apothecary."

Jonathan accepted the kindness of ladies of the

High Impropriety, while he lashed the hypocrisy of the religious, writing,

"I wish you a merry Lent. I hate Lent. I hate different diets and furmity and butter and herb porridge and sour devout faces of people who only put on religion for seven weeks."

Jonathan was not indulgent to all the sex, for, when the Duchess of Shrewsbury reproached him for not dining with her, he replied, "that he expected advances to be made by ladies and especially by Duchesses." He had a short and easy way with women. "Sing when I tell you," he thundered to the weeping Lady Burlington. His position was such that he decided the Dukes admissable among the Ministers and Wits, who met and dined as brothers. And woe betide offenders, for instance Lord Lansdowne: "I sent him a peppering letter and would not summon him by note as I did the rest; nor ever will have anything to say to him till he begs my pardon."

Jonathan insisted the Ministry should succor Wits even if they were Whigs. "Steele I have kept in his place. Congreve I have got to be used kindly and secured. Rowe I have recommended and got a promise of a place. Philips I could certainly have provided for, if he had not run Party mad, and I set Addison right at first." One time he visited a poor poet called Diaper, very sick, in a nasty garret, and gave him twenty guineas from St. John. Another called Harrison he visited with a hundred pounds, but arrived an hour after his death. Piteous twain of poets these, for this was all their future fame, that a certain Irish clergyman approached them in their last extremity, looking not unlike an uncouth vision of Death himself.

His charity was that of a patron, and his succor the pessimist's, who delights to return the drowning to a life which has only disappointments in store. He confessed with candor things that writers seldom confess: "I hate to have any new Wits rise, but when they do rise, I would encourage them; but they tread on our heels and thrust us off the stage." He perceived that his weakness toward the broken was only that feeling which is based upon an unbroken pedestal itself. His acid vision penetrated and dissolved the sorrow of others as keenly as the sources of his own security. He retained illusion or delusion in neither.

Pride and power brought him no happiness. When power ceased to be a vanity it became a vexation. Thought, as he had learned, brings thinkers to misery. The heights of theology and the steeps of devotion he eschewed, confining himself to the common code and daily drill of the

Church, whose cause he chose and championed like a side in politics. He would not perceive the theological taint of Popery in Anglicanism any more than Jacobitism in the Tories. His vision was overkeen. He had to blind himself when he wrote the *Tale of a Tub* rather than allow his Church a shred in common with the Roman. And his Tory friends blindfolded him rather than divulge their correspondence with the Pretender. Common unhappiness he soared above, but there can have been no chair-load of bitterer misery carried home from the tables of the great than Jonathan, even when hugging presentation flasks of Burgundy to his sides. He told Stella that he had to return early from fear of the Mohawks, who were said to include Bishop Burnet's son. "The dogs will cost me at least a crown a week in chairs. I believe the souls of your houghers of cattle have got into them and now they don't distinguish between a cow and a Christian."

Cares more deadly than Mohawks preyed upon his mind, not common cares, but the predestined curses which Destiny strewed like ashes upon his head. From time to time Ireland moved in his thought or slipped like a curse off his pen. Visitors and questers brought that country too easily to mind. One clergyman was plaguing him with a project for printing Bibles in Irish, "to make you

Christians in that country," he joked to Stella. He
entered more readily into plans for removing duty
off Irish yarn. Another day "the Bishop of Killa-
loe tells me wool bears a good rate in Ireland but
how is corn?" He need not have worried himself.
The English Government was determined to
destroy both Irish trade and Irish language.
Jonathan had written and even signed a Tract for
improving and correcting the English language,
and Irish with its fantastic poetry and outlandish
spellings had left him unmoved. But Irish trade
stuck in his watchful ire, and he could write, "I
have no shuddering at all to think of retiring to my
old circumstances if you can be easy, but I will
always live in Ireland as I did the first time. I will
not hunt for dinners there, nor converse with more
than a very few." His desire was always unto the
few.

He complained often of scurvy meals or scrub
acquaintances, but he dined perpetually with the
best. "When the Secretary showed me his bill of
fare, 'Pooh,' said I. 'Show me your bill of company.' "

Meantime the rolling thunder of great event.
The Peace of Utrecht was signed after interminable
intrigue in March of 1713. Nobody had guided
every step more closely than Jonathan, who even
laid down that the Emperor "having paid nothing

for the war shall get nothing by the Peace." Any
peace was a Tory triumph, and there could be no
Tory triumph without heavy debt to Jonathan.
But the rivalry of Harley, now Lord Oxford, and
St. John, who had joined him as Bolingbroke in
the Lords, was fatal.   Jonathan could pacify
Europe but not the Tory party. "It is impossible
to save people against their own will and I have
been too much engaged in patchwork already."
On the whole, he was satisfied with his work. The
obstructors of the Kingdom's happiness and of the
Queen's measures (otherwise Tory politics and
Jonathan's hopes) were rooted "in rage, rebellion
and revenge," he wrote to Archbishop King, who
had laid a wager to Jonathan against Peace before
August. His own reward was overdue. "Pray
make hay while the sun shines" wrote the worldly
Archbishop. The day the Dean of Wells died, he
frankly wrote to "submit my poor fortunes" to
Harley. He had been composing an Apologia for
his friends and as a *magnum opus* to his own
name, a History of these years of Queen Anne, but
he was impatient for recognition, security and
elevation. The Queen would not have him as
English Bishop, perhaps not even as Dean, for the
race was not to the swift nor the battle to the strong.
The red-haired Duchess of Somerset was stronger
than Mrs. Masham and Jonathan's male enemies

were legion. The Duchess resented a passage about Lord Essex in the Temple *Memoirs* and perhaps she had read the *Windsor Prophecy*. A Duchess may pardon being called a murderess, but "carrots" no woman can forgive.

Jonathan, still pretendedly careless but half-hopingly in suspense, was writing to Stella, "Bolingbroke made me dine with him this day (I was as good company as ever) and told me the Queen would determine something for me to-night. The dispute is Windsor or St. Patrick's. I told him I would not stay for their disputes." On the next day Mrs. (now Lady) Masham wept for "She could not bear to think of my having St. Patrick's." Unfortunately, for another motive the Queen could not bear to think of his having Windsor. "Do you think anything will be done? I don't care whether it is or not. In the meantime I prepare for my journey and see no great people." Harley sent to assure him that the Queen was resolved, though "some unlucky incident may yet come. Neither can I feel joy at passing my days in Ireland and I confess I thought the Ministry would not let me go but perhaps they can't help it."

It was necessary for Dean Stearne to be moved into a Bishopric if Jonathan were to take St. Patrick's. But the Lord Lieutenant Ormonde disliked Stearne, "so now all is broken again. This sus-

pense vexes me worse than anything else." The
month passed away. "I am not sure of the Queen,
my enemies being busy. I hate this suspense."
What enemies? The Duchess of Somerset waving
the *Windsor Prophecy* or Archbishop Sharp
thumbing the *Tale of a Tub*. But in vain, for
before St. George's Day the warrants were signed.
All came with a rush, Ormonde had been mollified
toward Stearne, and Stearne made Bishop of Dro-
more, so the Queen could sign and Ormonde send
over the order, and Jonathan Swift enter the
Deanery of St. Patrick's. It was really a more
subtle and greater triumph thought Jonathan
"that, I have made a Bishop in spite of all the
world, to get the best Deanery in Ireland."

On St. George's Day he dined for the last time
with Harley "and was so beDeaned. The Archbishop of York says he will never more speak
against me." In that day St. George and St.
Patrick lay down together. Jonathan rushed to
make a farewell to Court "and a thousand people
gave me joy; so I ran out. I dined with Lady
Orkney." She was a wise woman with whom to
discuss the future or past. For Lady Orkney and
Dean Swift lovers' oaths and the promises of
Princes derived from the same source.

All promotion is accompanied by expense and
irritation. Archbishop King was already madden-

ing the new Dean about Irish bricks and the project
of a steeple for St. Patrick's, and Dean Stearne
wanted him to purchase his old trash. "I shall buy
Bishop Stearne's hair as soon as his household
goods. I shall be ruined or at least sadly cramped
unless the Queen will give me a thousand pounds."
Enemies were foiled but busy. The ungrateful
Steele attacked him venomously alluding to the
Dean and poor Mrs. Manley as "an estranged
friend and an exasperated mistress." He called the
Dean a "miscreant," and miscreant meant mis-
believer. Steele's nature needed to avenge the
gratitude he owed the Dean for keeping him his
office. Jonathan understood Steele's savage desire
to be independent and with a soft word he departed
toward Ireland carrying his revenge in his saddle-
bags.

It was the first of June and he rode to Chester in
six days. In the old pink-stoned Palatine City,
where he had commenced, he closed his *Journal to
Stella.* His high politics lapsed and little avarices
reappeared. He wrote her not to take lodgings,
"the poor Dean can't afford it."

But the old feeling for Stella was bubbling to
the surface. He longed for something to sweeten
the dirty dregs which six days' riding away from
London could not wash out of his mind. It was
months and even years since he had seen her.

Writing had brought them closer, so close that
they shared the same handwriting. It had even
been accused that he addressed letters to himself in
his own hand. How faithfully he had written to
her and to Dingley all the while and rated them for
"sauceboxes and rogues." "Good boys must write
to naughty girls." He loved them both, surely
more than all his London life, perhaps Stella as
much as life itself. He had once written "you are
welcome as my blood, to every farthing I have in
the world." That was going deep, for it was
farthings which had kept him from marriage and
always would. And Dean Stearne's exactions and
his Archbishop's proposals made him grind his
teeth. Even as Dean he could not afford marrying.
He must be in love with Stella to think of it and
still jealous of Tisdall, whom he called a "puppy"
in his last letter in answer to Stella's last, which
caught him before sailing. "When I read that
passage upon Chester walls and just received your
letter I said aloud—'Agreeable bitch!'" which
more agreeable editors tone to "agreeable witch."

X

VANESSA AND THE DEAN

(1714-1723)

ON JUNE the thirteenth Jonathan was installed
Dean in Dublin. The sounds of political strife
died down or shifted. Echoes from England de-
velop preternatural distortion in Ireland. Clear
sailing, open intrigue or secret plotting in England
assumed Irish mystification, and transmogrifi-
cation. King William, with whom the new Dean
had once crossed argument and even asparagus-
stalks, was become a god of immortal and glorious
memory, reverenced by Irish Tories as deeply as
by Irish Whigs. The Pretender was dreaded for
more than a bogus bogey. The Arch-Tory of a
Pope with the French King made up this Trinity
of hellish plot in Dublin's scared eyes. The Dean,
who brought about peace with France and whose
closest friends were believed to be tools of the
Pretender, walked delicately.

He was wise to disappear into the enormous

Deanery and watch the times as carefully as critics were watching him.   He was received quietly but there had been a splutter of Irish pasquinades. Whigs prowled around his Cathedral like wolves. "I thought I should have died with discontent and was horribly melancholy while they were installing me."   He had to place his ladies in lodgings unassailable to scandal.   Before he had made new Irish friends, there was rumor of old ones falling in England. Bolingbroke, dashing centuries ahead of his time had proposed Free Trade between England and France.   The Whigs beat him in the House, and Harley sent an urgent appeal to the Dean, but he was among his streams at Laracor. He had hung up his inkhorn and pen by the willows that were therein, exchanging his great house in Dublin for "a field bed and an earthen floor." Not till September did Achilles leave his Deanery and the pamphleteer his tent to return to the scene of his unrepeatable triumphs.   One last triumph behind the scenes awaited him.   In November Primate Marsh died and King, who had shown hostility to Swift in October, was passed over for Dr. Lindsay who wrote to thank the Dean.   Besides King had ratted to the Whigs and Swift wrote to Doctor Stearne, "it was not to be done and you may guess the reasons."

The dissension between Bolingbroke and Har-

ley was extreme. Harley's political ideal was
composite, to be a Whig among Tories while remaining a Tory to the Whigs. The time had come
which allowed no compromise. The Queen sickened, and Harley was still vacillating. Harley's
favorite daughter died and the Dean consoled his
anguished patron, his intense sympathy arguing as
good a case for her peace in another world as for
the Allies in this. Harley with Nonconforming
conscience under his Tory buckler, fell for defense
upon the sturdy Dean, who sarcastically assailed
the Scotch Lords for "a poor, fierce northern
people" in *The Public Spirit of the Whigs*. Parliament tottered into wordy warfare, the Whig Lords
attacking the Dean, and the Tory Commons assail-
ing Steele. The Dean's comment on their poverty
before the Union, drove the Scottish Lords insane
with fury and Highland Dukes petitioned the
Crown for vengeance. The bewildered Harley
offered a three-hundred-pound reward for the
author and sent a surer hundred by a counterfeit
hand to the Dean for his printers. Harley was a
breaking reed, though dipped in the Dean's invigorating ink. Bolingbroke was rapidly cutting
away his ground. Only the old companionship of
the poetical and the political flickered against the
storm. Pope and Gay still met Harley and Bolingbroke under Doctor Arbuthnot's genial lead, but

the Dean could no longer hold Brothers or Scribblers together. In May of 1714 he fled, with a portmanteau of papers to sort and burn in an Oxfordshire Rectory. "I care not to live in storms," he wrote, "when I can no longer do service in the ship and am able to get out of it." With him he carried his promised contribution to the Scribblers' Club. No prophet could make him aware even in irony that this sketch of some ludicrous and imaginary Travels would outline all written of the time.

The Queen was nigh dead. Harley and Bolingbroke—"the Squire" and "the Dragon" were fighting for the Crown. The Dean called Harley "the Dragon" because he was "the mildest man that ever served a Prince." Only rumors reached him now—for the man, who has taken to himself Letters, shall live by letters. "The Dragon," the Dean heard from friends, "dies hard. He is now kicking and cuffing. . . . The Dragon holds fast with a dead grip." But the Dragon had lost his grip upon Lady Masham and, when he tried to move her, the moribund Queen turned on her death-bed and moved Harley. From the country the Dean prophesied that the game would be played into Lady Masham's hand. "She has very good sense but may be imposed upon." From afar off he could guess the moves like a blindfolded chess-player.

The game was played with astonishing speed. The Electress Sophia died of spleen on reading a rude letter from the Queen; news which reached the Dean at a farmer's house over a mug of ale. The Jacobites signaled to the Pretender and the Whigs to George, son of Sophia. Harley weakly offered a reward for discovering the Pretender. "As well discover the Longitude," cried the Dean. "This strain is a sacrifice to Hanover, the Whigs and the Queen's state of health. It will neither satisfy Hanover, silence the Whigs nor cure the gout." Before the end of July Harley was dismissed, on the ground of making uncongenial and tipsy appearances before the Queen. Lady Masham announced to the Dean the news with her own white hand: "I was resolved to stay till I could tell you the Queen had got so far the better of the Dragon as to take her power out of his hands. He has been the most ungrateful man that ever was born." The Dean did not think so, for he had written to the falling Minister: "the memory of one great instance of your candour and justice I will carry to my grave—that having been in a manner domestic with you for almost four years, it was never in the power of any public or concealed enemy to make you think ill of me, though envy and malice were often employed to that end. If I live, Posterity shall know."

The triumph of Bolingbroke was short. The
Queen was stricken two days later. The Protestant
Dukes closed round the last of the Stuart sovereigns, who delivered her white staff for the people's
good into the hands of Shrewsbury.

The passage of death darkened the Queen's
couch and the brilliant shadow of Marlborough
entering London darkened the white hopes of the
Jacobites, and the portentous Walpole utterly
crushed them. The Elector of Hanover was proclaimed King. Bolingbroke, desperate and defiant,
fled to the Pretender abroad, leaving every friend
suspect by his action. Harley preferred imprison-
ment and the Dean returned to Irish quarters of
exile.

Ormonde followed Bolingbroke before the fury
of a Whig Parliament. Harley was thrown into
the Tower. The Dean did not deign to show infidelity. He wrote to offer Harley service and
attendance. "Your life has been already attempted
by private malice. It is now pursued by public
resentment. Nothing else remained." Upon the
Dean swept the fetid tide of Whig virulence. All
the petty hate of the pamphleteers was loosed
against a political enemy who was down, and a
literary rival who was still supreme. His letters
were hereafter opened for traces of Jacobite plots
by his own Archbishop, who informed him of

rumors of Bolingbroke's return and pardon, and
with a deft dig added, "Certainly it must not be
for nothing. I hope he can tell no ill story of you."
The Dean furiously cleared his loyalty. Things
were not ripe for the Jacobites at the Queen's
death, he remarked. They were rotten. The Pretender would be worse than the worst Whig Ministry. He could not have shot a more Parthian
arrow. He came in time to see humor when they
opened the petition of a poor parson to him, for
to another letter he added—"Let the post-rascals
open this letter and let Walpole read it."

The Dean was peevish, splenetic and depressed.
He was more troubled at this turn of tide by his
affections than by his politics. The secrets of his
heart were more corrosive than the secrets of the
Tory Party. He was sorely troubled by a trick
which circumstance had played him, in spite of
circumspection. He had not believed it possible
that another woman could creep into his heart. A
woman daring enough to usurp his mind; a serious
pretender to the throne of Stella! Archbishop
King had divined his spleen and written, "An odd
thought came into my mind on reading that you
were among the willows, that perhaps your mistress had forsaken you."

The Archbishop expected a wedding but the
Dean looked through his recollections and pieced

together the threads of what seemed his Platonic bigamy. He had met a family of Vanhomrighs seven or eight years before in his London vicinity. They too had Irish interests. Widow, sons and daughters satisfied and pleased him. The clever boy Ginkel had drawn up the terms of a mock introduction to the beautiful Mrs. Long, since Jonathan demanded the first advance from ladies. Ginkel had forbidden his mother and "her fair daughter Hessy" to encourage the beautiful Mrs. Long to take airs toward the great Doctor, who quickly fell into the habit of calling and dining with them in town. It was so convenient when he was living at Chelsea to leave things in their house at St. James. He had taken to changing gown and periwig there. Could he have changed his heart there as well? No, no! and he trembled with anger and reproach. It was impossible, and he had kept Stella carefully acquainted with the new friends. "You know whom I have dined with every day since I left you better than I do." Stella sniffed them as people of no consequence. He had written toward the end of 1710, "I dined to-day with Mrs. Vanhomrigh," and mentioned "no adventure at all to-day."

Early next year he wrote that Mrs. Vanhomrigh had sent for him to see her eldest daughter, on the pretense that she was taken suddenly ill. On St.

Valentine's day he was asked to her birthday dinner. "That was our way of beginning Lent," he
commented. Did he tell Stella that Miss Vanhomrigh's name brought another Esther into his
life, or did it make a difference that this one was
called Hessy not Hetty? At any rate she was of
age and decided to go to Ireland to look after her
estates. It was curious that both Esthers were
drawn toward Ireland by inheritance of lands.
Could there be any other attraction? "I loitered at
Mrs. Vanhomrigh's and out of mere listlessness
dine there very often," he had once written, but he
protested, thought Stella, too much.

The Dean was worried. He had liked Miss
Hessy from the first for "a very ripe-witted young
gentlewoman." And she must have liked him
more than he had dreamed. Before she died, poor,
dear, beautiful Mrs. Long had written to warn him
that Miss Hessy was melancholy. Because he had
praised Hessy's mind for a man's and a politician's,
Mrs. Long had roguishly added, "How can I pretend to judge of anything when my poor cousin is
taken for an hermaphrodite?" The Dean had been
attracted by her masculine mind. It was an
awkward chance that she should have a feminine
body. He had not caused her melancholy and as
he had explained to Mrs. Long: "The poor girl
between sickness, domestic affairs and State spec-

Hester Vanhomrigh, "Vanessa"

From a picture in the possession of G. Villiers Briscoe, Esquire,

ulations has lost a good deal of her mirth. But I
think there is not a better girl upon earth. I have
a mighty friendship for her. She has good principles and I have corrected all her faults, but I cannot persuade her to read, though she has an
understanding, memory and taste that would bear
great improvement. But she is incorrigibly idle
and lazy, thinks the world made for nothing but
perpetual pleasure, and the Deity she most adores
is Morpheus. Her greatest favourites at present
are Lady Ashburnham, her dog and myself."

Mrs. Long had died a few days after reading
this, and Lady Ashburnham some years later. Except for the dog there was nobody left to suspect
the cause of Miss Hessy's melancholy. Jonathan
had dined three times a week with her and her
family and let her tease him for political secrets,
while making his coffee. He had teased in return
and she had threatened to follow him to Windsor
if he would not write. "Had I a correspondent in
China, I might have had an answer by this time."
Though she seemed to live in different worlds, she
pleaded for correspondence. She slipped down to
Windsor and he rebuked her: "You should not
have come, and I knew that as well as you." When
he was returning to Stella, he had scribbled to her
on the road from St. Alban's, and she had been
overjoyed, praying only for his health and comfort.

The Dean blessed her with "Adieu, brat!" but Miss Hessy was far gone into melancholy, and after three weeks sighed: "Oh happy Dublin, that can employ all your thoughts. Confess—Have you once thought of me since you wrote to my mother at Chester?" She had plied him with letters reminding him archly that the post would bring him none from the discreet Lady Orkney. She protested that she found no conversation on earth comparable to his. Surely his mortal headaches only showed that the gods envied his powers of thought. He had not replied, until he reached Laracor, whence he humorously essayed his rural news: "Go to your Dukes and Duchesses and leave me to Goodman Bumford and Patrick Dolan."

He had not bandied more than some shafts of irony in boredom. Later, when he was in retirement in England between the two Reigns, she had naughtily come to see him and he had written another rebuke: "You should not have come by Wantage for a thousand pound. You used to brag you were very discreet. Where is it gone?" When she proposed coming to Ireland, he had snubbed her direct: "If you are in Ireland while I am there, I shall see you very seldom. It is not a place for any freedom where everything is known in a week and magnified a hundred degrees." The peril of past flirtation hung between them. Meet-

ings must be left to Fate. He offered her perfect
esteem and friendship, hoping to leave matters
there. One reason for staying quietly in Ireland
had been to avoid Miss Hessy's cavalier raids in
England. Girl, woman or hermaphrodite, she was
very dangerous. He was really alarmed by her
invasion of Ireland.

The Dean had flirted with Miss Hessy over the
coffee and doubts whether he could cast her so
easily from his life assailed him. He declined to
consummate, though he was quite willing to embalm, their friendship. In a complimentary set of
verses he had begun at Windsor to study its mysteries and to assort its emotions. Sacredly private
though their friendship was, he took the precaution
to Latinize Dean to CADENUS, while Miss Hessy
Vanhomrigh was idealized into VANESSA. The poem
recounted their flirtation intellectually.

He tried to keep Vanessa in the world of
mythology, among his pleasant memories, in England, among manuscripts, on the slope of Parnassus, anywhere except Ireland. But before his
first winter was over, she had taken coach and ship
to Ireland with her orphan's liberty, her lovesick
loneliness and unending Irish lawsuits. To the
Dean's dismay she took lodging in an Alley near
College Green, and summoned her old friend to
visit her property at Celbridge. In alarm he wrote,

"I met your servant, when I was a mile from
Trim. I would not have gone to see you for
all the world. I ever told you you wanted discretion."

It was the Dean, not discretion that the poor girl
wanted. He still hoped to discourage her: "Does
not Dublin look very dirty to you and the country
very miserable?" The most he would promise was
a visit in Town. Meantime he would not let her
know where he was staying. He was becoming
angry: "a fig for all your letters and messages!"
And the comedy continued during the rest of the
year between an insanely distracted lady and a
sensibly perturbed Dean, sorry and angry in turns.
He saw her when business allowed him: "I will
give you the best advice, countenance and assistance I can." Friendship and tenderness he promised to the utmost. He was practical and stern, but
he was equally irresolute and threw her sops instead of satisfaction. She might have been content
with his Platonic companionship, but he had given
that elsewhere. Then Vanessa let her passion find
full vent. He was more anxious to discourage and
dissuade her than ever. To cut her off or cut her
out he neither liked nor dared. Somehow he had
awakened her passion and must bide consequences,
which tended to be complicated in a country which
already held Stella, and in a city full of what
Vanessa called "strange prying deceitful people."

That they were living among fools appeared no reason to Vanessa for avoiding her sage. "Pray what can be wrong in seeing and advising an unhappy young woman? I can't imagine." She poured forth: "You can't but know that your frowns make my life insupportable. You have taught me to distinguish and then you leave me miserable." To distinguish what? Vanessa threw hints to his memory or conscience, the two champion coward-makers. She threatened suicide:

> "If you continue to treat me as you do, you will not be made uneasy by me long. I am sure I could have bore the rack much better than those killing, killing words of yours. Sometimes I have resolved to die without seeing you more; but those resolves to your misfortune do not last long."

She implored assistance in dealing with cunning executors and importunate creditors. He saw, helped, comforted and rebuked her. Rebukes added fire to the frenzy, which his previous neglect had nourished but which some initial fault or mistake had sown. "When I begin to complain," complained Vanessa, "then you are angry and there is something in your look so awful that it strikes me dumb." The Dean was meshed in a net of worries and intrigues, assignments and refusals, all innocent seeming on his part. But the past held disturbing memories.

When her letters were handed to him in the midst of company, he was thrown into such confusion that he hardly knew what to do, and worse, the gossip of Dublin caught Vanessa's name, asserting that the Dean was in love with her and giving the particulars which gossip never fails to adduce. "I never feared the tattle of this nasty town," groaned the Dean. He hoped that "tattle by the help of discretion will wear off." The Goddess of Discretion might help in person, but without making Vanessa her neophyte. The agony and the misery and annoyance continued. She showered letters, while the Dean warded off her attentions as well as he could. Sometimes he wrote in his peculiar French. He could say more, and be less easily quoted. Four years of this cat and mouse pursuit passed, and in despair he allowed himself to say in French at least:

> "Believe me, if anything in the world can be believed, that I think whatever you could wish me and that all your desires will be always obeyed as commandments impossible to violate."

The Dean seemed to hope that the French language lent itself to discreet irony.

Vanessa would make no promises except to pester the Dean with letters. Did he "imagine that a woman would not keep her word whenever

she promised anything that was malicious." She
was willing to barter and bargain with him. She
would even desist interrupting his business with
letters, if he would throw away one hour on her at
some time of the day:

> "Once more I advise you, if you have any
> regard for your quiet, to alter your behaviour
> quickly, for, I do assure you, I have too much
> spirit to sit down contented with this treat-
> ment. Now because I love frankness ex-
> tremely, I here tell you that I have determined
> to try all manner of human arts to reclaim you
> and, if all those fail, I am resolved to have
> resource to the black one."

She suspected the presence and attraction of a
rival:

> "Pray think calmly of it. Is it not much
> better to come of yourself than to be brought
> by force and that perhaps at a time when you
> have the most agreeable engagement in the
> world? For when I undertake anything, I
> don't love to do it by halves."

Unfortunately circumstances had condemned the
Dean to love-making by halves. But this was a
letter he had to answer and with mingled reluctance
and relish he wrote:

> "If you write as you do, I shall come the
> seldomer on purpose to be pleased with your

letters, which I never look into without
wondering how a brat, who cannot read, can
possibly write so well. . . . But raillery
apart, I think it inconvenient for a hundred
reasons that I should make your house a sort
of constant dwelling place . . . for the rest
you need make use of no other black art besides your ink. 'Tis a pity your eyes are not
black or I would have said the same of them,
but you are a white witch and can do no mischief."

The Dean in a great rhapsody of irresolution sat
down to touch and retouch his Pastoral Poem on
CADENUS and VANESSA. It was high time that the
whole friendship should be embalmed and laid to
rest and Vanessa's mock passion prettily pretensed
and preserved in a roll of mock-heroics. He
sharpened pen and polished rhymes to praise and
please his *inamorata,* while discreetly veiling and
vaunting his own several behaviors.

He was already writing her rhymes and almost
enjoying the task;

> "For who could such a nymph forsake
> Except a blockhead or a rake?"

The Dean prided himself on being neither. He
added, "So drink your coffee and remember you
are a desperate chip" and again: "The questions,
which you were used to ask me, you may suppose to

be all answered just as they used to be after half-an-hour debate." He had not written for a long time, for she answered:

"I own I never expected to have another letter from you for two reasons, first because I thought you had quite forgot me and because I was so very ill that I thought I should have died . . . I have asked you all the questions I used ten thousand times and don't find them answered at all to my satisfaction."

The weary Dean again began:

"If you knew how many little difficulties there are in sending letters to you. You do not find I answer your questions to your satisfaction. Prove to me first that it was ever possible to answer anything to your satisfaction. I wish your letters were as difficult as mine for then they would be of no consequence, if they were dropped by careless messengers."

He begged her to call him CADENUS and to use strokes of her pen to express her loving epithets at the beginning or end of his letters. This privilege Vanessa found good beyond expression, promising to

". . . never quarrel again if I can help it, but with submission. 'Tis you that are so hard to be pleased, though you complain of me."

She was happy even when she could throw him into a huff:

" 'Tis the first time you ever told me so. I wish I could see you in one."

Though the Dean endured huffs and even terrors, especially when a drunken porter was imperiling his correspondence, he delayed and dallied. There were those terrifying and impossible questions she was always asking him. Could she want to be his servant or his mistress? Dared she ask him to ask her to be his wife? What was he intended to read between the lines of her letters?

He planned to satiate her mind and memory with verse and proposed writing another history of CADENUS and VANESSA from the beginning to this time as long as the first poem:

"It ought to be an exact chronicle of twelve years from the time of spilling the coffee to drinking of coffee, from Dunstable to Dublin with every single passage since . . . two hundred chapters of madness, the chapter of long walks, the Berkshire surprise, fifty chapters of little times."

Otherwise unrecorded!

All their little lover's secrets and scenes came to the surface of his memory with extraordinary tenderness. He devised indirect exchange of sentiments and from coffee extracted a mysterious sweetness dating from the happy London evenings

when she served him in her Sluttery, dunning him
for secrets, with "Drink your coffee, why don't you
drink your coffee?"   How it all returned to him!
All their fragile fresh love had been mixed in coffee
fumes until coffee symbolized all that had ever
passed between them.   When he had ridden away
from England, she had written to greet him at
Chester: "It is impossible to tell you how often I
have wished you a cup of coffee and an orange at
your inn."   Years passed and from Dublin to the
love-worn Vanessa the Vanessa-worn Dean wrote:
"We live here in a very dull Town and Cadenus
says he is weary of it and would rather drink his
coffee on the barrenest highest mountain in Wales
than be king here.   And you know very well that
coffee makes us severe and grave and philosophical."   He hardly wrote a letter without a drop
of coffee.   "I wish I were to walk with you fifty
times about your garden," he wrote, "and then
drink your coffee."   All this coffee may have been
innocent enough though Horace Walpole was to
comment: "I think you will see very clearly what
he means by coffee," and Dr. Birkbeck Hill con-
cludes: "Coffee certainly in all the letters to the
daughter had a hidden meaning."   But Vanessa's
coffee remains yet another of those secrets which
every reader of Dean Swift must solve for himself.

Business or discretion made meetings more and

more difficult. Vanessa began to sink into real distress and to complain of the prodigious neglect of ten long weeks, and to declare it was not in the power of art, time or accident to lessen her inexpressible passion. So violent grew that passion that her life became a languishing death ending in a cry, which might well float down the ages among the many pathetic shrieks delivered by womankind, but the shriek died into one of the world's great love-letters: "I firmly believe, could I know your thoughts, which no human being creature is capable of guessing at, because never any one living thought like you, I should find that you have often in a rage wished me religious, hoping then I should have paid my devotions to Heaven; but that would not spare you, for, was I an enthusiast, still you'd be the Deity I should worship. What marks are there of a Deity but what you are to be known by? You are present everywhere; your dear image is always before my eyes; sometimes you strike me with that prodigious awe I tremble with fear. At other times a charming compassion shines through your countenance which revives my soul. Is it not more reasonable to adore a radiant form one has seen than one only described?"

The Dean urged physical exercise against what he called spleen, purposely mistaking the organ affected in Vanessa. "Without health you will

lose all desire of drinking your coffee." He could
only threaten in answer to her complaining or beg
her to use her honor and good sense to avoid making them both miserable. Furious desire to be rid
of her burst into his script: "Settle your affairs
and quit this scoundrel island and things will be as
you desire." Perhaps it sounded harsh, for his pen
cooled and he added a flower in French, rather like
the last rose that a man throws into the grave of a
woman whom he has wronged: "Be assured that
never was anybody in the world so loved, hon-
oured, esteemed, adored by your friend as you."
It was supreme valediction, had Vanessa only had
the wisdom to leave the scoundrelly Island. His
mood, having changed violently in two successive
sentences, changed in yet a third; "I drank no
coffee since I left you nor intend till I see you
again. There is none worth drinking but yours if
myself be the judge." What meant this casual
reversion to the coffee motive in his hazy hectic
affair with Vanessa? Only Vanessa could inter-
pret his meaning. She had so long and so accurately surmised that his thoughts were unlike the
thoughts of any other in the world.

Vanessa lay under enchantment and would not
leave Ireland. The year 1722 found her still sighing, still complaining, still faint but still pursuing.
The Dean wandered through the country for

distraction or diversion. From Clogher he wrote
with little change in the ring of his phrases: "It
would have been infinitely better once a week to
have met Kendall and so forth where one might
pass three or four hours in drinking coffee in the
morning or dining *tête-a-tête* and drinking coffee
again till seven. I answer all the questions you
can ask me in the affirmative." Once more the
mysterious questionnaire, that catechism of life and
death to poor Vanessa. Once more the coffee
drinking as the cloak or symbol of stain or dalliance, and since the dining was *tête-a-tête,* it may
be presumed that "Kendall" was a family disguise,
borrowed like an old cloak from an uncle. Again
he enjoined reading and exercise upon the infat-
uated and begged her to "grow less romantic and
to talk and act like a man of this world." He
wished for her sake and his, that her new acquaintance were with her. It was tactless to wish her
and her five thousand pounds well married. Cynicism swallowed his remainder of spirituality:
"God send you through your law and remember
that riches are nine parts in ten of all that is
good in life and health is the tenth. Drinking
coffee comes long after and yet it is the eleventh,
but without the two former you cannot drink it
right . . . last year I writ you civilities and you
were angry. This year I will write you none and
you will be angry."

He still clung to the belief that she came as a
disciple to a tutor for the improvement of her mind;
that her languishing was only a lapse of the spleen
and that he had himself never loitered in her
direction. He showed her rough drafts and finished chapters of his present writing, the preposterous travels of a certain Captain Lemuel
Gulliver, which diverted and pleased her so much
that when she had some little success in Society
with one of the animals she met, she wrote that it
seized her fan and was so pleased that she feared
being carried to the top of the house and served as
Gulliver was served before he could escape the
monkey, which once took an unpleasant interest in
his person.

The Dean, amused by her letter, answered her
from the County Armagh: "I see every day as
silly things among both sexes and yet endure them
for the sake of amusements. The worst in you
and me is that we are too hard to please and
whether we have not made ourselves so is the
question. At least I believe we have the same
reason." This must have sounded like the pro-
verbial equation between goose and gander. Still
he insisted on differences. "We differ prodigiously
on one point. I fly from the spleen to the world's
end. You run out of your way to meet it." He
used the bad weather to read Voyages and History,

while she only brooded in her chamber. Nevertheless "the best maxim I know in this life is to
drink your coffee when you can and, when you
cannot, to be easy without it. While you continue
to be splenetic, count upon it I will always preach.
Thus much I sympathize with you that I am not
cheerful enough to write, for I believe coffee once
a week is necessary to that. I can sincerely answer
all your questions as I used to do. . . ." But
what questions, what kind of coffee and why all
this misery and makeshift while Vanessa languished? But the end was on the horizon, merci-
less and merciful, though neither could see Fate's
coming. An end of letter-writing came to the Dean
and an end of languishing to Vanessa. In August
of 1722 his last letter full of advice and persiflage
was written while traveling: "where I do not know
nor what cabins and bogs are in my way. I see
you this moment as you are visible at ten in the
morning and now you are asking your question
round and I am answering them with a great deal
of affected delays and the same scene has passed
forty times. . . ."

The Dean was dreaming as he rode on horseback between the big houses of the gentry. He
recalled all the scenes of their strange love and
faithless friendship: "Cadenus often thinks of
these especially on horseback as I am assured.

What a foolish thing is Time and how foolish is
man, who would be as angry as if Time stopped as
if it passed. But I will not proceed at this rate, for
I am writing and thinking myself fast into the
spleen, which is the only thing I would not compliment you by imitating. So adieu till the next
place I fix in, if I fix at all till I return and that I
leave to fortune and the weather." Fortune fixed
their next meeting place without help of terrestrial
weather. Their secret remains one that the gods
do not divulge nor can men discover. Vanessa
died not of broken heart, for that would have appeared too common and vulgar to Cadenus and his
pupil, but of an over-sensitive spleen aggravated
no doubt by Irish climate.

The date of Vanessa's death is clear, but whether
she sent Dean Price a page from the *Tale of a Tub*
as a token of final impenitence with "No Prayers,
No Price" written, is less certain than that she
wished to load her soul upon the shoulders of her
terrestrial god. Some say Vanessa died of Stella
and some say of Stella's lover, if lover he was of
either in any sense.

Vanessa's revenge was exquisite and, being
posthumous, unanswerable. In that May she made
Bishop Berkeley her executor, of whom the Dean
wrote: "he is a true philosopher but very visionary and endeavouring to quit one thousand pounds

a year for one hundred pounds at Bermudas." The Dean was no longer accounted a deity in her "sound and disposing mind," for he received no mention in her Will, though the Secretary of Harley and the Archbishop of Dublin each received twenty-five pounds to purchase rings. Altogether twelve persons were awarded rings. To have included one who had so persistently and negligently failed to provide a similar article of jewelry for Vanessa, would have indulged an irony too sharp even in the seriousness of dying. Her estate went to Berkeley to found his University in the West Indies, which often she had heard the Dean ridicule. It was better timed than she dreamed. On June first the Dean mentioned in a letter "Bermudas goes low." Five days later the Will was proved and Berkeley found his means.

But the poem of *Cadenus and Vanessa* was given, by her direction, to the world and failed not to convey the greatest pain possible to the person whom Vanessa believed to have supplanted her from beginning to end. The Dean's lines were now revealed to an amused and malignant Dublin:

> "The counsel for the fair began,
> Accusing the false creature Man."—

But the Defendant's counsel replied with arguments:

"Hence we conclude no women's hearts
Are won by virtue, wit, and parts:
Nor are the men of sense to blame,
For breasts incapable of flame."

The gods had conspired to raise one perfect
creature upon earth:

"Vanessa be the name
By which thou shalt be known to fame:
Vanessa, by the gods enroll'd:
Her name on earth shall not be told."

And could not until a rhyme could be found for
Vanhomrigh by some pronounced "Vanummery."
So perfect was this mythical maid that she needed
no spurious virtue known as blushing, which the
Dean dared call

"A virtue but at second-hand;
They blush because they understand."

Pallas and Venus, Love and Wisdom like rival
Queens contended for this creature, while among
earthlings

"Both sexes, armed with guilt and spite,
Against Vanessa's power unite."

Amid the Beaux, Dandies and suitors she apparently admitted the clergy:

"But this was for Cadenus' sake
A gownsman of a different make;
Whom Pallas once, Vanessa's tutor,
Had fix'd for her coadjutor . . .
Cadenus is a subject fit,
Grown old in politics and wit,
Caress'd by ministers of state,
Of half mankind the dread and hate."

But

"Vanessa, though by Pallas taught,
By love invulnerable thought,
Searching in books for wisdom's aid,
Was, in the very search, betray'd."

The pupil fell herself in love, whereat

"Cadenus felt within him rise
Shame, disappointment, guilt, surprise . . .
Appearances were all so strong,
The world must think him in the wrong;
The town would swear, he had betray'd
By magic spells the harmless maid;
And every beau would have his jokes,
That scholars were like other folks."

Altogether, the poem was a defense, condescending for the lady but high-pitched and exalted for
the swain, and the matter might have rested to the
satisfaction of both. But some demon of conscience, some devilry of remorse, some reckless

I received ye Letter when some Company
was with me on Saturdey night; and it put me
in such Confusion, that I could not tell
what to do. I here send you the Paper you
left me.   This morning a woman who
does Business for me, told me she heard I
was in — with one — neming you, and twenty
particulars, that little master and I visited
you, & that the A—B did so; and that you —
had abundance of wit &c. I ever feared the
Tattle of this nasty Town, and told you so;
and that was the Reason why I said to you
long ago that I would see you seldom when you
were in Ireld. and I must beg you to be easy if
for some time I visit you seldomer, and not in
so particular a manner. I will see you at the
latter end of the week if possible. These are
Accidents in Life that are necessary and must be
submitted to — and Tattle by the help of —
Discretion will wear off

Mondey morn.
10 a clock.

Letter of Swift to Vanessa

love of truth, some mocker clad in mystery added
the fatal and fantastic lines:

> "But what success Vanessa met,
> Is to the world a secret yet.
> Whether the nymph, to please her swain,
> Talks in a high romantic strain;
> Or whether he at last descends
> To act with less seraphic ends;
> Or to compound the business, whether
> They temper love and books together;
> Must never to mankind be told,
> Nor shall the conscious Muse unfold."

Sometime in her earthly state Stella was to read
these lines. With publication Vanessa's secret no
longer remained "to the world a secret yet,"
whereas Stella cherished one, for which Prince
Posterity would beat the gates of the tomb in vain.
The Dean had been aware of Stella's anguish and
on her birthday in 1721 clearly protested against
changing old Angels for new:

> "Nay, though the treacherous tapster, Thomas,
> Hangs a new Angel two doors from us, . . .
> We think it both a shame and sin
> To quit the true old Angel Inn.
> Now this is Stella's case in fact,
> An angel's face a little crack'd,
> (Could poets or could painters fix
> How angels look at thirty-six)."

Though the Dean would have resented the idea
that he was treacherous, should he have since hung
his sign from a heavenly mansion, it must bear different Angels on different sides. On earth he had
steered his bark as well as he knew between Stella
and Charybdis.

XI

THE KING OF IRELAND

(1720-1726)

THOUGH the Tories were scattered, their champion and chaplain still held his ground. Ormonde the impeccable and untarnishable supplanter of Marlborough became "a glorious exile" and fled across seas to join Bolingbroke under Stuart allegiance. His arms hung in the Cathedral, whence the Heralds removing them were faced and refused by the furious Dean: "I will never permit so gross an indignity to be offered to so noble a house." Free in conscience from all Jacobite taint, he asserted the right to be true to his friends. To Harley incarcerated in the Tower he wrote gallantly, "requesting leave to attend and accompany him there. It is the first time that I ever solicited you in my own behalf and, if I am refused, it will be the first request you ever refused me."

The Dean realized he had had his day. He had played the great game longer than is given to most

men. By way of burning his boats he burned his
letters from Ministers. He courted arrest and de-
fied triumphant Whiggery. He was made to feel
the venom, with which Irish poltroons reflect the
prejudices of their patrons in England. He was
hustled and hooted. He was lavishly libeled and
threatened with personal violence. He withdrew
behind the entrenchments of his petty kingdom.
After playing upon a Kingdom for chessboard, a
Deanery was small play and tiny occupation for
his grieving spirit. His giant mind was one
always pleased with bagatelle. Part of his gigantic
fund of mockery he reserved for himself and he
grinned to see himself marshaling Choristers instead of Wits and summoning a disobedient
Chapter instead of the well disciplined Scriblerus
Club. Instead of Marlborough looming in the
background he found Archbishop King, a Bishop
instead of a Knight. His Queen had been taken
and the only King on the board remained in-
accessible, unless the Dean evolved knowledge of
German. But he made no attempt to conciliate
the Hanoverian power and it was with despising
desperation rather than confident courage that he
faced the Dublin Whigs.

Health and spirits failing, he collapsed into a
corner of his vast unfurnished house. His life
seemed to have become a burden to others before

it became his own. Unloved and unsought, he observed that

> ". . . those with whom I now converse
> Without a tear will tend my hearse."

All whom he had loved politically were in danger of losing their Jacobite heads. The two women who loved him, as he had observed with no little terror and annoyance, were already close on each other's tracks. He would rather have stood naked and pilloried between onsets of Tories and Whigs than presided at a meeting of Stella and Vanessa. They garnished but they did not fill the unfurnished house of his mind. In the Dean's house were many mansions. The strong-room of power was closed, and the boudoir devoted to the Brothers and Scribierus Club, which he loved most, was separated by a corridor of sea. "When I leave a country without probability of returning, I think as seldom as I can of what I loved or esteemed in it to avoid the *desiderium*" he wrote to Pope, perhaps defining as far as possible in English that most pathetic and untranslatable of words, *desiderium*, in which desire is melted to anguish. *Desiderio desideravi*, with desire desired the Savior to eat the Last Supper. *Desiderio*, with desire the exiled have loved their ancient places, from which they have been removed. *Desiderio*, with desire poor Vanessa loved her Dean, and *Desiderio,* with desire her Dean recalled life and friends in England. The tedium and boredom of Dublin were only tempered by the humorous ferocity, for which that city is noted. Satire, gibe and squib, pasquinade and parody and broadsheet were poured upon the now defenseless Dean. One lampoon, *The Hue and Cry after Dean Swift,* was little less than a parody of the *Journal* he had written to Stella, drawn from repetition of intimate conversations or glances at private correspondence. The *Last Will and Testament of the Pretender* was published, bequeathing the Dean "liberty to write a second *Tale of a Tub* with as much blasphemy as he shall think proper."

The Dean welcomed his duties not because they were duties, but because they channeled the swirling eddies of his restless mind. He entered into every little care and minor custody in the Cathedral. He became intimate with sextons and the ancient Christian guild of grave-diggers. He shook his fist at Archbishop King, but he failed to frighten disobedient choir-boys even behind his imperious peruke. He allowed himself the most trifling amusements. How else could he lift the burdensome memory of the past or the vexatious anxiety, which he continued to feel for patrons proscribed, and flighted friends? The mighty pen

was hushed but not crushed. It was no longer
wise to whip the Whigs or to dig a Duchess or
to lash the Lord Lieutenant of Ireland. In secret
his pen tapped his overcharged cranium of much
morose and melancholic stuff in letters and correspondence with the English *literati* or more
secretly in sketching the fantastic Voyages of
Captain Gulliver. This he showed to Vanessa and
Stella. It amused him to compose with exquisite
care this parody he had promised to the Scriblerus
Club, even though the other members defaulted to
tedium, separation or forgetfulness. Sitting in the
damp and dreary Deanery without woman or child
to brighten his morning or console the fall of
eventide, he became more and more engrossed in
pages, which beginning as one of those literary
tricks, by which sages induce amusement in other
sages, swelled to a Philosophy for Fools. When
the mood allowed, he drove his undeviating pen
across the thick Irish foolscap. The beautiful
shape of his characters never altered, and the clear-
ness of his pencraft failed not. He wrote steadily
and steadfastly as though to harness his brain to
regular employ without letting circumstances and
memory lash it up heights and over precipices and
into gulfs. For fools and against fools he wrote.
Captain Gulliver embarked upon the famous Ship
of Fools . . . and kept a Log. . . .

There was an immediate household to command
and keep, a steward and a groom, footman, stable-
man and housekeeper, all the grandeur contained
in what the Irish call a Big House. Sometimes he
dined with Stella and Dingley and sometimes they
came to dine with him, but generally he sat alone
with a mutton-pie and half a pint of wine upon
his silent board.

The Dublin people watched his black looks and
black gown with dislike or disgust; dislike if they
were the Catholic natives, and disgust if they were
Protestants and Whigs. To the old Irish smarting
under the defeat of the Boyne and the laws, which
equally penalized their commerce with Heaven or
with earthly countries, the Dean was only another
proud, grasping, grinding Prelate arriving from
England to feast and fare upon the disappearing
fat of the land. He was a celebrated despiser of
their religion and a contemner of their darling
House of Stuart. He was a Whig to them except
in political label, though to the Irish minished and
menaced at every turn an Irish Whig or an English
Tory spelled slight difference. As a champion between slavery and freedom he barely figured even
in Celtic imagination.

From time to time the Dean rode morosely afield
through the desolate pastures of Meath or made
country-house visits as far as Clogher in the Pres-

byterian North or as distant from Dublin southerly
as Tipperary, which he described to a fellow Dean
years afterward in his best style:

". . . a bare face of nature without houses
or plantations; filthy cabins, miserable, tat-
tered, half-starved creatures, scarce in human
shape; one insolent ignorant oppressive squire
to be found in twenty miles riding; a parish
church to be found only in a summer day's
journey, in comparison of which, an English
farmer's barn is a cathedral; a bog of fifteen
miles round; every meadow a slough, and
every hill a mixture of rock, heath, and marsh;
and every male and female, from the farmer,
inclusive to the day-labourer, infallibly a thief,
and consequently a beggar, which in this
island are terms convertible. The Shannon is
rather a lake than a river, and has not the sixth
part of the stream that runs under London
bridge. There is not an acre of land in Ireland
turned to half its advantage, yet it is better improved than the people; and all these evils are
effects of English tyranny, so your sons and
grandchildren will find it to their sorrow."

Thus brooding silently and sullen, the Dean of
St. Patrick's rode the unfortunate Kingdom, troubled by revolving and wingless thoughts. He was
sorrowing for fallen friends and allies in England,
for Bolingbroke and Ormonde across the water.
He had brought his English hatreds to join fresh

hatreds in Ireland. He hated the beggary, the insolence, the poverty, the stupidity, the crass cruelty, the vapid folly of Irish life. He only waited the opportunity to push his inkhorn out of his snarling Snailery. Opportunity, however slow, was coming.

With some instinct for self-preservation the Dean sorted his principles. The Tories and the High Church foolishly tended to support the impossible Pretender. It was a question of clear thinking and clearer speaking. He had consistently scorned Pope and Pretender. The most malicious of his enemies had no more than galled his withers. The Irish Cause was more deeply associated with the Pretender than with the Tory High Church. Ireland was a lost and a losing Cause, most improper for an ambitious Dean. The Catholic Irish nation, whom he was pleased to consider the ancient savages of the land, had fallen with the Stuarts.

Nevertheless the quick eye of the Dean distinguished between the Stuart Cause, tied to the Pope, and an Irish Cause, separable from the Catholic Irish, associable with the Anglo-Irish interest and threatening a famous thorn to prick the English Whigs, the English Government and the detestable Walpole, to whom all power and glory had accursedly accrued.

Mortified by the slavery of the Catholics and servility of Protestants toward a Government in burlesque, the Dean sought common ground to rally all Irishmen except the actual placemen and phantoms of English rule. Carefully eschewing the mention of Pope or Pretender, the Dean issued a very modest *Proposal for the Universal Use of Irish Manufactures*. He summoned all people in Ireland to use only Irish goods. He instanced the late Archbishop of Tuam's pleasant saying that exports from England had better be burned, though out of humanity he excepted actual persons and out of humor English coals. The Dean trumpeted their wretched subjection abroad. In Scripture oppression made wise men mad. He hoped that Irish oppression "would in time teach a little wisdom to fools." The landlords were the greater tyrants because they were slaves themselves. As though universal oppression called down universal judgment from Heaven, he depicted an alarming state of the landscape:

"Whoever travels this country and observes the face of nature or the face and habits and dwellings of the natives, will hardly think himself in a land where law, religion or common humanity is professed."

Turning from the general panorama of ghastli-

ness, he ventured to state some ironical grievances
of poor England, how the Mayoralty of Dublin was
always executed by an inhabitant and often by a
native, whereby some worthy Englishman was
deprived of the salary, and how the Irish presumed
to dig their own coals or to send turf to market to
the discouragement of English trade.   English
Ministers looked upon the Kingdom of Ireland "as
if it had been one of their colonies of outcasts in
America."   The Dean kept within the pale of loyalty by proposing that both sexes in Ireland should
wear Irish manufactures to celebrate King George's
birthday.

At this turn of the Tory worm the Whig Government became indignant.   The adroit use of the
Irish Cause to embarrass their Government was
felt treasonable and treated accordingly.   To his
mingled fury and delight the Dean saw his printer
prosecuted before a Jury, who only out of weariness brought in a verdict against the heinous
proposal of aiding and restoring their own commerce.   In vain the Chief Justice swore that the
Proposal aimed to restore the Stuart cause.   The
Dean had laid his path too warily among the pit-
falls.   The Pretender could not even be made a
pretense.   The Dean turned to harry the Government on Finance, for "money is neither Whig nor
Tory."   He met proposals for an Irish Bank by

saying "bankrupts are always for setting up
Banks" and ridiculed the South Sea Bubble
schemes in England by devising a Swearers' Bank
in Ireland. He proposed adding a shilling to the
Revenue for every oath sworn. A gentleman
could afford an oath *per diem*. Irish fairs would
bring vast revenue. Heavy swearing would pay
for the Navy.

Walpole, having reduced the rule of England to
practical bribery, was puzzled by any power of
resentment or love of independence rising in Ireland. Irish offices, Bishoprics, privileges and
monopolies swelled a flow of political plunder as
unceasing as the River Boyne. The slow drainage
of Irish resources and Irish income might have
continued indefinitely until the lily-white hands of
a woman dipped for once too deep in the golden
sands. In the straightforward eighteenth century
the concubines of Kings were accepted as such.
Their expenses were assured and the asperities of
their position softened by covering titles. In this
case the Duchess of Kendal claimed especially generous treatment for accompanying King George
into England from Hanover and helping to make
exile in England bearable. It happened that Ireland needed copper coinage at the same time that
the Duchess needed coin of more valuable mint
and material. By a brilliant stroke it was arranged

to supply the two demands with the same patent. An ironmonger, William Wood, was given the right to coin a hundred thousand pounds' worth of copper coins for Ireland on condition of paying the Duchess ten thousand for the job. Neither the Irish Parliament nor the King's Deputy were consulted. The Houses passed respective protests. Wood was defiant. Memorials were presented and inquiry was opened. Wood, reliant upon Scandal and Jobbery as his great unseen supporters, desired the starveling Irish to swallow whatever fare he cooked for them.

Like an Irish Noah floating in his own ark, the Dean was not unobservant of the troubled waters. Without waiting for calm, he issued a Drapier's letter to the Irish people, packed with all his irony, scorn and ridicule. The Dean knew that a copper coinage was needed and that Wood's coins were not intrinsically trash. He knew Ireland had been far more seriously victimized by good money drained than by poorer sent in. He knew that job after job on a scale approaching the sublime had been perpetrated without revolting the Anglo-Irish or conscience stirring popular imagination. The Dean's political second-sight had revealed to him the ripe moment to strike. He struck with all the concentrated hate and cadenced restraint of his pen.

He wrote with magnificent confidence. If he loathed English jobmasters and tyrants, he scorned Irish slaves. He knew they would believe whatever he wrote. He met Wood's effrontery with effrontery of his own. He coined arguments against Wood's. He claimed safely that the Kingdom would be ruined by the halfpence, since it was ruined already. He claimed the poor would be undone, for the halfpence would run about like the plague. Shopkeepers would have to exchange good for dross. There was only one pennyworth of brass in twelve of Wood's pence. Wood's trash might as well be made out of old kettles. In vain the great Master of the Mint, Sir Isaac Newton, certified the particular excellence of the new coins. The Irish mob would have hooted the Law of Gravitation had the Dean so ordered. When he signed a notice postponing a solar eclipse, the expectant crowd is said to have dispersed.

The Dean intended trouble and there was no conflict he dared not risk. He said that he had preached the two sermons in his life against Wood's halfpence. The text "let us do good unto all men," which he expanded to the simple theory that "we are indeed commanded to love our neighbor as ourselves but not as well as ourselves." The Irish showed more loyalty and less public spirit than any other nation. He appealed to them to

prefer the interests of their Prince and their fellow-
subjects to that of "a destructive impostor." Ireland took fire and went up in one roaring hysterical
flame. The Dean did not allow it to die for lack of
fuel. The Drapier's letters lifted the Irish Cause
itself out of the smoldering mass of rejected halfpence. Were not the Irish as free as the English?
"Am I a freeman in England and do I become a
slave in six hours by crossing the Channel?"

Weeks passed and the turmoil increased. For a
miraculous moment Ireland was united. Fellows
of Trinity and City Butchers, the Lord Chancellor
Middleton and the mob, Archbishop and newsboys
combined to defeat Wood. The Drapier suggested
the circulation of the coins should be made uncomfortable to the circulators and it ceased. Walpole approximated the situation and his move was
as dexterous as any sarcasm of the Dean. He sent
Lord Carteret to Dublin with full powers. Now
Carteret was not only openly hostile to Walpole
but an admirer of the Dean. Walpole threw him
into the Irish maelstrom in time to meet the full
force of the Drapier's fourth letter declaiming Irish
Independence. Wood was already forgotten as "a
dog dissected alive." The case was between England and Ireland, and, for whatever motives the
Dean or his followers had espoused the quarrel of
the Centuries, it soared into the Empyrean of

Patriotism. The Anglo-Irish were declared free
by the laws of God, of Nature and of Nations. The
startling statement was made that "all government without the consent of the governed is the
very definition of slavery."   Carteret, who was
suspected of having revealed the connection of the
Duchess of Kendal with Wood's scheme, had the
duty of trying to induce the governed to swallow
their consent. He was required to appease waves
of his own making. He ignored the letter with
which the Dean met his arrival, and offered three
hundred pounds for discovery of the Drapier. The
printer was imprisoned. The Dean attended Carteret's *levée* and reproached the Viceroy for
imposing the wicked patent and imprisoning an
innocent printer. Carteret knew the reason of the
Dean's ardor and not unsympathetically parried
him with a line from Virgil: "The durance of
affairs and the novelty of my rule compel me to act
in this wise." In the classical eighteenth century
Virgil carried as far as Holy Writ. The Dean's
supporters were quoting the words, "Shall Jonathan die, who hath wrought this great salvation
in Israel?" And since the perils of the law menaced his devoted periwig, the quotation was continued, "God forbid: as the Lord liveth there shall
not one hair of his head fall to the ground."

The Chief Justice again attempted to browbeat

the Jury, but in vain. The printer was acquitted.
The Drapier became a toast and a tavern-sign, the
champion and the symbol of a nation, the rallying
standard of dispirited Protestant and of dispos-
sessed Catholic. The Dean of St. Patrick's offered
Walpole terms on condition they were left to
possess their brogues and potatoes in peace—and
the Drapier became King of Ireland.

But the scars sank deep into the Dean. He never
forgave anybody, Chief Justice or Master of the
Mint or the Mistress of the King for the parts they
played:

> "When late a feminine magician,
> Join'd with a brazen politician."

The rumor later that the King intended marrying the Duchess of Kendal with the prospect of
either bastardizing the Prince of Wales or making
the Duchess an honest Queen gave the Dean occasion for his most savage epigram. Whitshed, the
venal Chief Justice, he mortified through his motto
Libertas et natale solum, to which he chimed, "You
had good reason when you stole 'em."

"Liberty and Native Land" had rather been the
motto of the Dean, though Doctor Johnson would
have thought his patriotism only the refuge of another scoundrel. Who can deny that the Drapier

letters sowed the seed of modern Irish Nationalism or that his proposal to use Irish manufactures contained the germ of the policy called Sinn Fein? Only his wit survives from all the dust of that first political conflict between the two nations.   It was the Dean, who in answer to the toast of Irish commerce refused to drink to the memory of the dead and who urged the Irish to burn everything English except coals.   It was the Dean, who, while raising the Irish from being slaves and drawers of water, was not unwilling that they should remain "hewers of Wood."   The Dean felt in a position to carry argument, if not war, into the land of the oppressor.   The execrator of corruptions was ready to beard the Great Corrupter; the Dublin Drapier was unafraid of the Norfolk Squire; Swift sailed into the immediate orbit of Walpole, whose ecclesiastical henchman, Archbishop Boulter, sent warning of the coming of the terrible Dean and recommended, as though he were past praying for, that at least he be watched.   "We could wish some eye were had to him what he shall be attempting on your side of the water."   Walpole was not unwilling to meet his enemy in the way.   To the Dean, the lodestar of England was magnetic yet, and clouds of spleen and spite broke at the prospect of seeing his friends, like mariners after a storm.   Harley had died two years previously, obtaining a certain immortality by the manuscripts he had collected. Bolingbroke had returned from exile and Bishop Atterbury had taken his place. Arbuthnot, the beloved physician, waited to discuss certain marvelous manuscripts of Captain Gulliver's Travels, which were passing from hand to hand. Gay was offering a room in Whitehall and Pope had opened a retreat at Twickenham. Wits and writers were ready to choose the Dean as the Doyen of letters. The temptation to fence once again with the bad, bold Bolingbroke, to inspire the lovable Gay, to guide the rhyme-mongering Pope and to bask in the sweetness distilled by Arbuthnot overcame the Dean. "If there were a dozen Arbuthnots, I would burn my Travels," he cried. For the lack of one Arbuthnot God burned Sodom. As the world held but one Arbuthnot and his lodging was in London, the Dean was constrained to make another physical journey across the sea.

March of 1726 saw the Dean return to London and divide his time pleasantly between old friendships and his new book. On this occasion he found a phenomenon previously lacking in England. There was once more a Prince of Wales in the land. Through Arbuthnot's kindly influence he was introduced to the dapper little Prince and his big-souled Princess. Through the dullness of others or their own serene brightness they had

created a political opposition to the Whig King. So
often bit by Princes, the Dean was nine times shy
and it was necessary for the Princess to command
his presence nine times before he attended. Lately
there had been brought a "wild boy" from Germany, and the Dean supposed Her Highness to be
equally desirous to see a wild Dean from Ireland.
In that guise the Dean offered her some specimens
of Irish cloth and though the Princess did not become draped according to the pattern of the Drapier, she promised to remember the Irish Cause
when Queen. Another important acquaintance was
formed with Mrs. Howard, the mistress of the
Prince, whose Princess showed no jealousy of his
heartstrings, provided the strings of politics were
left in her fingers. The Howards had successfully
adventured to Hanover to meet the rising sun.
She was an intriguer, who once sold her lovely
hair to provide a political dinner, though she
showed an ugly neck. The Dean, writing her
character, said: "If she had never seen a Court she
might have been a friend." Mrs. Howard and that
other "unconscionable dealer," Walpole, thought
they understood each other, but both wrongly.

An interesting interview was made with Walpole. The official ruler of England was necessarily
anxious to meet the self-chosen director of Ireland.
Walpole as often wondered whether he could rule

England without the Dean as the Dean must have
weighed Walpole's worth in the Irish sovereignty.
They dined together by Walpole's invitation and
the Dean asked a further interview, at which he
stated the case for Ireland. The two protagonists
differed on every point. Walpole was clearly averse
to any view of Liberty propagated by the Drapier.
He would not bid for the Drapier's pen, and
the Drapier, though he could state his terms, would
not indicate his price. He only pointed out that
the glorious Revolution had brought great wrongs
upon the Irish Whigs, who celebrated it with such
zeal; a situation not lost on the cynicism of either.
Rumor spread that the most independent of Deans
had sued political pardon and proposed as Bishop
of Cloyne undoing his harm as Dean of St. Patrick's, but he cast the dust from indignant feet.

In August he returned to Dublin like a King to
his Kingdom, though it represented his intellectual
antipodes. The Corporation of Dublin welcomed
him in wherries, while the whole City received him
with gala and garland in the streets, and the bells of
the Churches rang to the glory of God and honor
of His Dean. But it was a sullen and saddened
champion they welcomed. His self-stabbing spirit
had been happier at his previous ignoble and un-
noticed arrival, when lampoons were affixed instead
of bunting. By Walpole's *non possumus* he knew

that the gulf had been entrenched between Ireland and England and that centuries must pass before the flower of Irish Freedom, sowed and watered in the Deanery Garden, shielded under his gown and defended by his pen and turning like a sword in every direction, could grow to maturity or harvest. Doubly seared he was at heart, for during all the time of his absence in England he had secretly known that Stella languished to death.

XII

1726

GREAT were the public triumphs of the Dean.
Overwhelming his private successes. In whatever
direction he threw himself, he seemed to achieve
portents, and to touch the stupendous. He kept
the Tories in power in England as long as he remained on the spot. Even from exile in Ireland
he had dealt the Whigs a reeling backhander. The
Lord Lieutenant confessed Government of Ireland
was by leave of the Dean. English rule in Dublin
was despotism tempered by his epigrams. The
Whigs made Protestants nervous with threats of
the "wooden shoes," which the Pretender and the
French King would compel. But the Dean had
made the flesh of Catholics and Protestants creep
with the ruinous possibilities of Wood's halfpence.

Dublin, from a hostile and indifferent place of
exile, had become his feudal fief. The Clergy had
rallied to the great restorer of their cloth. Arch-

bishop and Lord Chancellor followed the Drapier.
Politicians obeyed his broadsheets and lampoons,
while the mob undertook his defense from violence
or arrest. Carteret informed Walpole he must
send ten thousand soldiers, to lay hands upon the
Dean. And the Dean found new worshipers like
Doctor Sheridan, whose town wit and country
place were at his disposal. Vanessa had died, but
Stella kept mysterious guard on his unbesiegable
heart. Stella and Dingley lay at his beck and call.
Power and influence lay in his pen. All the terrors
he could covet as a cleric, a man of letters or
political leader were in his ink. The Lord
Lieutenant was his admiring friend. Walpole
having intruded his Whig understrapper, Archbishop Boulter, into the Primacy, Ireland lay
poised between Archbishop and Dean. It would
have been no compliment to add the Dean to that
Bench of Nobodies and Somebodies, whom he insisted were not the true and good men chosen in
England for the Sees, but highwaymen, who had
robbed their papers on Hounslow Heath.

But the Dean was never happy, nor amused.
Amusement he called "the happiness of those who
cannot think." Happiness is the achievement of
minor successes by little minds. He had tasted in
some degree all that men value most and all had
turned bitter on his tongue. He no longer needed

to be miserly, but he was more miserable than ever. He had made a host of followers, but he was more than solitary. Stella had weaned him from misogyny, but he had fallen the deeper into misanthropy. The country, which he loved, offered him no relief from exile, and the country, which loved him, he disliked. He loathed Englishmen in power and scorned Irishmen thereof, sitting "like a toad in the corner of my great house with a perfect hatred of all public actions and persons." During lonely and sleepless nights, dreary and dreamless days he turned to unfailing founts of patience and power, his pen and ink. Between tracts and lampoons, Chapter meetings and Castle *levées,* he amused himself with the ever imaginary Voyages of Captain Gulliver.

No change in latitude healed or changed his sultry mind. No traveling from Ireland to England, no riding and visiting through Ireland afforded peace or rest. Religion supplied no consolation in this world, nor did the duties of Dean suggest conjectural rewards in the next. His ingenious and restless mind was only eased or satisfied away from the petty planet and its puny habitants. The mind of the Dean vacated the Deanery and drifted into seas unknown, uncharted and certainly undescribed.

His young imagination had fed in Sir William

Temple's library upon real Journeys into Siam and
Ethiopia and Morocco. He had perused every
Voyage, which had since fallen under his eye, and
enjoyed the pleasant and irresponsible scope they
gave to discovery and delusion. Eighteenth
century travelers did not hesitate to embellish and
enshrine their travels and, provided they had disappeared for a decent number of years, they were
accorded a cultivated and uncritical audience. The
Dean read a new book called *Robinson Crusoe* with
the utmost good humor, and fell into the accurate
and conscientious style of the author, "the fellow
that was pilloried, I have forgot his name." Publishers, he perceived indulgent to the adventurous
and the readers glad to be gullible. He decided
to incur adventures such as few writers had ever
imagined or publishers had yet dreamed. He indulged deep in geographical joking and commenced to write of a Voyage to Lilliput. As he
played with the subject, he began playing with
himself. He entered into the clothes and character
of his Captain Gulliver. He interwove his own life
like an underlying parable. Gulliver's early
journeys to sea corresponded with his first flights
from Moor Park, where, like Gulliver, "my hours
of leisure I spent in reading the best authors
Ancient and Modern." Captain Gulliver did not
join in the controversy, but returned to sea.

The Dean saw himself rising above earth until the jostling crowds had shrunk from feet to inches. They were the same folk except that their proportions and circumstances were miniature. Their passions and ambitions were identical, but they appeared petty. Their desires and possessions, their grandeurs were indistinguishable from those of the English Court, but theirs were the pomps of dolls and the desires of dwarves. By applying his friend Berkeley's Theory of Vision the Dean found all the magnitude and magnificence of the life which he had craved, coveted, embraced and lost, reduced to insect focus. The only question was which end of the telescope he applied. It stood him instead of philosophy to recall London as an ant-heap instead of an arena. What a relief to his disappointed spirit to realize that the whole Court was a box of marionettes, and that events, which had frayed his mind's edge, did not matter. The few hundred miles which England occupied in space resembled a few hundred yards. England was Lilliput!

However, on with Gulliver! The Dean described himself lying on the Lilliputian shore stung by the arrows of scores of Lampooners and Pamphleteers. Later Gulliver, like the Dean, was placed under the royal protection, and when some Lilliputians renewed their puny attack, the Colonel

in charge ordered the ringleaders to be handed into
his power, whereat Gulliver was content to release
them with a severe fright, an act of clemency, which
was represented very much to his advantage at
Court. Was the Dean thinking of the day when
Bolingbroke used his power to pick up and squeeze
some noisy Pamphleteers including the most
mordant of the Dean's vilifiers? He had liked to
attribute their release to his personal magnanimity.
And the Dean remembered nights of London
entertainment when Gulliver wrote:

> "I now considered myself as bound by the
> laws of Hospitality to a people who had
> treated me with so much expense and
> magnificence."

When Gulliver was drawn prisoner to the
Emperor of Lilliput, the Dean stamped him with
mysterious figures, making him identical with himself. Gulliver was fastened with fourscore and
eleven chains and six and thirty padlocks. Now
the anonymous author of the *Tale of a Tub* stated
that he had written fourscore and eleven Pamphlets
for the service of thirty-six factions. Gulliver was
accommodated with an ancient Temple, esteemed
to be the largest in the whole Kingdom, which had
been polluted some years before by an unnatural
murder and since secularized and stripped of orna-

ments and furniture. This Temple Gulliver used
as his kennel, but was the Dean not thinking of the
polluted and vandalized Cathedral of Canterbury
where he had been promised his first prebend?

George the First, with whom the Dean knowing
no German could no more converse than Gulliver
with his Lilliputian Majesty, was the Emperor of
Lilliput.   The Dean could safely indulge the
King's character, his courage and horsemanship,
his simple dress and sense of economy, while
literary prudence inspired a flattering picture "of
his countenance erect, all his motion graceful and
his deportment majestic."   Uncouth and unattrac-
tive as King George was, it was not merely sarcasm
of the Dean to refer to "his body and limbs well
proportioned," but part of his greater satire that
admiration or disgust was only a question of scale.
The beautiful, when enlarged, becomes monstrous,
while the ugly equally reduced becomes fairylike.
It was a satiric and social reading of Doctor
Berkeley's Theory of Vision.

With infinite zest and caution the Dean proceeded to describe the Ministers of Lilliput and
Gulliver's endearment to the natives. The scene
of boys and girls playing hide-and-seek in his hair
was a secret reminiscence of those far days, when
his best periwig was kept at Mrs. Vanhomrigh's
and the Vanhomrigh children played with a strange

curate from Ireland. But the whole world was
intended to recognize Flimnap, as the Walpole of
Lilliput and "my friend Reldresal" as a sort of
Lilliputian Carteret. Politics in Lilliput were
reduced to dancing on the tight rope. Skill in
trimming and balancing made their political art.
Needless to say, there was no Minister who had not
received falls at some time or another. Flimnap
himself had been saved on one occasion by falling
upon one of the King's cushions. This allusion to
political succor once afforded by the Duchess of
Kendal to Walpole must have given the Dean a
chuckle sufficient to purge his momentary melancholy. To call the King's concubine a cushion was
perhaps not courteous, but she had abetted Wood.
The Dean was enjoying himself immensely and
continued to tease the worthy Walpole, who had
recently revived the Order of the Bath to mark his
political purchases. He described how the King of
Lilliput, tested the dexterity of his Ministers, by
making them creep or leap under or over a stick;
to be rewarded by threads of Red or Green or Blue.
The Blue of the Garter had been recently assumed
by Walpole, while the Red of the Bath adorned his
many minions. The Dean remembered the restoration of the Green ribbon of the Thistle, as Queen
Anne's inducement to the Scotch Lords to enter
the stables of Union.

The General of Lilliput, described as a great patron of Gulliver, was no doubt, Ormonde, while Gulliver's mortal enemy, Skyresh Bololam, masked the Earl of Nottingham, who had preened himself also on naval knowledge and was known as "old Dismal." The Dean hated him well, since he had been pleased to express fears in the Lords' lest one who was not even a Christian should be promoted to the office of Bishop. "Admiral of the Realm but of a morose and sour complexion" was an indelible description. Following the agreement concluded between Gulliver and the Emperor, the former was allowed to visit the Emperor's Palace, which, with its outer Court forty feet square, and two Courts between gates and walls, was roughly designed upon Windsor Castle. To look into the Royal Apartments Gulliver used stools, which he cut from trees in the Royal Park, a hundred yards away. The Dean was thinking of his past visits to Windsor in the time of Queen Anne and his first acquaintance with Her Majesty, who had not received him as genially as Gulliver was received by the Empress of Lilliput, being "pleased to smile very graciously upon me and gave me out of the window her hand to kiss." The abhorrence of the Empress for Gulliver allegorized the Queen's horror at the *Tale of a Tub*. Gulliver passed on without further account of the Kingdom, except the promise of "a greater work with a particular account of their Wars and Politics," referring to the *History of the Reign of Queen Anne,* which the Dean treasured under hand.

When Reldresal was complimenting Gulliver on his newly gained liberty and assuming some merit himself, the Dean was thanking Carteret for standing between him and prosecution during the Drapier storm. He amused himself translating the feud of Whig and Tory into the Lilliputian struggles between High and Low-Heels, the Parties of Slamecksan and Tramecksan. The Emperor showed the lowest Heel of all, but the Heir Apparent, like the new Hanoverian Prince of Wales, was allowed a tendency toward High Heels, otherwise High Toryism.

Lilliput nourished a rivalry with the Empire of Blefescu, wherein the Dean pleasantly sketched the troubles between England and France, dating from the religious controversy whether eggs should be eaten at the Big or Small End. A previous Emperor (presumably Henry the Eighth) had cut his finger eating an egg according to the ancient practise and issued an edict changing the mode of egg-eating. The Easter-egg or the mode of Sacrament, whether Catholic or Protestant, had led to six rebellions (from the Pilgrimage of Grace to the last glorious Revolution). One Emperor (Charles the First) had lost his life and another (James the Second) his Crown in the subsequent controversies. Eleven thousand martyrs had died rather than break their eggs at the wrong end and countless Big-Endian exiles had taken refuge in Blefescu. The remainder had been rendered incapable of holding office by penal law. Hardly eleven thousand Catholics had been really put to death and the Dean strangely omitted the few hundred Protestant or Small-End martyrs. By a daring parody of the famous text from which the rival doctrines of the Communion service are based, he quoted the Lilliputian Koran, in which the great Prophet Lustrog required all true believers to break their eggs at the *convenient* end. No doubt the cynical Dean intended to advise Christians to follow the doctrine convenient locally and even in Rome to do as the Romans do.

Having settled the strife of Christendom, he passed to the wars of England with France. How Gulliver reduced the entire forces of Blefescu and was created a Nardac, the highest of Lilliputian titles, was a squinting dream of Marlborough winning his Dukedom by the prostration of France. It was followed by a rapid transformation of Duke to Dean, when Gulliver proclaimed the opinions of the author of a celebrated Pamphlet on *The Conduct of the Allies,* for "so unmeasurable is the ambition of Princes that the King of Lilliput seemed to think of nothing less than reducing the whole Empire of Blefescu into a Province and governing it by a Viceroy; of destroying the Big-Endian exiles and compelling that people to break the smaller end of their eggs. But I endeavoured to divert him from this design by many arguments drawn from the topics of policy as well as justice. And I plainly protested that I would never be an instrument of bringing a free and brave people into slavery." The Junto of which Gulliver complained, was the same malicious group who hated the Dean and opposed certain "conditions very advantageous to our Emperor," wherewith Gulliver modestly did not trouble the reader, since they were the Dean's own.

The Ambassadors of Blefescu generously invited Gulliver to visit their country and, if perhaps the Dean was never invited to France except by Bolingbroke, certainly he was there much admired. The French Ambassador used to compliment the Dean "like a Dragon." Needless to say, Flimnap and Bolgolam misrepresented Gulliver's intercourse with the Blefuscudians as much as Walpole and Nottingham endeavored to involve the Dean with the Jacobites in the eyes of their sovereign; especially Walpole, who like Flimnap "had always been my secret enemy though he outwardly caressed me more than was usual to the moroseness of his nature," and took the first occasion to advise Gulliver's dismissal.

Gulliver's vindication of the Court lady, Flimnap's wife, who was said to have taken a violent affection for his person and to have come privately to his lodging, recalled Walpole's trouble with his first wife as well as the Dean's alliance with the dashing Lady Masham; "I own she often came to my house but always publicly nor ever without three more in the Coach, who were usually her sister and young daughter." In real life it was a brother and a son, but this was, perhaps, a paragraph intended for Stella's anxious eye. But there was also a remembrance of Bolingbroke's later effort to bribe away the Duchess of Kendal from Walpole, for Gulliver wore sometimes the Dean's clothes and sometimes Bolingbroke's.

Gulliver's conclusion was a reflection of the Dean's relations with the Treasurer at the time of rewriting, since "I lost all credit with him and found my interest decline very fast with the Emperor himself, who was indeed too much governed by that favourite." The climax of Gulliver's misfortunes came with the Articles of Impeachment secretly exhibited against him by Bolgolam and Flimnap, which read like a satire upon the accusation of treason made against Bolingbroke

and Harley. Gulliver's sentence of blinding instead of death referred to Carteret's modification
in the proceedings threatened against the Dean.
Through Carteret or another the Dean may have
received the hint, which he sharpened into the sarcasm that "it would be sufficient for you to see by
the Eyes of the Ministers, since the greatest Princes
do no more!"

Gulliver's flight to Blefescu was Bolingbroke's
to France, but the overturned boat, in which he
escaped was the Ark of St. Patrick's, which safeguarded the Dean's exit from the Lilliputian intrigues in the Court of St. James. "I told the
Emperor that my good fortune had thrown this
boat in my way to carry me to some place, from
whence I might return into my native country and
begged his Majesty's orders for getting materials
to fit it up together with his license to depart;
which, after some kind expostulations, he was
pleased to grant."

In such moments the Dean accepted Ireland as
his native country. The sheep which Gulliver
brought home and hoped would prove advantageous to the woolen manufacture in his "native
country" recalled the Dean's proposals on behalf
of Irish Industries. The materials which he begged,
the thousand pounds for installing himself in the
Deanery, promised but not given, still rankled.

Having inspected the personal pettiness of politicians and people of England through his Lilliputian prism, the Dean reviewed the grossness of all mankind by voyaging to the other end of the perspective. In Brobdingnag he found a race of human beings, gigantically magnified. The Dean was remembering the ignoble change in his fortunes when he left the field of his English achievements for Irish obscurity. Gulliver was thinking the Dean's thoughts, when he wrote:

> "I reflected what a mortification it must prove to me to appear as inconsiderable in this nation as one single Lilliputian would appear to be among us."

At first sight the Brobdingnagians esteemed him as much as a weasel or "any hateful little animal which we have a mind to destroy."

From a copy of Sturmy's *Mariner's Magazine,* the Dean copied out the vivid language describing a storm, the sea itself "grown very hollow" and the technical processes of the ship "spooning" and turning to windward. Deftly he introduced the nautical terms to delight possible sailor readers or to puzzle the lubber.

Gulliver was given his true value as soon as he reached Court, for the Queen purchased him for the sum of a thousand pieces of gold, which was another

backward glance at the money promised by Queen
Anne. The delectable picture drawn of the witty
Queen of Brobingnag, who graciously extended
her finger-tips instead of her foot to the osculation
of her visitor, was the Dean's compliment to his
newly-made friend, the Princess of Wales, whom he
saluted as "the ornament of Nature, the darling of
the world, the delight of her subjects, the phœnix
of the Creation." But the King of Brobdingnag
reflecting the ideal patriot King, of whom Bolingbroke wrote and Swift dreamed, carried a memory
of King William, "a prince of much gravity and
austere countenance," who had been educated in
philosophy and mathematics. Gulliver's first interview recalled the famous interview which Jonathan
had received from his first dread sovereign. His
Brobdingnagian Majesty "could not conceal his
astonishment" and put several questions, to which
he even received rational answers. The royal love
of Music connoted the Hanoverian Prince of
Wales, who had joined in the general craze for
Handel and music, which the Dean enjoyed as
much as a Moscovite.

Gulliver disliked the music in vogue but scoffed
at contemporary science more. The Professors of
Brobdingnag classified Gulliver not under occult
causes but as a *lusus naturae* or jest of nature "to
the unspeakable advancement of human knowl-

edge." At heart the Dean considered Nature neither occult nor a joke, though possibly he might have allowed her like womankind to be a combination of both.

While he was placing the final touches to this Voyage, one very dear to him was sickening and threatening to sink into a gulf which to the Dean was final. To Stella, under the guise of his Brobdingnagian nurse Gulliver paid exquisite compliment. On Stella was modeled the daughter of Gulliver's new master, who cared for him so tenderly and tried to spare her precious charge in every way:

"A daughter of nine years old, a child of toward parts for her age, very dextrous at her needle. She was likewise my schoolmistress to teach me the language. When I pointed to anything, she told me the name of it in her own tongue."

Like Stella and the Dean in sweet distant days, Gulliver and his nurse presented each other with endearing names, "Grildrig" and "Glumdalclitch." This was a delightful memory of the "little language," which once passed between them, and an inversion of their relations in the schoolroom. Stella's dying eyes could not have been deceived by the balm in the manuscript spread like ointment unto her burial.

Moor Park in Sir William Temple's day inspired
Gulliver's complaint of "my master finding how
profitable I was like to be," as well as the longing
expressed in the words, "I had a strong hope, which
never left me, that I should one day recover my
liberty." The Dean felt that his allusions to Stella
and the Princess of Wales were too thinly disguised
and expressly excepted them both from the strong
Brobdingnagian odor, of which lesser carnivores
are sensible in the larger, for their "persons were
as sweet as those of any Lady in England."

All the while Stella was desperately ill and sinking dispiritedly. Her fate weighed not a little on
the Dean's mind, for she had suffered both in health
and repute by her devotion for him and he composed a most loving epitaph for her under the veils
of Glumdalclitch, when he confessed that

> "I should be guilty of great ingratitude if I
> omitted this honourable mention of her care
> and affection towards me, which I heartily wish
> it lay in my power to requite as she deserves
> instead of being the innocent but unhappy
> instrument of her disgrace as I have too much
> reason to fear."

It amused the memoried Dean to float backward
in time, and with godlike afterthought and divine
revengefulness to remember his enemies and
friends. Especially ungrateful and embittered was

the enemy he selected in Steele to personify the
huge and vain Dwarf, who became so jealous of
Gulliver and attempted to play such wicked tricks,
"against which" Gulliver complained "I could only
revenge myself by calling him brother and chal-
lenging him to wrestle." Steele, strutting vain-
gloriously attacked the Dean as unfairly as the
Dwarf, who dropped Gulliver in the cream;
whereat the Brobdingnagian Queen, like Queen
Anne of bountiful but moribund memory, "would
have immediately cashiered him, if I had not been
so generous as to intercede."

The drift of story-telling carried the Dean
onward, and he lowered the tangle of his memories
like a net into the tide. Here, there and in every
corner flashes of his past life flitted phosphores-
cently under the darkening eddy. At one time he
recalled his wonderful influence on the Court
ladies, by making them assist and forward Gulliver
in his cockle-boat. "My business was only to steer
while the ladies gave me a gale with their fans."
At another time he recollected that the Fitzgeralds
had crossed his path and summoned their legendary
and historical monkey to leave their coat-of-arms
in order to snatch and carry Gulliver upon the roof.

Vanessa's lawsuit as well as his own confirmed
his growing hatred of lawyers, for Gulliver wrote
of "having been formerly almost ruined by a long

suit in Chancery which was decreed for me with costs." And the Reverend Jonathan bitterly remembered the posts, which had been offered to him in penury, when he had refused to join the company of "slavish prostitute Chaplains to some Nobleman."

The King of Brobdingnag finally passed into the Dean, and his questionnaire of Gulliver became savagely ironical. Even the crop of Peers, whom Harley had created to save his Government and beat Marlborough, only left a sediment of scorn in the Dean's mind, for the King asked:

> "What qualifications are therefore necessary in those who are to be created new Lords, whether the humour of the Prince, a sum of money to a Court Lady, or a Prime Minister or a design of strengthening a Party opposite to the Public interest?"

His long-fed, long-fanned hatred for standing armies, and National Debts opened the query, "Who were our creditors, and where should we find money to pay them?" The benevolent Brobdingnagian

> "wondered to hear me talk of such chargeable and expensive wars: that certainly we must be a quarrelsome people or live among very bad neighbours and that our Generals

must needs be richer than our Kings. He asked what business we had out of our Islands, unless, upon the score of Trade or Treaty or to defend the coasts with our fleet."

The centuries still seem to echo the Dean's anger against standing armaments and floating debts!

The King's conclusion that "the bulk of your nations be the most pernicious race of little odious vermin that nature ever suffered to crawl upon the surface of the earth" was intended to remain with the Dean's compliments as a general indictment of the human race and not to the score of his dear English alone.   But then the King spoke from the superior civilization of a people, who utterly declined to learn the secret of gunpowder, who had made writing legal commentaries a capital crime and considered that:

"Whoever could make two ears of corn or two blades of grass to grow upon a spot where only one grew before,"

deserved better than all the politicians together.

The Dean searching the earliest notes he had made of his Voyages, found the parody he had made for the Scriblerus Club of an unfortunate Kingdom ruled like Plato's Republic by Professors.   So his cynical imagination brought him to a

Kingdom of Laputa, which was provided with a
Flying Island, into which pulleys facilitated his
arrival.

The King of Laputa took Gulliver in hand, and
had him measured mathematically by Quadrant
and Compass for a suit of clothes, which were
found quite out of shape owing to a mistake in the
arithmetic. This was an unkind dig at Sir Isaac
Newton, whose calculation of the earth's distance
from the sun had been recently upset by a printer
adding an accidental cipher. Laputa bore vague
resemblance to Academical and scientific England.
Sir Isaac's absence of mind suggested the use of
Flappers for calling the attention of the learned,
while the fear aroused by Halley's comet in England touched the mirth of the Dean and he very
safely ridiculed the idea "that the earth very nar-
rowly escaped a brush from the tail of the last
comet, which would have infallibly reduced it to
ashes, and that the next, which they calculated for
one and thirty years hence, will probably destroy
us."

The mighty phenomena of Nature did not
affright a Dean, who stood in no excessive awe of
the supernatural. One rare and overwhelming
scene from the pageant of the Heavens had occurred twice in his lifetime, the Total Eclipse of
the Sun. His impressions, whether gleaned in 1715

or 1724, gave him the idea for the description of the
Flying Island. Certainly it tallies accurately with
modern accounts of a total eclipse, "when all on a
sudden it became obscured as I thought, in a manner very different from what happens by the inter-
position of a cloud. I turned back and perceived a
vast opaque body between me and the sun moving
forwards towards the Island (on which Gulliver
stood). It seemed to be about two miles high and
hid the sun six or seven minutes . . ."

The ladies of Laputa lamented being held to one
place, like the ladies of England, of which the Dean
would as gladly have written as Gulliver: "I think
it the most delicious spot of ground in the world."
In a previous voyage Gulliver animadverted upon
the slanting handwriting of the English ladies.
From Laputa he criticized their contempt for their
husbands and their preference for Continental
gallants: "for the husband is always so rapt in
speculation that the Mistress and Lover may proceed to the greatest familiarities before his face."
Somewhat prophetically, the Dean gave these
sky-starers credit for charting three times as many
fixed stars as were known to their English compeers
as well as for discovering the two Satellites of Mars
then unknown to Europe.

The Flying Island in its depressions and oppressions mimicked the action of England upon

Ireland, for whenever his subjects grew rebellious,
the King of Laputa hovered above Balnibarbi
depriving them of sun and rain and afflicting them
with disease and death. In an extreme case he
crushed them by depressing the adamantine bottom
of his Flying Island, as was threatened over the
affair of Wood's halfpence, had it not been that
Dublin, being one of those cities, which "abound
in high spires, a sudden fall might endanger the
bottom or under surface of the island," to-wit upon
the sharp spire of St. Patrick's. And like the Irish
under the Dean's tuition, the subjects of Laputa
"of all this are well apprized and understand how
far to carry their obstinacy where their liberty or
property is concerned."

Balnibarbi was Gulliver's melancholy dream of
Ireland and Lagado a dingy vision of eighteenth-
century Dublin, "which is about half the bigness of
London but the houses very strangely built and
most of them out of repair. The people in the
streets walked fast, looked wild, their eyes fixed
and were generally in rags. We passed through
one of the town gates and went about three miles
into the country, where I saw many labourers
working with several sorts of tools in the ground,
but was not able to conjecture what they were
about, neither did I observe any expectation either
of corn or grass although the soil appeared to be

excellent." Munodi, his cultured host and con-
ductor, "had been some years Governor of Lagado,
and by a cabal of Ministers discharged for
insufficiency," whereby the Dean signified Carteret.
When they came after three hours' traveling "into
a most beautiful country, farmers' houses at small
distances neatly built, the fields enclosed, contain-
ing vineyards, corn grounds and meadows," the
Dean was sketching the choice estates, which he
had visited in the Pale or in Ulster. Munodi's
house represented the magnificent Georgian mansions beginning to adorn a countryside of bog and
cabin. All this rising prosperity, Munodi mentioned sadly, he would have to destroy unless he
wished to incur censure from the ruling powers of
Laputa.

The principal institution in Balnibarbi was an
Academy and founded by persons who had paid
visits above upon business or diversion and returned to contrive prosperous new rules and
methods, of which the only inconvenience was that
none could be brought to perfection and the country languished in consequence. This Academy
Munodi was unwilling to visit but he sent Gulliver
in charge of a friend as a credulous person and
one who had "been a sort of Projector in Younger
days."

In other words the Dean recalled his membership

of that sapient University of Dublin, which had done so little for him in his youth or in his prime. He made it the target not only for his satire upon the sciences as taught in Trinity College but upon the contemporary schemes and bubbles, swelling and breaking in the brains of Englishmen. Accordingly the Warden or Provost showed Gulliver round the chambers of various Experimenters, some of whom gave signs of being inspired by Rabelais. Here was demonstrated the original scheme for extracting sunbeams from cucumbers and bottling them against the Irish climate. Here ice was being calcined to gunpowder and the process was proceeding of making fire malleable. Here were devised the advantageous devices of plowing with hogs or spinning silk with spiders. Here were assistants of the Universal Artist condensing air into a dry tangible substance by extracting the niter, while others were softening marble to pillows. That great Artist hoped within reasonable time to breed naked sheep, which in view of the Woolen Laws of the kingdom would have been sublimely suitable to Irish pastures.

Gulliver could only approve the project for treating the humors of the political body by the same medical pharmacy as the natural body with a view to shortening debate and dispatching business. The project would "curb the petulancy of

the young and correct the positiveness of the old,
rouse the stupid and damp the pert." For the
public good legislators were directed to vote to the
direct contrary of their speeches. There was only
a division of opinion whether it were best to tax a
man's vices by his neighbors' opinion or his qualities according to his own. Gallants for instance
could be taxed on the favors they had received
from women by their own vouching. The taxes
on women's chastity were not worth collecting, but
their own opinion of their clothes and beauty
would yield considerable revenues. To so excellent
political projects the Dean was inspired to add a
proposal for encouraging the race of Discoverers
and Informers, who had been busy of late against
his Tory and Jacobite friends. Bishop Atterbury
had been tried for treason and exiled on evidence
of letters which mysteriously mentioned a spotted
dog. Gulliver accordingly devised a Dictionary
for Informers. The Dean's irony colored the
traveler's simplicity sufficiently to suggest that:

A lame dog could be twisted to signify an
Invader,
A sieve—a Court Lady,
A plague—a Standing Army,
Gout—a High Priest,
A bottomless pit—the Treasury,
A sink—a Court,
A running sore—an Administration!

These synonyms supplied red-hot by the Dean possibly turned Gulliver's mind toward his own beloved country for he "began to think of returning home to England," and visiting Glubbdubdrib, the Island of Sorcerers, on the way. The Governor of this Island had the power to call up spirits and Gulliver was invited to name and question any of the mighty dead and to depend upon their answers, "for lying was a talent of no use in the lower world." Gulliver summoned Alexander the Great, Hannibal, Cæsar, Pompey and Brutus, of whom "Cæsar freely confessed that the greatest actions of his life were not equal by many degrees to the glory of taking it away." Whether the Dean shared Gulliver's tyrannicide opinions or not, the Drapier was not displeased "with beholding the destroyers of tyrants and usurpers and the restorers of liberty to oppressed and injured nations." Howsoever far Gulliver might travel, the uttermost parts of the sea were haunted by the specter of the island, which the Dean dared not name.

The seances in Glubbdubdrib enabled Gulliver to introduce Homer to his commentators and Aristotle to Descartes. The memory of the *Battle of Books* returned to the Dean like a smell from the garden of his youth. Aristotle predicted that the Doctrine of Attraction, otherwise Newton's Gravitation, would be exploded and that "new systems of Nature were but new fashions, which would vary in every age, and even those, who pretend to demonstrate them from mathematical principles, would flourish but a short period of time." By the necromancy of his pen the Dean could lean back in his chair and question the history and learning of the past. With cynical insight he gleaned the secret and contemptible motives to which great enterprises and revolutions owed their success. In the pedigrees of Kings and the nobility, which he raised in ghostly succession from the grave, he revealed fiddlers in the royal descents and "an interruption of lineages by pages, lacqueys, valets, coachmen, gamesters, captains and pickpockets," sufficiently to make his aristocratic or eugenic friends think.

Corruption in politics and degeneracy in blood preyed upon the mind of the Dean till *Gulliver's Travels* became tinged with the spleen of melancholic loathing and distressful distastes. The vision of antiquity revealed not only racial decay but how disease "had altered every lineament of an English countenance, shortened the size of bodies, unbraced the nerves, relaxed the sinews and muscles, introduced a sallow complexion and rendered the flesh loose and rancid," dismal details, which could be realized by summoning from the dead some English yeoman of the old stamp.

The Dean sickened while he was writing and the floodgates of despair and abomination flowed into his desolation. The old pains of giddiness and the horror of deafness took hold upon the Dean in fits. The sound of turning waters surged through his groaning skull. Upon those waters Gulliver pursued Voyages like an observant madman. Henceforth Gulliver was a pessimist.

He came to the immortals called Struldbruggs, the ghastly ghosts of themselves encased in flesh and blood, endowed with eternal life but not with youth. Filled with envy against others were the unenviable Struldbruggs and principally envious of "the vices of the younger sort and the deaths of the old." By reflecting on the former, they found themselves cut off from all possibility of pleasure, and whenever they saw a funeral they lamented and repined that others were gone to an harbor of rest. The only law tempering their curse was one granting automatic divorces at fourscore on the ground that "those who are condemned without any fault of their own to a perpetual continuance in the world should not have their misery doubled by the load of a wife."

Thence Gulliver tacked into realities by journeying to Japan. Here a Dutch disguise was necessary, since Christianity had recently been abolished and only the Dutch were permitted entry

on condition they trampled a Crucifix. Tales of
Japanese persecution had reached England, but the
Dean was thinking more of his own hatred for the
Dutch and obliquely of the insinuations, which
had been made against his own orthodoxy by Nottingham and Steele. Accordingly Gulliver petitioned the Emperor of Japan to be excused the
anti-Christian ceremony, until the Emperor "began to doubt whether I was a real Hollander or no,
but rather suspected I must be a Christian." It
was a shrewd touch, for the suspicion had been
stronger in the other direction.

The Dean made up his mind to throw over-
board the whole human race and dispatched Gulliver upon his last dread and direful voyage. He
determined to recreate men in the image of brute
beasts. The Creator had made them a little lower
than the Angels. The Dean remade them con-
siderably lower than horses. In the land of the
Houyhnhnms Gulliver found civilized and loqua-
cious steeds holding in subjection and contempt a
race of debased men, for whom no word would
suffice but Yahoo. The filth and misery, in which
the Yahoos had their life and being, were outwardly sketched from the unhappy natives of Ireland. The beggars of Brobdingnag, who "watching their opportunity crowded to the side of the
coach and gave me the most horrible spectacles

that ever an English eye beheld," had been a
reminiscence of Dublin. The Yahoos of these
God-forsaken lands conveyed his most horrible
memory riding through the Irish countryside.
The poor creatures half naked and unnourished,
for whom the Dean's fierce pen had striven to carve
out some economical charity or commercial hope,
had sat as their models. Apart from their
souls and ideals, the bodily condition of the Irish
nations was not far different from those which
appalled Gulliver. His masters, the Houyhnhnms
of the unspellable and unsayable name, were more
than performing horses or uncultured squires.
They were a race of equine philosophers, who
learned with horror of the state of England, after
Gulliver had learned their language sufficiently to
absorb the views of the Dean, with which these
quadruped prodigies were mysteriously endowed.
Horrified were Houyhnhnms to hear of such things
as wars of religion, "whether the juice of a certain
berry be blood or wine"; or of wars waged by
Princes sometimes "because the enemy is too
strong and sometimes because he is too weak."
Penal Laws also puzzled poor Houyhnhnms, and
Gulliver's master was at a loss that Law "which
was intended for every man's preservation should
be any man's ruin." On the other hand a cup of
coffee sounded a miracle of civilization, when Gul-

liver assured them "that this whole globe of earth
must be at least three times gone round before one
of our better female Yahoos could get her breakfast
or a cup to put it in." Of all his home-Yahoos the
most hateful to Gulliver were lawyers, against
whom he loosed every vindictive memory. He described how by sheer falsehood hired lawyers
might argue him out of possession of his own cow
and "never desire to know what claim or title my
adversary hath to my cow but whether the said
cow were red or black, her horn long or short,
whether the field I graze her in be round or square,
what diseases she is subject to and the like, after
which they consult precedents, adjourn the cause
from time to time and in ten, twenty or thirty years
come to an issue."

The Dean continued to prompt Gulliver to
describe an English Prime Minister as a passionless person, who "never tells a truth but with an
intent that you should take it for a lie nor a lie
but with a design that you should take it for a
truth." Lying was unknown to his horsey hosts,
who circumlocuted it as "the thing which was not."
Gulliver learned that in their refinement they
controlled their breeding by limiting themselves to
one child of each sex and their domestics to three.
Males and females received the same education.
As for the poor human Yahoos, asses, which had

been recently introduced into Ireland, were described as preferable both in smell and sound besides being more tame and orderly. Gulliver did not hesitate to use the dried skins of Yahoos to make shoes. The Dean, remembering that the castration of priests had actually been included in the English penal laws, presented the idea to Gulliver as a means of ending the Yahoos without taking life. A reminiscence of Irish outlaws and Rapparees and their practise of houghing cattle colored the fear expressed by the Houyhnhnms that Gulliver might be able to seduce the lower Yahoos into the woody and mountainous parts and bring them in troops by night to destroy their cattle.

Maddened, deafened, disappointed and tortured, the Dean poured the vials of his hate into the spleen of the ingenious Captain Gulliver until there was no insult nor horror left imaginable of the human race. He was feeling in a specially Irish mood when he recorded that "The original progenitors of the Yahoos may have been English, which indeed I was apt to suspect from the lineaments of their posterity's countenances although very much defaced." Only by frequently using a looking-glass could he habituate himself to tolerate the sight of a human creature. And not unlike the English gentleman who places his horses above his

women, Gulliver, on his return, found himself
preferring the company and even the odor of his
favorite quadrupeds. In his random thoughts the
Dean once put horses and women upon a level, at
least he made equal "the powers in their mouths and
in their tails." A French satirist observed that the
more he knew men, the more he liked dogs. An
Irish Dean not unnaturally preferred horses. It is
possible that Swift felt at such paradox with his
age that he had conceived some kindliness for animals whose lot was then unconsidered torture. At
least in his correspondence with Knightley Chet-
wode he described going without dinner rather
than disturb a cat which had kittened in his oven,
and he cherished the horse, he called after Bolingbroke, preferring to lay his whip on his groom. The
fate of eighteenth century post-horses was to die on
the road whether they were Peterborough's or
Archbishop King's. Swift was the first writer to
investigate or imagine the feelings of the horse, if
it was only for the pleasure of contrasting the de-
grading touch, which Gulliver found in the em-
brace of his human wife, after returning from
Horseland. "Having not been used to the touch
of that odious animal for so many years I fell in a
swoon for almost an hour." Such was the pretty
result of *Gulliver's Travels.*

XIII

THE SINKING OF THE STAR

(1724-1728)

GULLIVER'S TRAVELS were a success before being printed and were destined to become a classic before the author's name was generally known. Vanessa had read them. Stella had listened to them. The letters of friends touched upon these amazing *Travels*. His conversation and correspondence assumed Gulliver. In 1724 he wrote, "I have left the Country of Horses and am in the Flying Island where I shall not stay long." He wrote to Sheridan; "you will every day find my description of Yahoos more resembling." In the next year he retired to Sheridan's house at Quilca and transcribed the *Travels* complete. "They are admirable things and will wonderfully mend the world." Burying himself in the Irish back-country amid unknown tongue gave him the illusion of voyaging into the strange and foreign. To Pope he wrote:

"I have often reflected in how few hours with a swift horse or a strong gale a man may come among a people as unknown to him as the antipodes."

Quilca came as near any spot to bringing him peace, the peace of pleasant activities. Meditative happiness was never possible to his now questless spirit. Quilca and Laracor he loved as he had once loved Moor Park. Here he had been able to house Stella outside the reach of rumor and beyond the stings of spite. Dame Street in Dublin might have been named after Dame Gossip herself. Dublin was always hating and hateful. Dublin he called "doghole" or "rathole" and cursed her for a city situated "in that odious country and among that odious people." Living in Ireland was like living in a "coal-pit." Stella's health worried him. Under her raven hair she was pale and bloodless. He had taken care over her exercise in the past, over her riding and her walking—the Dean's infallible remedies for pallor or for spleen. "Spend pattens and spare potions. Wear out clogs and waste claret," he had urged of old time. He had claimed to "row after health like a waterman and ride after it like a postboy." Stella had kept up her riding until her horse's gait became uneasy to bear. Scorning scorn and gossip, they drew closer and closer. When the Dean was ill, Stella nursed

Esther Johnson, "Stella"

him in the Deanery. When Stella languished in
decline, she was revived by his invigorating visitation. He recalled the quiet paces and happy
pastimes which they had shared at Laracor or
Quilca, where his restlessness found rest and his
loneliness a dwelling. In a letter to Sheridan he
remembered the days when he and Stella went
a-riding or a-fishing or playing poetry together:

> "You will find Quilca not the thing it was
> last August. Nobody to relish the lake; no-
> body to ride over the Downs; no trout to be
> caught; no dining over a well; no night heroics;
> no morning epics; no stolen hour when the
> wife is gone; no creature to call you names.
> No blind harpers."

As for Dublin,

> "we have new plays and new libels and nothing
> valuable is old but Stella."

Again with merry complaint from the country:

> "what carking and caring there is among us
> for small beer and lean mutton and starved
> sheep and stopping gaps and driving cattle
> from the corn. The ladies' room smokes. The
> rain drops from the skies into the Kitchen."

The ladies were with him constantly, and rays of
Stella began to be reflected in the letters of distant

friends. Bolingbroke wrote, "Your Star will probably hinder you from taking the same journey." And again, "with what pleasure should I hear you *inter vina fugam Stellae moerere protervae.*"

At last he sped to England with the completed manuscript of Gulliver, leaving Stella installed in the Deanery. She was sinking, languishing, even dying in his absence and would not let him be told. But he dragged the truth from a faithful henchman, writing in desperate agonies:

> "Pray write to me every week, that I may know what steps to take; for I am determined not to go to Ireland to find her just dead or dying. Nothing but extremity could make me so familiar with those terrible words, applied to such a dear friend. Let her know I have bought her a repeating gold watch, for her ease in winter nights. I designed to have surprised her with it; but now I would have her know it, that she may see how my thoughts were always to make her easy."

Poor Stella! with so few nights or days left to check upon her gold watch. Poor Dean! with so small a toy trying to ease his own grief! At Sheridan's advice he returned, scarcely concealing the terror of seeing her die. When he returned, she revived and spent her last but not unhappy autumn with him in the country. Unrecorded this

last happiness and melancholy. Their last winter
followed, the same Dublin quarters, the same
weekly dinner, the same friends and the same expectation and delight over the coming book which
he had written for her, insomuch as he had put his
soul into its pages and his soul was Stella. Under
the white mask of her uncomplaining face even
Dublin held its jadish jaw, and averted wolf-eyes
from the slow and silent tragedy, which nothing
was destined to abate.

The Dean suffered intensely after his manner.
The ghost of Vanessa unexpectedly threatened his
devoted periwig, albeit was sheeted in literary
form. Some one, not Bishop Berkeley, had found
and was printing and publishing his lines to Vanessa, which he insisted:

> "no friend would publish, written fourteen
> years ago at Windsor and shows how indiscreet
> it is to leave anyone master of what cannot
> without the least consequence be shown to the
> world."

But Stella had forgiven him, though Vanessa had
not, and, even when *Cadenus and Vanessa* was
published to the world, Stella only remarked that
the Dean had been known to write finely upon a
Broomstick!

An overwhelming publication was breaking on
the horizon. Early in November of 1726 the peri-

wigged features and bland eyes of Captain Lemuel
Gulliver of Redriff appeared upon the frontispiece
of his *Travels into Several Remote Nations of the
World.* The exactitude of dates and painstaking
details conferred a certain credential on the journeys performed in his name. The legend beneath
the portrait *"ætat: suæ* 58" was the age of the Dean
himself, when he was adding the last touches in
1725. In the following year he had returned to
England and a chosen friend had dropped the
Travels from a hackney carriage at the publishers
in the dead of night. The Dean had wondered if
he would find a printer who would risk his ears.
Motte the printer risked his ears, but not every
word that the Dean had written. In great rage the
Dean speedily found how mangled and murdered
a copy had been printed and wrote to say so under
the name of Sympson, a family connection, under
whose cloak was written the Introduction to the
Travels. The Dean had never given his name nor
received proofs to correct, so that the printer performed his own correcting with a wholesome desire
to keep enough ear for a pen-rest. The talented
author of *Robinson Crusoe* had lost his aforetime
for injudicious writing. Rather than incur the
pillory by giving offense, Motte changed the colors
of the English Orders, which the Dean had satirized
in Lilliput, from their true Blue, Red and Green

to Purple, Yellow and White. Walpole, who had
revived the Red of the Bath, was to be dreaded.
Omitted was Gulliver's entire account of the King
of Laputa's attempt to reduce his rebellious subjects in Lindalino, "the second city of the Kingdom," who had complained of great oppressions
and instead of sending petitions had erected Four
Towers to menace the adamantine bottom of his
Flying Island. "This incident broke entirely the
King's measures and he was forced to give the town
their own conditions," as completely as King
George's Government had been compelled to sur-
render to the Four Letters of the Drapier.
Gulliver's hints of rebellion and regicide were
enough to frighten the printer, who introduced re-
visions in Gulliver's account of England to his
Houyhnhnm master. For instance, the character
of the Prime Minister Motte attributed to "some
European Courts" rather than to England
particularly. The Dean had called Prime Ministers Buzzards. Motte changed this to "great
statesmen," and carefully omitted the sacred name
of Germany as well as the appellation of "beg-
garly" to Princes in Northern Europe, who let
their troops upon hire, since some such Prince had
come to the English throne. The Dean had written
of spies and discoverers being "under the colours,
the conduct and pay of Ministers of State," whom

Motte preferred to call "dextrous persons in sufficient power both to protect and reward them."

The misprinting was dreadful and the Dean fumed and fashed, reading and rereading the first copy and scratching corrections. The second volume was worse than the first. Every cause for offence to ruling power was blotted out. "The admirable instance of a Cow was reduced with flatness and softenings from a satire against Law in general and not only against Attorneys and Pettifoggers." The sting was extracted from some passages, the style debased, the humor lost and the matter made insipid in others.

His very attack against the House of Lords had been miserably watered. He had written that a "weak diseased body, a meager countenance and sallow complexion are the true marks of noble blood." The printer, terrified of the Peers, had changed these into "the no uncommon marks of a great man." And the bitter suggestion that a healthy robust nobleman was generally taken to be the son of a Groom or Coachman had been watered into concluding "his real father to have been one of the inferiors of the family." The final sentence was entirely deleted, to wit, that "without the consent of this illustrious body no law can be made, repealed or altered and these nobles have decision of all possessions without appeal." The Dean made

corrections in his friends' copies and reintroduced
his stings upon lawyers in Lord Berkeley's.

The Dean's anger was tempered by the sponta-
neous song of success which arose from literary and
social England, though he had written to vex rather
than divert the world. If the printer vexed him in
return, the critics afforded him that diversion which
writers of mystery love. Some sought Lilliput on
the map. A shipmaster remembered Gulliver well
but insisted that he lived in Wapping not Rother-
hithe. An Irish Bishop pronounced *ex cathedra*
the book to be full of lies! The *Travels* were read
from the cabin to the Cabinet.

The delight and praise of the Dean's friends was
extravagant. Some strange flatterers came to tail.
The terrible Sarah, now Dowager Duchess,declared
she could dream of nothing else. "She has now
found out that the whole of her life has been lost in
caressing the worst part of mankind and treating
the best as her foes," reported Pope. Walpole
stayed mum. It was Walpole's ears and not the
printer's which tingled. It would have been no revenge to pillory a poor printer because he himself
was gibbetted for all time. The Prince of Wales
condescended to be highly and mightily amused.
The Princess of Wales showed charming appreciation and Mrs. Howard wrote imitations to the Dean
signing herself "Sieve Yahoo," and accepting his

definitions of Court Ladies and the human race.
To Mrs. Howard he pretended ignorance and even
posted her his own delicious criticism; "I am not
such a prostitute flatterer as Gulliver, whose chief
study is to extenuate the vices and magnify the
virtues of mankind and perpetually din our ears
with the praises of his country in the midst of
corruption and for that reason alone has found
many readers and probably will have a pension,
which I suppose was his chief design in writing!"
A touch as exquisitely humorous as any in the book.

The Dean began to take a serious view of Mrs.
Howard's influence and abilities. Through her he
hoped for Irish Bishops of Irish manufacture.
Through her the Princess already wore Irish plaid,
which he had sent as his livery with private word
to tell no politicians lest they made a law to cut the
fingers of Irish weavers! European fame reached
him and he decided to visit France for the sake of
the waters at least. At periods he was attacked by
his old pains. Giddiness troubled his poise and
deafness withstood even the deafening praises of
his friends. In April he left Dublin for England
and found his Lilliputian admirers at his Brobdingnagian feet. He was offered literary commands
and political campaigns. Pope and Gay arranged a
literary body-guard, while Bolingbroke and Pulteney urged him to lead a forlorn hope against

Walpole, since the King was tottering in health.
Mrs. Howard appeared suitable to be his Bellona.
The Dean was actually sharpening his travel-worn
pen against the detested Prime Minister when the
King died.   The Dean on the point of leaving
England wrote, "If the King had lived but ten
days longer, I should now be in Paris."   In the
confusion of thought and confounding of persons,
which are occasioned by a changing throne, the
Dean was persuaded by Mrs. Howard to stay and
watch his chances.   He wrote to her, "I had not the
least interest with the friend's friend's friend of
anybody in power."   He felt he had been used like
a dog by the sweepers at Court and stated, "I will
never venture to recommend a mouse to Mrs. Cole's
cat or a shoe-cleaner to your meanest domestic."
He kissed the hands of Caroline, though "Her
Majesty said I was an odd sort of a man, but I
forgive her, for it is an odd thing to speak freely
to Princes."   Mrs. Howard pretended to mistake
the shape of his script, whereupon he replied how
easy it was to mistake "untoward" for Howard or
"well pull" for Walpole or "monster" for Minister.
But Mrs. Howard's political predilections proved
greater than her influence.   The Queen and Walpole undertook to govern England, leaving Mrs.
Howard to the King and the Dean to himself.   Of
Walpole's renewed power he noted only that "he

has held the longest hand at hazard that ever fell to any sharper's share, and keeps his run when the dice are charged."

To be left to himself was a terrible fate. His agonies bodily and mental had returned as well as agonies between the two which conspired to give him the most melancholy apprehension for his reason. Lucid and logical though he remained in his own mind, his insanity took the form of belief that he was becoming insane. Dizziness and deafness stunned his brain or set it buzzing. And in the midst Stella fell a-dying once more. The Dean prayed for his own death.

"These are the perquisites of living long; the last act of life is always a tragedy at best, but it is a bitter aggravation to have one's best friend go before one."

To Sheridan he uttered epistolary groans, "Here is a triple chord of friendship broke." To the faithful Worrall he wrote, "I have these two months seen through Mrs. Dingley's disguises." Stella must make her Will. Stella must not die at the Deanery. He can not watch her die. They were cries of distraction and he implored Worrall to burn his letter.

In September he threw English dust from his

feet for ever and rode to Holyhead. He missed the
packet boat and occupied himself scribbling while
sub-lunar tides flowed and ebbed. In his own
mind the last tide was ebbing and he wrote a
humorous final notice to that Posterity whom he
had saluted in his first famous work, to the effect
that he would disappoint his imitators of their
immortality by ignoring their names. With a last
shaft at his first adversary he mentioned that
"Bentley and several others will reap great advantage by those who have not observed my rule." He
begged Heaven to forgive Pope, who had immor-
talized so many dunces in his Dunciad! He himself would allow none to rise to fame upon the
wings of his resentment. His mind had flowed its
full course. It could cover no fresh ground and
began rushing back to sea, churning the flotsam
and floating thought it had detached during a lifetime. Henceforth he could only play or trifle upon
the old personalities, the same prejudices, the same
old ideas. Upon Ireland or Walpole, upon his miseries and indignities, upon surviving friends or
sinking enemies, upon his own independence and the
general slavery, he rang his last railing notes.
There was nothing left but Ireland, and Ireland
appalled him like some Inferno of Dunces, a night-
mare imaginable to Dante and Pope together.

"Remove me from this land of slaves,
Where all are fools and all are knaves;
Where every knave and fool is bought,
Yet kindly sells himself for nought."

The next moment he was cursing the Captain for incivility: "I come from being used like an Emperor to be used worse than a dog at Holyhead." It was doglike usage, which had driven him there of old, whether to escape the education of a dog in Ireland or the doglike treatment he once imagined at Moor Park. Before leaving England and Wales for ever, a jumble of dreaming came upon him. He saw himself back in St. Patrick's. In the Gallery were Bolingbroke and Pope, the Infidel with the Papist! The Dean could not find his surplice, for the doors were shut and the way blocked with vergers, but Bolingbroke was preacher! The Dean dreamed sending for him to his stall, which the Trinity students had inconveniently broken down. Squeezing into the rabble he managed to hear Bolingbroke's sermon. His prayer was good, but he quoted from one of Wycherley's licentious plays. In his vexation the Dean awoke.

His next sight of St. Patrick's was with eye of flesh. Stella lived and lingered. The Dean wrote to English friends that he had returned to his

maintenance and convenience in Ireland. To Pope
he slipped a more frenzied note:

> "I have often wished that God Almighty
> would be so easy to the weakness of mankind
> as to let old friends be acquainted in another
> state; and if I were to write an Utopia for
> Heaven, that would be one of my schemes.
> This wildness you must allow for, because I
> am giddy and deaf . . ."

Extreme temperance had availed not against
giddy fits. He has given up his Bohea Tea. He
ate only the "easiest meals," "I never eat fruit nor
drink ale," and even "I take no snuff." Doctor
Arbuthnot still plied him with Peruvian Bark and
Dust of Valerian, with lavender drops and warm
gums, with absinthe and aloe, with bitters and
tonics, with antispasmodics. In vain! for, as he
had foretold by pointing to a tree decayed in the
top, his illness was under the skull, not in the blood
or the belly.

There were not six males he cared to meet in
Dublin and necessarily one-sixth that number of
females. Only correspondence with England
made life seem a phantom of itself, but before the
year had failed, the Dean discovered he had a new
correspondent though an old admirer. A flattering
letter from Paris arrived begging guinea subscrip-

tions from Ireland: "let me indulge the satisfaction
of talking of you as posterity will." It was signed
Voltaire. "The more I read of your works the
more I am ashamed of mine" was his final opinion.

The Dean had little heart to make new acquaintances, for Stella had entered passive agony. Days
without health and nights of pain remained her
portion. In his strange and selfish love the Dean
had promised himself not to see her die. He had
written to Sheridan that he could not "bear it like
a philosopher nor altogether like a Christian." The
philosopher weighs the happiness of the past and
the Christian that of the future, but the Dean could
poise neither in his broken balance. The day came
when he visited her and said some prayers he had
written for her, after which he did not return.

The prayers expressed human agony rather
than divine platitudes. His was really the agony
of despair and the valediction of a Voltaire. He
never expected to see the dead again. Stella was
come to her utter end. When the doctors offered
to pull her uphill, she answered sadly that she
would be out of breath before reaching the top. It
was one of the *bon mots* collected in writing by the
Dean in a collection, which rather fitted his remark
that "very little wit is valued in a woman as we
are pleased by a few words from a parrot."

The beginning of the year brought the end. It

was the evening of Sunday, January twenty-
eighth, and whether Stella's dying was the reason
or not, there was company at the Deanery.   Perhaps the Dean had gathered friends round him,
fearing Death without, and Madness within.
About eight of the clock, a servant brought the
news; Stella had been two hours dead.   Late into
that night the Dean strove to soothe and comfort
his rending mind with his all-but-almighty pen.
The quill, that could inflame nations and rouse the
living, could not raise the dead.   Nevertheless he
wrote what he wished the centuries to know and
esteem of Stella, and of her relations with him;
how he had known her from her sixth year and
brought her and Dingley into Ireland in her
twentieth on an adventure resembling a frolic, until
censure was blown over by her excellent conduct.
In other words all scandal had been abated under
Stella's unselfish obedience and the Dean's selfish
discretion. . . . He was still writing when St.
Patrick's struck midnight and he noted the hour
as he used in his letters to Stella when the watch-
men cried the night from the London alleys . . .
oh, so long ago!

To that patient and pathetic character he could
have borne beautiful testimony, but he wrote only
in praise of her advice and judgment, of her feminine dignity and brilliant conversation, of her

clever repulse of coxcombs, of the adoration of her servants, though "her demeanor was so awful that they durst not fail in the least point of respect." This wit and awfulness, this scorn of scoundrels with the devotion of inferiors, Dean and Stella had in common, though he recorded "a gracefulness somewhat more than human" and "a conjunction of civility, freedom, easiness and sincerity" which were not among his own social gifts.

The night passed, and he wrote, "my head aches and I can write no more. . . ." A day passed, and a night, and a day. The Dean was too sick in body or heart to attend the funeral, only writing to his agonized self:

> "It is now nine at night, and I am removed into another apartment that I may not see the light in the church, which is just over against the window of my bedchamber."

In his agony he took courage by remembering her courage; how she had once met and shot a house-breaker mortally with her pistol; and how the Duke of Ormonde used to toast her health on that account; and how she had never cried out upon any accident in coach or on horseback. And again he wrote of her contempt for coxcombs and detestation of Bishops, who (unlike her dear Dean) had sacrificed truth and honor to their ambition.

Sooner would she have "forgiven them the
common immoralities of the laity."   To philosophers also, she had given their due meed and
measure.   She "could point out all the errors of
Hobbes."   She understood Plato and Epicurus
and "judged well the defects of the latter."   In one
aspect of the Platonic philosophy the Dean had
certainly instructed her by a path of hard example
as well as by precept.   They had shown that a
shining unsensual Platonic love was possible between a beautiful and fascinated woman and a
passionate man as strong of frame as of intellect.

The Dean continued to extol her virtues.   She
was well read and the best of critics, though "sometimes too severe."   The Dean had found her so to
the benefit of his readers.   She had an eye for
Physic and a finger in Anatomy, as she had shown
by her care and nursing when he was sick.   "She
preserved her wit, judgment and vivacity to the
last but often used to complain of her memory."
It was clear that she complained of nothing else,
still less of the Dean's memory, if there was
anything for him to remember. . . . When he
had time, he added to his remarks; that her charity
to the poor became a tax upon the furnishers of
women's fopperies; that she wore no lace for many
years; that she had perfected the art of making
agreeable presents; that she needed no one's lib-

erality but detested the covetous; that she detested
dirt and informed a coxcomb that "neither virtuous
nor even vicious women love such kind of conversation"; that she made men her company and
Bishops her visitors; that she suffered fools, not
gladly, but because "it prevented noise and saved
time"; that she loved Ireland better than the Irish-
born, and, "detested the tyranny and injustice of
England in their treatment of this kingdom"; that
expectant female visitors were disappointed when
"they found she was like other women." The
Dean had discovered otherwise. Poor Stella had
scarcely found him like other men. . . . She bequeathed her soul to God, her body to the vaults of
St. Patrick's, a bond of thirty pounds, her strong
box and all her papers there or elsewhere to the
Dean. "In the name of God. Amen. Esther
Johnson, of the City of Dublin, Spinster."

If Vanessa had died a published Martyr and
Confessor of her passion, Stella figures in Love's
Calendar as a secret Martyr no less—and Virgin.

XIV

(1728-1734)

WITH Stella sank the last flickering light of
happiness behind the dreary windows of St. Patrick's Deanery. The Dean fled for months into the
country remaining at Market Hill with new
friends, the Achesons and Leslies, to whom he gave
a faded immortality in his poems. Then he returned to Dublin as to a tomb. The third in the
Platonic partnership, Rebecca Dingley, survived
like the husk after the kernel, like the stalk after
the flower, like the smoking wick after the extinc-
tion of the lamp. She lingered like a caricature
of the past into older and older age, grotesque for
those who would see, and garrulous unto those who
could hear her. She continued to live in lodgings
about the Cathedral precincts and to haunt the
place where she had found human companionship
and from which she now espied divine peace. The
Dean had never found her ought but a dull toler-

285

able old body and ridiculed her with his old housekeeper in lines to the tune of *Commons and Peers:*

Dingley and Brent,
Wherever they went,
Ne'er minded a word that was spoken;
Whatever was said,
They ne'er troubled their head,
But laugh'd at their own silly joking.

Should Solomon wise
In majesty rise,
And show them his wit and his learning;
They never would hear,
But turn the deaf ear,
As a matter they had no concern in.

He now watched with cold pity this sniveling,
snuff-taking phantom of his life in England passing in and out of his Irish Cathedral, whether to
hear Stella's old master assert prayers or to be near
the grave of her sweeter half. Toward Christmas he
sent her frigid cheer and formal charity and once
in a while he would invite himself to dine with her
but upon condition that he selected the hour and
forwarded wine and viands, and that she was "disposed to be easy and cheerful." With what
trembling fussiness the old soul swept her chamber
and brushed her wits to make play for the terrible
old Dean! But alone he watched her slow decay,
writing ten years after Stella's death: "she is quite

sunk with years and unwieldiness as well as a very scanty support. I sometimes make her a small present as my abilities can reach, for I do not find her nearest relations consider her in the least." This characteristically he wrote to a cousin of Dingley. Seven years later she became church dust and a portion for rats.

The Dean, having conceived a fixed idea that his own relations had treated him wrongly, was anxious to compel others to honor theirs. He called various descendants to subscribe to the preservation of ancestral tombs in his Cathedral. When refused, his wrath became spiteful. He wrote several solemn hints to Lord Burlington requesting funds to repair the great tomb erected by the first Earl of Cork. He appealed to Lady Catherine Jones to repair the monument of Lord Ranelagh, for the ancient Jones family was then in the Peerage, and one whom the Dean called "rascal" had been Dean before him. The Dean went wild at Lord Burlington's refusal to answer, as though the request came from one "of your hedge chapters in England." Did His Lordship think that the Chapter of St. Patrick's would cheat his posterity by helping themselves to three and sixpence a head *per annum?* By Gay he sent word: "pray tell him this in the severest manner and charge it all upon me and so let the monument perish." Threats passed to vengeance when Lady Holderness declined to provide a monument for her grandfather, the Duke of Schomburg killed at the Boyne, whom Orange balladry made Patroclus to the Dutch Achilles. To the Dean's fury this was also refused and he wrote to Carteret that, "if for an excuse they pretend they will send for his body, let them know that it is mine, and, rather than send it, I will take up the bones and make of it a skeleton and put it in my registry office to be a memorial of their baseness to all posterity." Sometimes morbid and often mordant, the Dean on this occasion was both. Finally he achieved vengeance by composing a Latin snarl to direct the erudite passers-by to the alien admiration rather than to the consanguinary ties which surrounded the ashes of the Duke;

"PLUS POTUIT FAMA VIRTUTIS APUD ALIENOS
QUAM SAGUINIS PROXIMITAS APUD SUOS."

Though the Latin had been modified by friends, the Dean true to his practise of pillorying a defaulting or cheating shopkeeper in the newspapers, inserted a paragraph in the Press to the scandal of the Duke's kin and the anger of King George, who damned the Dean for embroiling him with the King of Prussia. "It is dangerous writing on marble," wrote the Dean and decided to write his next bitter epitaph for himself. Mrs. Howard wrote thanking

Providence that a lasting monument had been raised to his own imprudence.

When love's suppleness forsakes the spirit, the prejudices and hatreds of a lifetime become ossified. With blindfold vigor and sterile sarcasm the Dean plunged deeper into personal or public feuds. There was always Walpole and English statecraft to bite, and bark at; Irish Bishops and placeholders to gibe and gibbet.

Instead of composing Memoirs he preferred to annotate the pages of others with vitriolic punctuation. Macky's or Burnet's contemporary accounts were scored with screams from his pen. Take the Dukes of Queen Anne's time: Somerset had "hardly commonsense," Richmond was a "shallow coxcomb," Bolton "a great booby," Grafton "almost a slobberer," Montagu "an arrant knave," Portland was "as great a Dunce as ever I knew." Clarendon's *History of the Rebellion* he seared with curses upon the Scotch for hell-hounds and fanatics. He could seldom control himself to finish such a sentence as "let them wait for Cromwell to plague them and enslave their scabby nation." As for their Covenant "the Devil their God had taken it!"

As for Bishop Burnet, the "Jackanapes" and "Puppy," his book was full of vulgar expressions and coffee-house scandals. The Dean detected "the style of a gamester" and once an Irish Bull; ridiculing such phrases as "cut out for a Court," "left in the lurch" or "pardoning Planet" as evidences of illiterate origin. Under the suggestion of Archbishop Sancroft's nepotism he wrote "false as Hell," and to Burnet's famous eulogy of King William that "he had no vice but one" the Dean added that "it was of two sorts . . ." What "no more Synods?—dog!"

And Time bred the Dean new enemies like Lord Allen and Sergeant Bettesworth, who seemed to have been born to receive the squirting vials of his wrath. The quarrel with Bettesworth became famous. That he was a fuming, bullying, blatant Whig was enough to draw a shaft from the Deanery. The Dean's brain had become beset with trifling and rhyming versification, perhaps saving him from more serious and painful thinking. He wrote that, when not considering how to die, "I trifle more and more every day and I would not give three pence for all I read or write or think." He developed extraordinary ingenuity for fitting rhymes and casting verses. He told Pope that his poetical fountain was drained and rhymes were as hard to find as guineas, but he still skewered jingles "such as Dublin third-rate rhymers might write for nine hours a day till the coming of Anti-Christ." He ranged:

> Tyrants with "high rants,"
> Dublin with "trouble in,"
> Cudgels with "judge else,"
> Malthouse with "fall to us,"

and a thousand other jangles until it became a mental aberration. The most unrhymable names and words in English went round and round his mill till they collected their syllabic mates.

Even in his sleep the mighty engine of his brain revolved vacuously under its roof, grinding stuff of which one curious memento remains. One night in 1733 he woke at two of the morning and in the dark scribbled lines which survive, though perhaps hardly their meanings;

> "I walk before no man, a hawk in his fist,
> Nor am I a brilliant whenever I list."

It is interesting to touch the first screw which became unloosed.

In the same year he fired his famous rhyme at "the booby Bettesworth,"

> ". . . though half a crown o'er pays his sweat's worth."

His victim swore to clip the Dean's ears and set out to harangue him personally. Of the interview the Dean sent an amusing account to the Duke of Dorset. The angry Bettesworth repeated the in-

sulting lines and "said I was mistaken in one thing,
for he assured me he was no booby but owned himself to be a coxcomb." The Dean informed him of
his invariable rule neither to own nor disown writings laid to his charge and the Sergeant-at-law,
whom the Dean pretended to take for a
regimental, retorted that the Dean resembled his
own Yahoos in squirting at others from security.
The Dean felt bound to inform the Lord Lieutenant that Bettesworth had "since related to five
hundred persons above five hundred falsehoods of
this conversation," and the Dean's friends formed
a society to protect his peace and person.

The Dean was more amused than otherwise by
Bettesworth. It required a Bishop really to raise
his full odium and to draw such rhyming proph-
ecies as:

"One thousand seven hundred and thirty-five
when only the Devil and Bishops will thrive;
One thousand seven hundred and thirty-six
when the Devil will carry the Bishops to Styx;
One thousand seven hundred and thirty-seven
when the Whigs are so blind they mistake Hell
    for Heaven;
The last is the period two thousand and one
when Monarch and Bishops to Hell all are
    gone."

And he added "when that time comes pray remember me."

Bishops almost drove him to insanity. The best of them, he concluded, only acted out of ignorance or hope of promotion. He would not even look into a Bishop's coach for terror of the sight which might strike his eyes. If he spared his eyes, he never spared his pen. The virtue of the saintly Berkeley he contrasted with the licentious Hort in the real humor of a Classical Burlesque. Pallas in the name of chastity implores Neptune to drown

> "A wretch! whom English rogues, to spite her,
> Had lately honour'd with a mitre."

But Venus interposes to save her darling, safely wagering,

> "At sea or land, if e'er you found him
> Without a mistress, hang or drown him. . . .
> If Hort must sink, she grieves to tell it,
> She'll not have left one single prelate:
> For, to say truth, she did intend him,
> Elect of Cyprus *in commendam.*"

To the Cyprian Goddess a compromise is proposed,

> "But if you'll leave us Bishop Judas,
> We'll give you Berkeley for Bermudas."

Pallas in consequence ". . . who conceived
    a hope . . .
Believed it best to condescend
To spare a foe, to save a friend;
But, fearing Berkeley might be scared
She left him virtue for a guard."

How he loathed Bishop Hoadly whom he wished
hanged fifty times to save the life of his predecessor! How he loathed Bishop Evans, who had
spread the first tales of his marriage to Stella! To
Evans he concluded a letter: "I hope your Lordship will please to remember in the midst of your
resentments that you are to speak to a clergyman
and not to a footman," which was the exact
attitude of English-born Bishops to Irish curates.
They were the great appointees of the State, dom-
ineering the small and petty fry called by God to
perform all the pastoral service. It must be remembered that every country and period is
Bishoped as it deserves. Eighteenth-century
Bishops were proud and pompous, avaricious and
sometimes scandalous because wittingly the society would have it so. England sent "worthless
Bishops all bedangled with their past illiterate
relations and flatterers." The Irish Bishops
treated their clergy as their clergy expected and
often merited to be treated. Swift regarded a
chaplain as a valet who laid out the family prayers

and cleaned up theology like a pair of Sunday boots for his master. He boasted himself that he kept some poor parson to drink the foul wine for him. Even for Archbishop King he preserved a lingering distaste, though King had stood by him in the Drapier troubles and been rewarded by "an excellent new ballad." But the bitter pen gave vent to spleen at last, writing to say that "from the very moment of the Queen's death Your Grace has thought fit to take away every opportunity of giving me all sorts of uneasiness." When the Irish Bishops promoted Bills for what Swift considered the "enslaving and beggaring the clergy," he burst into furious rhymes about Satan their Archbishop:

"And He was a primate and He wore a mitre,
Surrounded with jewels of sulphur and
   nitre. . . .
Could you see his grim grace, for a pound to
   a penny,
You'd swear it must be the baboon of Kilkenny."

This was a personal allusion to Bishop Tennison of Ossory, while another epigram described Archbishop Hort of Tuam, who was more fond of Court than of Choir, as,

"His station despising, unawed by the place,
He flies from his God to attend to his Grace."

That Judas had a Bishopric to lose, and that the same plant could be woven to provide a Bishop's sleeve or a criminal's cravat pointed the savagery, with which Swift reasoned that,

> "Those former ages differ'd much from this;
> Judas betray'd his master with a kiss:
> But some have kiss'd the gospel fifty times,
> Whose perjury's the least of all their crimes;
> Some who can perjure through a two inch
>   board
> Yet keep their bishoprics, and 'scape the cord:
> Like hemp, which, by a skilful spinster drawn
> To slender threads, may sometimes pass for
>   lawn."

To Archbishop King the Dean announced his impenitent independence and undying championship of the Irish cause; "My Lord I have lived and by the Grace of God will die an enemy to servitude and slavery of all kinds." He continued in intervals of bespitting personal enemies to fight those of Ireland. Court interest and place-mongering drew clerical and episcopal supporters to the hated lead of Archbishop Boulter, Walpole's dull ecclesiastical double in the Irish Primacy. The Dean never really fleshed his claws in this secret enemy more than by writing that "a Boulter by name is not bolter of wit." The Primate by proclamation lowered the Gold to suit the Silver. This early

policy of Bimetalism was furiously opposed by the
Dean, who rang a muffled peal and hoisted a black
flag on his Cathedral. The Primate did not often
dare to lift his voice against what Carteret called,
"orders fulminating from the sovereignty of St.
Patrick's," but at a banquet of the Lord Mayor
of Dublin he accused the Dean of enflaming the
populace. The Dean answered as furious as just;
"Enflame them! Had I lifted my finger, they
would have torn you to pieces." The Dean insisted
that he had only refrained, lest History should
record the odd figure of a Primate destroyed by the
people over a job! He then stalked from the Lord
Mayor's board.

The last interview with Walpole had showed
that the Prime Minister at St. Stephen's, London,
would make no offer to the Dean of St. Patrick's,
Dublin. Walpole would take no advice because
his policy toward Ireland was fixed. Little lay between Ireland and a policy of stunting starvation
and exterminating exodus except the Dean's quill
pen. As a hen would have gathered its chickens
under its feathers, the Dean had tried to instruct
the various Irish like "a brood of goslings to stick
together while the Kite is in the air." He considered that the laws of Political Economy worked
reverseward in Ireland as long as government itself
was unnatural, Ireland being "the only Christian

country where people contrary to the old maxim are the poverty and not the riches of the nation." Hibernian prosperity was as strange as the winter-flowering blossom of the Glastonbury thorn. For Ireland all the year long was winter.

The combined weakness, imbecility and coward-ice of the old Irish and the Anglo-Irish squires or clergy left him in despair. Famine in 1729 was slaying the children of the soil no less than ruining the lords of the land. Nothing and less than nothing was done. Deliberate indeliberation was the Walpolian policy. The Dean wrote a Tract for the gaiety of nations and the anguish of his own, the famous but explicitly *Modest Proposal* to make Irish children a benefit instead of a burden to their parents by using them for food as yearlings, instead of selling them full grown to the Barbadoes. If ten shillings could be fixed as the price of a child's carcase on the table, the Dean pointed out that there would be an end of causing abortions and murdering bastards. The innocent lambs would be allowed their year of life. Every child would make two good dishes and even on the fourth day should taste good enough boiled with salt and pepper. The skins, like those of Gulliver's Yahoos, could be flayed for ladies' gloves or gentlemen's summer-boots. This proposal he considered "would be a great inducement to marriage." Hus-

bands would become as fond of their wives as of
their mares in foal. By one hint only did he relieve
the reader from the rack, by changing metaphor
and suggesting that the Irish landlords, having
"already devoured most of the parents, seem to
have the best title to the children!"

Across centuries the *Modest Proposal* chills the
blood. It was written in ghastly earnest and there
was no reply. Walpole could not have enjoyed a
surer sign that his policy was a success and that the
unmanageable Drapier was beaten to despair. No
less ironical was his answer to the *Craftsman* suggesting sending surplus Irish to America as a
screen against Indians. Carteret's friendship was
only a sop to the Dean, who impotently confessed
Carteret had "a genteeler manner of binding the
chains of the Kingdom than most of his predeces-
sors." His last power lay with the mob, who protected him from violence and threatened his
enemies. He poured forth his thoughts on Ireland
to English friends:

"This kingdom is now absolutely starving,
by means of every oppression that can be in-
flicted on mankind. Shall I not visit for these
things, saith the Lord."

He became "an interceder for the City of Dublin" and tried to induce the Duke of Chandos to

return some old Irish records to Ireland. He wrote begging Mrs. Howard to remind the Queen that she had ordered him, "if I lived to see her in her present station, to send her our grievances, promising to read my letter and do all good offices in her power for this miserable and most loyal kingdom." He freely pardoned Mrs. Howard her bad advice to himself and sympathized, perhaps a little ironically in her fall from Court favor.

There are times when a gentle rider seems to use the spur like a caress, and Swift concealed a little dig when he congratulated her on being delivered from a favorite's toil. He recounted that he had known three ladies to suffer the same fortune and, since "ladies are very often good scaffoldings, I need not tell you the use that scaffoldings are put to by all builders as well political as mechanic." But to Gay he confided that Mrs. Howard was "good for nothing but to be a rank courtier. I care not whether she ever writes me or no. She has cheated us all and may go hang herself and so may her mistress. A pox on her for hindering me from going to France and in a most treacherous manner, when I laid it on her honour." A month later he wrote her joy of becoming Countess of Suffolk and tried to make his peace with the Queen, offended by the Schomburg inscription. And then the Queen forgot her promise to hear him on Irish miseries. On the Queen's account he told her "I will trust your sex no more." He forgot his idealization of Caroline in Gulliver and to Addison's fulsome account of her beauty he scribbled, "I have bad eyes."

With the eighteenth century the cause of Ireland sank like a dark cloud into the West, illuminated only by occasional flashes from the Dean's lightning mind. Despair and disgust had conquered the Irish Prometheus. An occasional half-tragical, half-comical groan broke from his heart. "A leather coinage will be all we want, separated as we shall then be from all human kind. We shall have lost all, but we may be left in peace, as we shall have no more to tempt the plunderer." He sent Pope word that he was being cured of Irish politics by despair. By one last satiric touch he directed his body to be buried at Holyhead, "for I will not lie in a country of slaves." His *Story of an Injured Lady* reads more like a final dirge for Ireland than a brand thrown to enflame nations. England, the "too fortunate lover," he accused of treating the Lady Erin as a conqueror and bully, who claimed "vast obligations in sending her so many of his own people for her own good and to teach her manners," whereas it was suggested that it had been better for him had she been sunk into the sea. Across two centuries his diagnosis of Irish

economics remained verifiable. "We must send all
our goods to his market just in their naturals, the
milk immediately from the cow without making
into cheese or butter; the corn in the ear, the grass
as it was mowed, the wool as it comes from the
sheep's back." The Dean had only futile and bitter
memories of his struggles to rouse home producers
in Ireland. Once he had arranged for the Archbishop and his clergy to wear gowns of Irish stuff,
but the weavers themselves had failed to bring
samples. By his personal power and neither for
love nor money, he had induced the Queen and the
mistress of the English King to wear Irish tweed.
He had protested when the Dutch sailors carried
away the fish harvest under Irish eyes; "I laughed
to see the zeal that Ministry had about fishing at
Newfoundland, while no care was taken against
the Dutch fishing just at our doors." In an out-
spoken recital to an Irish exile, Captain Wogan, he
summed up his rewards as an Irish patriot:

> "I have in twenty years drawn above one
> thousand scurrilous libels on myself, without
> any other recompense than the love of the Irish
> vulgar, and two or three dozen signposts of the
> Drapier in this city, beside those that are
> scattered in country towns, and even these are
> half worn out."

The Dean should have added the solatium he

received in the year of the *Modest Proposal* when
the Corporation of Dublin offered the champion
of their liberty the Freedom of his City in a gold
snuff-box. A foolish Lord Allen, who had fawned
upon the Dean without receiving much in return,
upbraided their act in honoring a Jacobite and
enemy of King George. The Dean mauled him
under the name of *Traulus* in a Dialogue purport-
ing to be between the Dean's two friends Tom
Sheridan and Robin Leslie, who only accredited
madness to a Peer who wants "to foul the man he
chiefly flatters." The Dean mercilessly drew
stinging attention to the "motley fruit of motley
seed," the mixture in Allen's blood betwixt a Fitz-
gerald dam and base paternity:

> "Who could give the looby such airs
> Were they masons, were they butchers?"

He defended himself with ease against the
hornets, who

> "Still swarm and buzz about his nose
> But Ireland's friends ne'er wanted foes.
> A patriot is a dangerous post,
> When wanted by his country most; . . .
> His guilt is clear, the proofs are pregnant;
> A traitor to the vices regnant."

Henceforth the Dean crawled on his trail within
the Cathedral precincts, growling or picking

quarrels. He wrote a sulky challenge to Lord
Palmerston to shake off any gratitude he retained
for the Temple family. He snarled at his own
Archbishop. He was hurt when the Duke of
Dorset failed to answer his letters and he wrote to
Lady Elizabeth Germaine attributing the ducal
manners to His Grace being busy or a gartered
Duke or Lord Lieutenant or over noble or even to
the Dean's own obscurity. It did not strike him
that the Duke possibly found him a bear or a bore.

The Dean's state of mind and decline were reflected in the odd companionship he chose and
collected. His curiosity for the vulgar and his
self-torturing prying into senile horrors led him
to adopt a seraglio of distressed and distressing old
women, whom he christened Pullagowna, Stum-
panympha and Cancerina. Cancerina he buried
without a coffin but without fees. "I now hate all
people I cannot command." Accordingly he
gathered about him the devoted buffoon, the bask-
ing butt and the flattering poetastress. When he
was not sour and savage, he frittered himself into
fretfulness and frivolity. "Valetudinarians must
live where they can command and scold. I must
have horses to ride. I must go to bed and rise when
I please and live where all mortals are subservient
to me. I must talk nonsense when I please and all
who are present must commend it."

In return he became fatuous on behalf of
creatures like Mrs. Barber whom he commended
to England as "the best poetess of both kingdoms."
Mrs. Barber took some political and indecent verses
of his secretly to London. The printer and Mrs.
Barber were arrested on account of a *Poem to
Young Lady,* mentioning:

> ". . . How the helm is ruled by Walpole,
> At whose oars, like slaves, they all pull."

The same poem revealed the Dean's theory of his
art and mission as a consecrated poet and divine:

> "Thousand sparkles falling down
> Light on many a coxcomb's crown.
> See what mirth the sport creates!
> Singes hair, but breaks no pates."

Walpole mooted the Dean's arrest and Dublin
was indignant at the betrayal of his printer, which
lay between Mrs. Barber and the wretched clergyman Pilkington, whom the Dean had also laden
with recommendation and drawn thereby caution
from Bolingbroke that "the fellow wants morals,
and, as I hear, decency." He, who had once
skimmed the cream of London to make his dining
agreeable, was content to sup the dregs of Dublin,
relieved by the transitory gleam of the dying and
beautiful Miss Kelly or the fulsome verses of Lord

Orrery, which their recipient generously wrote would turn his enemies' hatred to envy. Orrery, a Wit among Lords, fawned to the Lord of Wits.

Swift complained that he only knew "a few middling clergymen and laity." He paid an old parson's wife a shilling to play backgammon. No Lord Temporal nor Lord Bishop did he visit. He boasted he was "as much a monk as any in Spain" and again on condescending to "unStoic" himself for a dinner: "I am very much a monk and of so severe an order that I hardly know what an invitation is." Giddiness was his growing portion and even prolonged headaches had not the normal effect of halting the ache at heart. He hated being out of reach of his bed and slowed attendance at Church for fear of being caught in a fit during prayers. If he walked and rode and lived temperately, it was for glee of keeping out his successor as he wrote: "If I were well and was temperate, I would counterfeit myself sick as Tobie Mathew Archbishop of York used to do, when all the Bishops were gaping to succeed him." He began to grow shrunken to "the ghost of a ghost of what I was," until he felt "not an ounce of flesh or a dram of spirits left." From across the seas Doctor Arbuthnot still plied him with drugs and simples, prescribing cinnabar and castor in *bolus* and tiny portions of *tinctura sacra*. Unfortunately, all the cinnabar in

Jonathan Swift in Later Years

the world would not avail against his deafness.
Something more miraculous than *tinctura sacra*
was needed to still the labyrinthine vertigo which
rocked his brain.   In vain the Dean took garlic
steeped in honey for his hearing.   He still heard
the noise of seven watermills churning in his ears
and he could distinguish only voices of feminine
trebles or masculine counter-tenors, which necessarily limited conversation.

Abandonment of Hope seemed inscribed over
the Deanery and the Dean himself with seeming
infidelity to his post wrote that he had "given up
all hopes of Church or Christianity."   He did not
resent attacks upon Christianity so much as upon
the Church.   "Although Tithes be of divine institution they are of diabolical execution," he wrote,
and when Bishops supported the Dissenters on the
Test he screamed, "if, I shall pray God to forgive
them, His divine Justice will not suffer Him!"   Bolingbroke thought he "would make both divines and
free-thinkers clamorous" by his insistence that
Revelation and Reason were separate and that
Revelation was the only mark of Christianity.   But
was the Dean himself not on the side of Reason?

Bolingbroke thought he was, and derived more
good from Swift's trifles than from all the profound
Divines.   They remained strangely satisfied with
each other, the Dean and Deist, free-thinker and

free-lance. The Dean's fatalism hailed Bolingbroke's star. "He is a controller of fortune and
poverty dares not look a great Minister in the face
under his lowest declension." Bolingbroke was
always suggesting an English living, and the
Dean's proud spirit would have preferred to be a
chaplain to St. John than to Saint John. A gen-
uine and apprehensive materialism underlay the
Dean's creed. It was not in irony only, always,
that he wrote about money as "the great divider of
the world and uniter of people" or argued that
"avarice and hardness of heart are the two happiest
qualities a man can acquire, who is late in his life,
because living long we must lessen our friends and
may increase our fortunes." He put his gospel of
"bread and butter" to the Duchess of Queensberry
thus:

> "From hence and hence only arise all the
> quarrels between Whig and Tory, between
> those who are in the Ministry and those who
> are not, between all pretenders to employment
> in the Church, the Law and the Army."

He had an itch for saying what people then or
since have preferred not even to think.

The Dean was less consumed by his search for
God than haunted by an excusable dread of poverty. It is true that he never became rich in his

efforts not to become poor, for he boasted he had not been "master of thirty pounds for thirty days this thirty years." The power of giving alms and dispensing influence buoyed him better than vaulted bullion or millions invested in Bubbledom.

His belief appears to have been at best the wise agnosticism of a mind to which belief and unbelief were equally open. He accepted what previous Divines and Statesmen had thought and settled for him. He fell back upon apology rather than exploration, as "one appointed by Providence for defending a Post." In his *Letter to a Young Clergyman* he said:

> "I am not answerable to God for the doubts that arise in my own breast, since they are the consequence of that reason which He hath planted in me."

He prudently advised not meddling with religious mysteries. "If you explain them, they are mysteries no longer. If you fail, you have laboured to no purpose." In his sermon on the Trinity he observed that:

> "God commandeth us to believe a fact that we do not understand. And this is no more than we do everyday in the works of nature."

Miracles he reduced to reason. He suggested softening Christ's Divinity to the Chinese. He was offended that Paul's allegories were made articles of faith. He hated Dissent more than he loved God, and enjoyed the self-criticism, which he applied generally, that "we have enough religion to make us hate, not enough to make us love." Morning Prayers, which he read secretly to his servants, were his daily drill in the virtues required by the State. The Sacrament, which he distributed so reverently, was the Test against Dissenters. He was too big mentally to be bigotedly intolerant. He offered the Sects their spiritual ease without political power. Deists and Infidels he only attacked when they attacked, and for the love of counter-attack. As for Atheists, even "to say a man is bound to believe is neither truth nor sense." To his own earth-bound mind he was indulgent in the words. "I defy any law of God or man obliging him to comprehend Omniscience or Beatific Vision." He attacked the "Nothingarian by Creed," because he saw nothing to be gained in either world by abandoning religion.

All that can be said of his final stage was that in his own words he despaired of Christianity and Church, though he remained like a mute gargoyle on guard outside. From time to time with belching mouth he flushed the ecclesiastical gutters, but he retreated into his old irony that "cast Wits and cast Beaux have a proper sanctuary in the Church."

And to this he added the melancholy teaching that "both wit and beauty will go off with years and there is no living upon the credit of what is past." All was Vanity in the end as in the beginning.

His religious state was one that neither friend nor critic nor himself, who was neither, could venture to penetrate. "God be thanked that I have no flock at all so that I neither can corrupt nor be corrupted." He associated himself with the Divine refusal to bear with mankind:

> "Which God pronounced He never would,
> And soon convinced them by a flood,"

though the Dean's deluge took the form of ink. From that flood of his abuse few indeed were saved. Doctor Sheridan was perhaps his Noah, but there was no room in his Ark for Sheridan's wife, whom the Dean hated for a slut. On his last visit to the Sheridans the Dean wrote from Cavan:

> "This is the dirtiest town and except some few, the dirtiest people I ever saw, particularly the mistress, daughter and servants of this house."

Sheridan brought him to meet and entertain the most distinguished citizens. "There were sixteen of them and I came off rarely for about thirty shillings. . . . The cursed turf is two hours kindling and two minutes decaying." The day came when even Sheridan was no longer wanted at the Deanery. And so it went on.

There arose something from the dark bottom of his heart in his advice to Sheridan, "it is safer for a man's interest to blaspheme God, than to be of a party out of power." Of the latter state the Dean had had his share and, if he would not curse God, he cursed his day, studying on every succeeding birthday the Third Chapter of Job, and uttering imprecations upon himself.

"Let the day perish in which I was born,
Let darkness and the shadow of death stain it.
Let a cloud dwell upon it and let the blackness of
     the day terrify it.
As for that night let darkness seize upon it.
Let it not be joined unto the days of the year.
Let it not come into the number of the months.
Let that night be solitary,
Let no joyful voice come therein. . . . Let the
     stars of the twilight thereof be dark. . . ."

The star of his twilight had already set, and there were other verses which rang truer from his Dublin dunghill than from Job's.

"Why died I not from the womb? . . .
For now should I have lain still. . . . There
the wicked cease from troubling; and there the

weary are at rest. There the prisoners rest
together; they hear not the voice of the oppressor. . . . For my sighing cometh before
I eat, and my roarings are poured out like the
waters. For the thing which I greatly feared
is come upon me, and that which I was afraid
of is come unto me."

The poor and the Irish were always with him.
It was all become desperate and to the Lord Lieutenant Dorset he would not even "prescribe a dose
to the dead." He told Bolingbroke that he became
"every year more angry and revengeful, and my
rage is so ignoble that it descends even to resent
the folly and baseness of the enslaved people among
whom I live." And again he said, "time and the
miseries I see about me have made me almost as
stupid as the people I am among." He felt like a
vermin-eaten lion prisoned behind his Cathedral
bars, for "the zeal of liberty hath eaten me up and I
have nothing left but ill thoughts, ill words, and ill
wishes, and like roaring in the gout they give me
some imaginary ease."

But vainly, like Job's, were his roarings poured
forth like the waters. "We return thrice as much
to our absentees as we get by trade, which I have
been telling them these ten years to as little purpose
as if it came from the pulpit." To Gay he laughed
in irony that "the English sea-publicans grumble,

if we carry our own nightgowns unless they be old." Whether Irish conditions had become worse, the Dean's obsession grew no less. Why, if a salmon were left at the Deanery its entrails would be searched for letters! He saw only "a mass of beggars, thieves, oppressors, fools and knaves," and he shouted, "you have twenty merchants in London who could each of them purchase our whole cash." Thieves were encouraged by the premium of a free passage to more favored parts of the earth. "Whole boatfulls go off with pomp and mirth and music and drink as a Governor sent to the West Indies." As for the beggars, he drew up a workable scheme for giving them badges within the Liberties of St. Patrick's, and returning those imported from England "in justice a dozen to one." As for the local oppressors, "take notice that a squire must have some merit before I shall honour him with my contempt for I do not despise a fly, a maggot or a mite." Life seen through the windows of the Deanery, dusty panes and laughterless caverns and childless corridors was a gaunt and terrible thing. The atmosphere was that breathed forth by a Minor Prophet taken to bitter brooding and ceaseless scolding. He cried to Pope: "You advise me right not to trouble myself about the world but oppression tortures me." It began slowly to kill him no less.

Few institutions caused the Dean more hysterical
wrath than the famous Irish Parliament, the
College Green Club. Though the name of Swift
stands in golden letters upon the roll of Irish
patriotism, it is curious to find how he scorned the
ewe-lambs of modern Nationalism and imprecated
against the old Irish and their language, the Catholic Creed and the old Dublin Parliament. "I
detest hearing the slavish practices of those misrep-
resentative brutes," he told Pulteney, whom he
hailed as *"ultimus Britannorum,"* that they "will
imitate yours in everything as a monkey does a
human being." Nor were his hopes higher for
English freedom, since "we see the Gothic sys-
tem of limited monarchy is extinguished in all
the nations of Europe. It is utter extirpated
in this wretched kingdom and yours must be the
next."

Walpole swelled upon the Eastern horizon like a
black cloud. The Dean once swore he would
mount an equipage if the good news ever came of
Walpole's fall, and he encouraged Gay to write the
Beggar's Opera which contained a skit compounded
of Walpole and the Irish highwayman, Captain
Maclean. The success of the piece delighted the
Dean who wrote to the author: "The Beggar's
Opera has knocked down Gulliver. To expose
vice and to make people laugh with innocence does

more public service than all the Ministers of State from Adam to Walpole."

In all the correspondence which he poured forth like waters, muddy and bitter in turns, there seldom flickered a lighter touch or ripple. One night he heard the bells of St. Patrick's ring late and sent his servant to inquire whether for joy or sorrow. His letter recorded his comic joy that a new master was chosen to the Corporation of Butchers! For the Duchess of Queensberry he composed an early specimen of an Irish *bull,* writing, "I never saw you except once in the dark, to use a *bull* of this country." When he and Sheridan hobnobbed or scribbled it was in burlesque and they went to extremes of pedantic trouble in squeezing Latin into English shapes or the reverse. It was the descent of Jove and Juvenal to Pierrot and Pastiche. It was the Marathon runner taken to acrobatics. It was Hercules juggling with Apples of the Hesperides or playing pushpenny with the grooms in the Augean stables. It was Gulliver gaga. The Dean was doting. He had once called Life "a ridiculous tragedy, which is the worst kind of composition." His own words were upon him and worse, for the remainder of his existence became a ghastly decomposition.

XV

GOLGOTHA THE PLACE OF THE SKULL

(1734-1745)

DEAFNESS gathered as thick upon the Dean as
the sands of Time himself throttling some old
post stuck into the shore. He could hear only the
suck and the squelch of many waters like the constant ebbing of tides. He had to abandon for good
any thought of a London winter, preferring "a
scurvy home where I can command people to speak
as loud as I please."

Bolingbroke's suggestion of a poorer English
living, the Dean humorously insisted must be
made up out of the Duchess of Queensberry's pin-
money. He kept his fewer lighter moments for the
distant great. His English correspondence
afforded a secret channel running clear and free
under the besetting sands of deafness and the eddies
of dizziness. His pen wrote letters but no more
books. The *Last Four Years of Queen Anne* lay
finished beside him but unpublished, chiefly at the

entreaty of Harley's son. Two unfinished treatises hung their fire, one upon the platitudes of polite conversation and the other upon impolite servants. Before he presumed to offer directions to servants, he studied some very careless and filthy specimens. A lifetime's observation passed into a few coarse pages. It was never finished. There was nothing to be finished now except life itself. "I have neither spirits to write or read or think or eat," he wrote. He felt a Lilliputian shrinking, "I am the most insignificant man of this most insignificant country."

He retained his curious interest in madness and in the fate and care of the mad. Madness has always been a fascinating subject, whether it be attributed to a substraction of the human or, as in the East, to an addition of the divine in the intellect. The motive of madness ran through his writings and the *Tale of a Tub* contained a digression on the subject.

A strange prevision appeared in his early attack on the Dissenters that "some think that when our earthly tabernacles are disordered and desolate, shaken and out of repair, the spirit delights to dwell within them, as houses are said to be haunted when they are forsaken and gone to decay." The Dean's decay was near. In 1732 Sir William Fownes wrote to him about the misery of the lunatics during his Mayoralty of Dublin. Two years

later the Dean made a Will bequeathing his whole
fortune to found a madhouse, which he called
"settling my perplexed affairs like a dying man."
Seven years later he was himself accounted legally
mad by a *Commission de lunatico inquirendo*.

In the unique lines upon his own death he put
this Testament into one stanza:

> "He gave the little wealth he had
> To build a house for fools and mad;
> And show'd by one satiric touch,
> No nation wanted it so much."

As for Death, to which Deans, cabbages and
Kings are all susceptible:

> "I was forty-seven years old when I began
> to think of death, and the reflections upon it
> now begin when I wake in the morning, and
> end when I am going to sleep."

With dehumanized, but not humorless, passion
he imagined the comic scenes following his de-
cease:

> "And Lady Suffolk, in the spleen
> Runs laughing up to tell the queen.
> The queen, so gracious, mild, and good
> Cries, 'Is he gone? 'tis time he should.'"

With one ear pricking his shroud he overhears
society ladies playing cards:

"Receive the news in doleful dumps:
'The Dean is dead (Pray what is Trumps?) . . .
Six deans, they say, must bear the pall:
(I wish I knew what king to call.)' "

Pope he prophesied would grieve for a month,
Gay a week and Arbuthnot a day; but Death is
not mocked and only Pope had survived from the
famous trio to die while the Dean himself was
dying.   Dear "volatile" Gay was the first to go.
"Any lady with a coach and six horses would carry
you to Japan," the Dean wrote him fantastically. A
heavier coach carried him farther than even the
geography of Gulliver, but from his dying pillow
Gay called for Swift.

All his brilliant friends were fast dying like the
trail of bright ashes which follows a falling star. In
1729 died Congreve, whom the Dean had loved
from his youth and deplored in his broken age for
squandering away a good constitution.   The beautiful and brilliant Congreve's eyes by one of
those accidents which final Fate reserves for her
favorites, were held by cataracts lest he should look
on the beauty of his Duchess of Marlborough, the
younger; for Congreve died like Gay—the play-
thing of a Duchess.   Gay's last letter of gossip to
the Dean had told him, what he knew before, that
"the great are ungrateful."   Soon afterward came
a letter from Pope, which the Dean dared not read

"by an impulse foreboding some misfortune."
Gay had been added to the gaieties of Heaven.

Arbuthnot had sent his last prescriptions, Dust of
Valerian, Peruvian Bark and such like electuary
and tinctures, but the Dean was ill beyond posset
or apothecary. In 1735 died the beloved physician.
In the same year died Peterborough, "the ram-
blingest lying rogue on earth." The Dean's dear
hang dog and beloved vagabond, Peterborough,
as the great exception to all Court experience,
had been made a General for courage, an Ambassador for wisdom and most remarkable of all an
Admiral for "skill in maritime affairs."

In 1734 died dear Lady Masham, upon whose
skill with Queen Anne had depended the fates of
England and the Dean. And the boy, which
Swift had once grudged her bearing in her political
heyday, became a rake running the town. Long
gone was the dear and wise Lady Orkney to find
her sweet William beyond a wider stream than the
Boyne. Whether Mrs. Howard was living the
Dean cared not. Her mistress Queen Caroline had
died at the hands of royal doctors, who had treated
common appendicitis for royal gout. The Dean
would not forget how she had forgotten him until
the time came to forget her entirely. "They have
neither memory nor manners," he wrote of both.

And long, long time before had died Addison

and Prior, Harcourt and Harley, and the shadow
which the great John, Duke of Marlborough, had
thrown over Europe was swallowed in the shadows.
With insult the Dean had followed the Duke's
hearse impugning his courage in his unpublished
History and in a poem forbidding widows and
orphans to sigh:

> "True to his profit and his pride,
> He made them weep before he died.
> Come hither, all ye empty things!
> Ye bubbles raised by breath of kings!
> Who float upon the tide of state;
> Come hither and behold your fate!"

It was perhaps the only poetical image he ever
conceived and it covered the fate of most of his
friends.   Of the galaxy, through whom he had
once steered the State, only St. John Bolingbroke
survived, and where was Bolingbroke, "methinks I
am inquiring after a tulip of last year?"

The time was come for the Dean to recall the
lines he had rhymed upon his own Death.   They
contained his Irish epitaph:

> "The Irish Senate if you named,
> With what impatience he declaim'd!
> Fair Liberty was all his cry,
> For her he stood prepared to die."

His swan song he reserved for the Irish Parlia-

ment under title of The Legion Club, dedicated to
the Demoniac in Scripture.   The politicians had
roused him out of the ordinary by a Bill to relieve
Landlords from the Title of Pasturage due to the
Church.   Irish Pastors thought themselves in more
need of pasturage than their flocks.   Attempted
diminution of Church revenue was a red rag to the
Dean and he screamed his wild scorn at the House,
which he described to all time as:

"Not a bow-shot from the college;
Half the globe from sense and knowledge."

He drew upon all his clever jingling power,
upon his wickedest wit and his flow of scrofulous
and scarifying shrieks.   He continued to write,
until the poem itself became the work of a demoniac, not without an unwitting strain of prophecy on the future of the Irish Parliament:

"Let them, when they once get in,
Sell the nation for a pin;"

He painted a club of hobgoblins and horrors
rather than men, pressing distorted phrase and
ordurous fury to their limits until the need of
another art dawned upon him and he invoked a
satirist whose pencil truly matched his pen:

"How I want thee, humorous Hogarth!
Thou, I hear, a pleasant rogue art."

A merry rhyme, but the Dean was writing his
last page. For the last time the shapely writing
ran across the paper and the ink twice made of gall
soaked into the good rag paper. The poem was
finished to the bitter dregs.

"I concluded, looking round them,
'May their god the devil confound them!' "

But the imprecation fell back upon the impre-
cator. God or devil touched the maddened brain.
Something broke or burst within his screaming
skull and the Dean of St. Patrick's put down pen
and tossed aside the sheet. The old dizziness
drained the fibers running through his head, and
deafness was rolled about him tenfold and the
waters rushed through and through the aching
labyrinth of that mighty mind; mighty no more.
A joint letter with Mrs. Whiteway announced this
"very masterly poem" to Sheridan. If the printer
was condemned for it, "Mrs. Whiteway is to have
half the profit and half the hanging." But the
Dean never wrote again without blots and
bungling.

It seemed as though the words of Job the
Patriarch were upon him. His birthday prayer

had been ironically heard. His day was now
stained by the darkness and by the shadow of
night. Darkness itself was seized of his night. "'Let
no joyful voice come therein," he had required, and
when the shouts of the faithful adoring mob pierced
the haunted corridors of the Deanery and even his
deafness, he gave orders that his anniversary was
not to be celebrated. " 'Tis all folly. Better let it all
alone." Better indeed, since, to raise the grisly
curtain once, the *Hardwicke Papers* relate that
"his madness appears chiefly in the most incessant
strains of obscenity and swearing." Henceforth
no woman could remain under his roof and poor
Mrs. Whiteway was withdrawn, though in 1738
she delivered what the Dean would have called one
of her gasconades, "the miseries of this poor kingdom have shortened his days and sunk him even
below the wishes of his enemies," but she was sure
that like a second Cato he would remain at his post.
Henceforth without Mrs. Whiteway to remind
him, he no longer said his prayers.

From darkness and pain he returned to days of
lucidity but of expectant torture. Last notes were
written to the faithful Mrs. Whiteway in 1740 to
say, "the whole of last night I was equally struck as
if I had been in Phalaris' bull and roared as loud
for eight or nine hours. I am at this instant unable
to move without excessive pain although not the

one-thousandth part of what I suffered all last night," and again, "all I can say is that I am not in torture but I daily and hourly expect it. I hardly understand one word I write. I am sure my days will be very few. Few and miserable they must be." It was a Saturday and he barely expected to survive over Sunday, but five more years of agony awaited him until his brimming brain was peacefully housed in the Cathedral Golgotha.

Few friends visited him and each time he was hopeful that it was for the last time. "Good night, I hope I shall never see you again," he used to say with a truthfulness not recommended in his hints for Polite Conversation. He became ungovernable and by affidavits of the year 1742 we learn that, driving with one Wilson, a Doctor of Divinity, he mistook him for the Devil and properly ordered him back to Hell and moreover scratched his face and tore off his wig and thrust fingers into his eyes. But the Dean's servant stated that Mr. Wilson had demanded to be made sub-Dean and being refused began to curse and to strike his fellow-Divine. A month later it was necessary to appoint a Commission of Inquiry and take Statute of Lunacy against the Dean of St. Patrick's. No less than twelve Members of the Legion Club sat to try the Very Reverend Demoniac. But many were good friends of him and their finding found him to be of "unsound mind and memory and not capable of taking care of his person or fortune," and this was affirmed by a Jury of honest shopkeepers, whose names and trades have been recorded. There was a Chandler and a Brewer and a Currier and a Hosier. And between them they found the poor Drapier mad!

Henceforth he was restrained within the Deanery. In awe and pity men watched him, when no woman could bear to stay under the same roof. He would only eat by himself the food which was left for him. For hours and hours he would tramp the corridors and stairways seeking peace in vain from room to room. Very few, and all sad, were any words he said at long intervals. Once, catching glimpse of himself in the glass, he murmured or was said to have murmured to himself, "Poor old man," and on St. Patrick's Day of 1744 he was recorded to have used the divine formula, "I AM WHAT I AM." It was his last most terrible satire.

One final spasm of pain smote him. Like Job his body was covered with boils. One of his eyes swelled to an egg and five pairs of hands could scarce keep him from tearing it out. The eye sank back into the tortured skull and he himself into apathy. Mrs. Whiteway was the last one he knew. "To be sure, my old friend," he said and collapsed.

The Dean was not really mad, not utterly distraught, not a lunatic. His brain was cloaked by many waters and his skull was clouded with total deafness. His memory moved within its own phantasmagoria, though the words, which he would say, failed his lips and those, which he could say, failed his thought. "I am a fool," he said and relapsed into silence beyond words; into sadness without hope; into emptiness beyond words.

As he lay back in his odorous couch or sat dry-rotting in his armchair, the curtains would lift from his mind and upon the tiny stageboard of his skull the characters who had played in his life, shot once more like tiny Lilliputians into his swooning sight.

Afar back they entered from over Time's edges; his accursed uncle and his beloved mother and his old nurse reading him the Bible. How her sentences flowed like trickling water through his tired head. He could see the Castle at Kilkenny and himself scribbling among schoolboys like a tiny marionette until the greater shadow of Dublin Castle blotted them all out and he saw the Fellows of Trinity like horrible grubs moving blindly behind bookshelves until the day they hatched into white-winged Bishops.

Every figure was minutely recognizable. There was dead Doctor Ashe correcting his papers as of

old and suddenly swelling into lawn sleeves and
floating away to Clogher. He looked again and
saw a risen Congreve sitting in the Rose Tavern
with the first ribaldries of youth breaking from his
amorous lips. His were lips to make little women
laugh and love-locks to wipe away their little
tears. Behind Congreve sat the Dean's ludicrous
old cousin, Dryden. The old shriveled beau was
shrunken to an ant's face and his fingers were as
thin as that insect's antennæ. He was too tiny to
be hated! And there was Doctor Bentley, like a
horrible black-beetle nosing the dustheaps of the
past; not worth stamping upon!

The Dean was dreaming and dreaming. Suddenly he saw Sir William Temple lying dead with
a sun-dial piercing his heart as though Time had
shot his bolt visibly, and in a corner of the room
there was Aunt Giffard and her parrot making her
famous puddings in haste for the funeral! . . .
And there was King William carried upright in his
coffin to the funeral and behind him all the pageant
of Sovereigns, whom the Dean had ever known,
King William himself advanced in silken scarf and
polished armor, smaller than ever. For scepter he
was carrying proudly a stick of asparagus and for
Orb a tulip bulb from Holland. The Dean's eyes
looked eagerly for some promised prebendary to
drop from his folds, but the King looked away.

The good Queen Anne followed with her eyes of
Bounty and a sedan-chair packed with her dozen
dead babies, and the Dean shuddered remembering
he had once advised children for food. From her
hand dropped State papers; appointments for
Bishoprics thought the Dean and clutched a flying
document, but it was only the "profane strokes"
from the *Tale of a Tub* and he drew back as though
he had touched a hornet. George the First followed, arrayed as the King of Lilliput with Low
Heels and George the Second with High Heels.
They gibbered a little German and were gone to the
sound of a musical box, or was it the sound of
many waters which rushed back into his head. For
days the Dean sat like one dead. . . .

When he opened his eyes again he could see the
Court and all the great folk whom he had known
in London, all the august Statesmen and Augustan
Scribblers of Queen Anne. There was Lord
Somers with his soft voice covering his mastered
passions and the gallant Godolphin! He had written a song to his mistress on a playing card and
was affixing it to his White Rod. There was Lord
Halifax offering him the Deanery of Hell, which
not unnaturally lay in the Whigs' gift. There
was the wicked Lord Wharton in his white Presbyterian mask enticing young men through pleasure parties unto blackest Whiggery. There was

the tall, thin, dismal-faced, honey-voiced Nottingham, dark as a Spanish Jew, and the peacock Duke
of Somerset with his carrotty-haired Duchess; all
three reviling Doctor Swift but in such distant
tones that the Dean could not overhear a sound.
And there was the old Duke Midas of Marlborough with his Duchess Sarah; the one like
tempered steel in the Inferno and the other bursting
with sparks. The godlike Duke was advancing in
mail of solid gold, while she danced around like a
frantic Fury scattering pieces of money from her
skirts. Like a cruel gnome hovered the Prince
Eugene, and the Dean overheard him engaging
Mohocks from the streets to murder Harley and
prevent the Peace with France. And there was dear
Harley lying murdered and the assassin twisting
like a rat on a pitchfork, run through by Bolingbroke with his sword-arm while his other clutched a
naked wench from the streets. At last among
friends, and the Dean rushed toward the bedside.
Thank God Harley moved, Harley lived! From
the Statesman's fingers fell a paper. There should
be no harm seeing what it was. It might be the
belated Bishopric. No! It was only the Treaty of
Utrecht beautifully written in the Dean's own
hand!

Again half a time forward and a long time back.
Again he fell into oblivion and the dream of death.

Harley, his beloved Harley, was lying dead and a
horrible swollen toad with the Blue Ribbon of the
Garter across his back was squatting over him. It
was Walpole!   Walpole surrounded by faces
which resembled toads, all the rulers of England
and of Ireland during a generation. Walpole, the
Great Corrupt, and all his corruptibles, with red
and blue ribbons round their necks.

"To Cerberus they give a sop,
His triple barking mouth to stop;
Or, in the ivory gate of dreams,
Project excise and South-Sea schemes."

No one was fending or fencing them off except
the remnant of writers and Wits. The Dean tried
to cheer and egg them on. There was the lean-
carcassed, hollow-faced Prior screaming French to
a customs officer. Pope, immortal contemner of
mortal man, was there, and the light fantastic Gay
and the blessed Doctor Arbuthnot. The Dean
could have cried aloud to them, but his voice
choked and the most violent vertigo was vented
within his skull again. On, on against the hosts of
the corrupt! But Arbuthnot was too busy mixing
a drench and Gay was fluting a song from the *Beggar's Opera* and Pope was stealthily filching and
collecting for publication all his letters, which were
floating over the Deanery floor. The young god

Congreve was seducing an Angel upon his knee
and there was Steele starving and stinking in a
corner. . . .

Once more cloud gripped his brain and darkness
drove out the day.   Once again a time forward and
a time back.   The great Court favorites passed him
by; all the serried mistresses of Kings taking the
Dublin packet-boat to cross the Styx!   Lady Orkney sunk in fat and wrinkles with her dragonish
squint worthy of the Pit waving to him.   There
was the gorgeous and gorging old Duchess of
Kendal offering Charon one of Wood's halfpence,
and the lovely Mrs. Howard bartering her golden
hair for the trip. . . .

When the Dean looked again out of his sobbing
skull, was it weeks or was it months?   For he had
forgotten Time as Time seemed to have forgotten
him.   He only perceived that he had crossed to
Ireland.   He saw the long line of his enemies and
a mob of friends.   He felt neither good nor evil to
either.   He was so far beyond.   They were so
small and tiny.   There were all the Bishops of his
time, bestial and bibulous, their white lawn sleeves
glistening with the whiteness which corrodes and
corruscates the sepulchers of liberty and justice.
There was the sniveling Scotchman, Burnet of
Sarum.   There were Hort and Hoadly and the
baboon Bishop of Ossory and that dull brute, Arch-

bishop Boulter, balancing gold and silver in his pawn-broker's scales. There was a whole pack of Irish Bishops dressed as Highwaymen with black masks to cover their bloated faces and pirates' hats balanced on top of their smooth Court wigs; and against them only stood one lone Dean, who had no allies but the wise and the mad, the Wits and the half-wits. Enemies were rising against him on every side, Politicians and Lawyers; the blustering Sergeant Bettesworth, the brawling Lord Allen and the blundering impostor of a blackguard Wood. He could see Wood scattering his damned halfpennies among the crowd to make popularity, but the noble mob of Ireland refusing and throwing the trash back in his face sticky with Liffey mud.

He could see his enemies crowding the Parliament Hive like a Legion of Demons. It was surely time to invoke the Devil to carry away and confound his own. The Dean raised his hands in prayer to the Demon and uttered his own lines of cursing, "may their god the Devil confound them." . . . Dark inky waters descended upon Dublin. The House and the whole content of the House were swept away. There fell a sound of roaring waters and the Dean heard his own solemn voice responding through the darkness: "For the thing which I greatly feared is come upon me and that which I was afraid of, is come unto me." Could it be so? Oh Demon! Oh God! Oh God-made Demon; Oh Demon-God! Was he mad, mad, mad, at last? This time his whole shuddering brain quailed in his skull and his mind staggered into the void out of which it was fashioned. . . . His stale and silent corpse was left dying . . . till it became stark.

It was the twenty-second of October in 1745. The great bell of St. Patrick's was tolling and the bells of the City of Dublin were answering the metallic dirge. The sound of voices and of feet never ceased in the narrow streets and alleys about St. Patrick's Cathedral and Deanery. Mourners and mutes filled the rooms and corridors of the Deanery. Day and night they kept watch over a white-haired and eyeless body. It was toward midnight of the third day before the clergy of the Cathedral with torch-bearers and corpse-carriers came and fetched the broken clay and the blasted brain to burial. Crowds had glimpsed their patriot's face lying in his hall. "He had on his head neither cap nor wig." He was laid out and coffined without spices. Thus then without balm to body or to mind was buried the Dean of St. Patrick's—Jonathan Swift.

It was midnight, and there was much going to and fro and fuss to hide away an empty skull behind crumbling stones which were to reveal no ordinary epitaph; UBI SÆVA INDIGNATIO ULTERIUS COR LACERARE NEQUIT. The heart of Jonathan Swift, the Dean of this Cathedral, was no longer lacerable to savage indignation beneath the marble pall he had inscribed to all mortal time with a further challenge to any passing champion of Liberty, for Liberty rather than Christianity had been his religion. ABI VIATOR ET IMITARE SI POTERIS STRENUUM PRO VIRILI LIBERTATIS VINDICEM! Tyranny was the unforgivable sin and he hated the chains of oppression more than the shackles of sin. He professed Christianity, but he was Liberty's Confessor.

The Commission of Lunacy had gravely concluded their report: "It does not appear to us who is his next heir." It was true in every sense. Without a predecessor he had left no successor. He was no ordinary man, was this Jonathan Swift, for, as it is said that it takes all sorts of men to make a world, it took all manner of worlds to make this man; and none may profitably ask into which world he finally went, nor question either the Divinity or the Demon concerning his ways, for he was of neither unless he was of both. Ask perhaps the spirits of Literature, which he adorned, and ask in words from among the earliest he himself wrote as a young and hopeful grasping youth:

> "Say Muse, for thou, if any, know'st,
> Since the bright essence fled,
> Where haunts the reverend ghost?"

Where indeed? But if the Muses did not come to escort him homeward, the spirit of Vanessa was crouching that night outside the Cathedral porch to kiss his lonely feet and within the Great Aisle the spirit of Stella waited to touch and soothe his empty skull before their three ghosts passed together into the void. Beyond words and beyond the worlds whatsoever love and suffering had ever been theirs became part of the Starlight.

ALAS POOR STELLA

INDEX

INDEX